JAPAN'S 'INTERNATIONAL YOUTH'

Japan's 'International Youth'

*The Emergence of a New
Class of Schoolchildren*

ROGER GOODMAN

CLARENDON PRESS · OXFORD
1993

Oxford University Press, Walton Street, Oxford OX2 6DP

Oxford New York Toronto
Delhi Bombay Calcutta Madras Karachi
Kuala Lumpur Singapore Hong Kong Tokyo
Nairobi Dar es Salaam Cape Town
Melbourne Auckland Madrid
and associated companies in
Berlin Ibadan

Oxford is a trade mark of Oxford University Press

Published in the United States
by Oxford University Press Inc., New York

First published 1990
First issued in Clarendon Paperbacks 1993

British Library Cataloguing in Publication Data
Goodman, Roger
Japan's "international youth": the emergence of a new class of schoolchildren.
1. Japan. Children, social life
I. Title
952.0480854
ISBN 0-19-827897-7

Library of Congress Cataloging in Publication Data
Goodman, Roger.
Japan's "international youth": the emergence of a new class of schoolchildren/
Roger Goodman.
p.   cm.
Includes bibliographical references.
1. Education—Japan—Case studies.   2. Schoolchildren—Japan—Social
conditions—Case studies.   3. Returned students—Japan—Case studies.   4.
Reverse culture shock—Japan—Case studies.   5. Student
adjustment—Japan—Case studies.   I. Title.
LA1312.7.G66 1990   371.8'0952—dc20   90–33969.
ISBN 0-19-827897-7

1 3 5 7 9 10 8 6 4 2

Typeset by Pentacor PLC, High Wycombe, Bucks
Printed and bound in Great Britain
on acid-free paper by
Biddles Ltd, Guildford and Kings Lynn

For Carolyn

Acknowledgements

Any book which has taken as long as this one to prepare will inevitably incur innumerable debts and I am glad at last to have the opportunity to acknowledge these here.

David Brooks and Judith Okely taught me the principles of social anthropology and encouraged my progression to postgraduate research. N. J. Allen and James McMullen of Oxford University, who supervised the doctoral thesis on which this book is based, were not only generous in their encouragement, but also gentle in their criticism. Peter Rivière and Brian Moeran provided constructive suggestions for developing the thesis into a book. Much of this manuscript was written in the supportive environment of the Nissan Institute for Japanese Studies in Oxford, where I benefited greatly from the help and encouragement of its staff and director, Arthur Stockwin. Similarly, I am grateful for the support and advice of Ronald Dore at Imperial College, where I completed the final version. Many others have also given freely of their time in discussing aspects of the project and, in particular, I would like to thank Bruce La Brack, Opal Dunn, Joy Hendry, Michael Houser, Nagashima Nobuhiro, Okano Masazumi, and Marguerite Wells.

My original research was made possible by generous support from the Economic and Social Research Council and the Japan Foundation Endowment Committee. But without wholehearted co-operation from a school with returnee children, I could have achieved little. I wish, therefore, to express my gratitude to the staff, students, and parents of the school which I have called Fujiyama Gakuen. I am particularly grateful to its principal, who had both the confidence, and the interest in academic scholarship, to allow me to spend a year researching freely in his school. Without exception, the staff at Fujiyama Gakuen were extraordinarily generous with their time and they made this project not only possible but also fascinating and enjoyable. I will always value the warmth of their friendship. Similarly, I want to thank all the students at the school who taught me far more than I could ever teach them. It is my sincere hope that all those at the school feel that I have represented them both fairly and accurately.

I also am keen to thank the teachers, especially the heads of the international education departments, who took the trouble to explain their educational programmes for returnee children when I visited the following schools: International Christian University Kōtōgakkō, Dōshisha Kokusai Kōtōgakkō, Gyōsei Kokusai Kōtōgakkō, Ochanomizu Fuzoku Chūgakkō, Tsukuba Daigaku Fuzoku Kōtōgakkō, Keimei Gakuen, and Canadian Academy. Among the scholars in Japan who gave generously of their time, I should like to thank particularly Professors Hoshino Akira, Kobayashi Tetsuya, Minoura Yasuko, Anne Murase, Nakanishi Akira, and Uehara Asako. Onoda Eriko deserves a special mention for all her help and advice throughout the project. I should emphasize, of course, that I alone am responsible for all the faults and mistakes which remain in this text.

On a personal note, I would like to express my appreciation to Watanabe Junko who, while working at the Japanese Ministry of Education, took infinite trouble to arrange my fieldwork and showed a great interest in my work. The early death of this genuinely internationally-minded educationalist, just a few weeks after I arrived in Japan, was the saddest aspect of the whole project.

My greatest debt is to Carolyn Dodd. She encouraged me throughout, not only improving the manuscript through her own knowledge of Japanese society, but also giving me the belief that what I was undertaking was both possible and worthwhile. In every way, her support has been invaluable.

R.J.G.

Essex
1989

Contents

Figures

Tables

JAPAN: PREFECTURES (excluding Ryūkyū Islands)

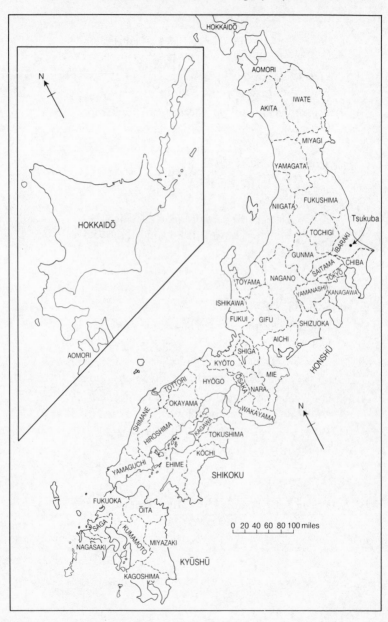

Abbreviations for Journals and Newspapers Cited in the Text

AEN	*Asahi Evening News*
AS	*Asahi Shinbun* (Asahi Newspaper)
DY	*Daily Yomiuri*
EK	*Europa no Kurashi* (Living in Europe)
J	*Japan* (Embassy of Japan, London)
JEJ	*Japan Education Journal*
JT	*Japan Times*
JTW	*Japan Times Weekly*
KEJ	*Kodansha Encyclopaedia of Japan*
KSK	*Kaigai Shijo Kyōiku* (Overseas Children's Education)
KSKK	*Kaigai Shijo Kyōiku Kenkyū* (Research on Overseas Children's Education)
MDN	*Mainichi Daily News*
MS	*Mainichi Shinbun* (Mainichi Newspaper)
NKS	*Nihon Keizai Shinbun* (Japan Economic Newspaper)
TES	*Times Educational Supplement*
TS	*Tokyo Shinbun* (Tokyo Newspaper)
YS	*Yomiuri Shinbun* (Yomiuri Newspaper)

(When articles are bylined, the name of the author is also included, e.g. Houser, *TES*, 26 March 1982.)

A Note to the Reader

All Japanese names are given in the Japanese fashion with the family name first. The Japanese Ministry of Education is called by its Japanese name, Monbushō, except where reference is made to a work it has published in English under the title of Ministry of Education, Science and Culture.

I have not followed the standard romanization for words in the Japanese language which have been taken from western languages, i.e. *manyuaru* (for manual) or *karuchā shokku* (for culture shock). To be strictly logical, I should perhaps also give the original pronunciation for the many Chinese loan-words used in Japanese, but my main purpose is to avoid unnecessarily confusing people who cannot read Japanese who might well also be interested in the number and form of such western loan-words in the discussions that follow. As a result, loan-words from western languages are romanized (i.e. written in the roman alphabet) in their original form, but italicized, e.g. *manual; culture shock*.

Macrons have been used to make long vowels in Japanese. The only exceptions to this rule are in well-known place names which have long vowels in Japanese, such as Tokyo, Osaka, and Kyoto.

To avoid confusion, non-private schools in both Japan and Britain are referred to as state schools. In Japan, these include both national and local establishments. Similarly, all non-private universities in Japan are called state universities. Private schools in Britain are referred to as public schools, even though they have recently begun to refer to themselves as 'independent schools'.

Billion is used in the American sense of one thousand million. I have decided to express all monetary values in yen when discussing the financial situation in Japan since translations into pounds or dollars are rendered almost meaningless by the rapidly changing exchange rate between the countries. For the purposes of comparison, however, £1 was around ¥320 in 1985 and ¥230 in 1989; $1 about ¥245 in 1985 and ¥140 in 1989.

Unless it is otherwise made clear, the pronoun 'he' is used generically to refer to both males and females.

1
Introduction

No Japanese dares leave his Country, and if he does, he must never return. They are so wedded to their own Customs and Opinions, and so jealous of having new or foreign Customs introduced, that they will not send Embassies to other Kings or States, or suffer their Merchants to have Commerce out of their own Dominions.

Thus wrote Alexander Hamilton (1930: 165) in around AD 1700, when Japan was already fifty years into its 250-year period of self-imposed isolation from the rest of the world. As can be seen all around the world, however, the Japanese no longer keep themselves to the shores of their own country. They can be found travelling on business or tourism in all corners of the world and as the Japanese economy gains in strength, so the numbers of Japanese overseas increase. In the 1970s, however, there began to appear in Japan a series of books which suggested that Japan's attitude towards those who had been overseas had not substantially changed from that described by Hamilton. This literature concentrated, in particular, on the experience of Japanese children who had gone overseas owing to their parents' work and had then returned to Japan. A term coined for such children—*kikokushijo*—quickly became common usage as the media began to discuss these children with increasing regularity.

Bookshops in major urban cities began to advertise special sections under the title *Kikokushijo Mondai* ('The Returnee Children Problem'). Educators began to hold seminars to discuss how to help such children. Researchers set up units to examine their problems and the Japanese government invested in schools which established programmes to aid the readaptation of such children to life in Japan. The vast majority of the literature on the *kikokushijo* set out to measure just how serious their problems were when they returned to Japan. How long did it take them to readapt to Japanese society? What specific problems did they face? Much of the literature also attempted to explain why it was only natural that these children—who had received part of their education over-seas—should have problems when they re-entered Japanese society.

The media showed particular interest in the plight of the *kikoku-shijo*. *Kawaisō* ('how pitiful!') became a common reaction to their treatment. They were even written about in foreign publications, where they were generally known as 'returnee schoolchildren' or simply 'returnees'.

This book is an examination of the whole '*kikokushijo* phenomenon' which first really came to public attention in Japan in the mid-1970s. The first three chapters are, in essence, an examination of the subject as far as it has been studied both inside and outside Japan. As Ebuchi Kazukimi (1986*a*: 236–7) shows in a recent survey, the literature on *kikokushijo* has essentially been divided into two parts: one which examines the special education systems which have been set up for the *kikokushijo* and one which examines and explains the types of problems which *kikokushijo* encounter on their return to Japan. Chapter 2, however, first examines the experience of the children before they return to Japan. This experience is extremely varied, depending on a wide variety of different factors: where the children went, how long they were overseas, what type of education they received there, and how much contact they had with the local communities. There are also, of course, differences depending on their age, their gender, and their own individual personalities. Yet all such children, when they return to Japan, are classed as *kikokushijo*. They all tend to have the same qualities ascribed to them as a result of their overseas experience; they all tend to be perceived as suffering from the same problems; and they are all eligible for the special treatment provided by the schools and universities, the counselling centres and support groups for *kikokushijo*.

Chapter 2 also introduces many of the main actors involved in the *kikokushijo* issue—the Japanese government, Monbushō (Japanese Ministry of Education), the mass media, the schools, the universities, the commercial education interests—and, perhaps most significantly, it also introduces the parents of the *kikokushijo*. These parents clearly come from a high stratum of Japanese society: they are almost all white-collar workers and many of them are diplomats, journalists, academics, and businessmen who work for the biggest (and in Japan the most powerful) companies.

Chapters 3 and 4 examine the different reasons which have been given to explain why *kikokushijo* have problems when they return to Japan. These are generally divided into two types: problems due to Japan's cultural system and problems due to Japan's educational system. The cultural explanations are examined in Chapter 3, which also introduces many of the ideas that Japanese tend to take for granted about their own society. These ideas are widely dispersed throughout Japan in the form of books and articles known as *Nihonjinron* (theories of Japaneseness). They concentrate on the homogeneous, exclusivist, conformist, harmonious image of Japanese society and they contrast Japan and the Japanese with other (particularly western),[1] societies. The *kikokushijo* who have been in the west, therefore, are seen as heterogeneous, independent, and argumentative. Small wonder, it is argued by those who have studied them, that they have problems on their return to Japan. Indeed, they argue, such problems are to be taken for granted. In this context, then, the job of the researcher is simply to measure and record these problems and to suggest means for their alleviation, not to question whether such problems really exist. *Kikokushijo*, it is argued, suffer from all kinds of mental and physical problems on their return to Japan owing to the very nature of Japanese society, as a result of which they may even come to suffer from *futekiōbyō* (non-adaptation disease).

It is also taken for granted that Japan's educational system will cause *kikokushijo* as many problems as the cultural system. Some authors link the two closely together and show how the educational system works to create the cultural values of conformity and homogeneity. Everything is done to minimize inequality in the educational system and to ensure that those who rise to the top rise through their own merit. What constitutes this merit, however, is cause for heated debate: many argue that success in the Japanese educational system is simply a test of perseverance and rote-memory, that children's creative urges are denied. Since the early 1970s, there have been increasingly strident demands for reform of the educational system, yet Monbushō has been slow to change a system which many recognize has played an important part in Japan's post-war economic growth—the so-called 'Japanese miracle'. Everyone receives the same treatment within the Japanese educational system; everyone must take the same examinations at the same time—everyone, that is, except *kikokushijo*. Because the problems of *kikokushijo* on returning to Japan have been so well documented, it has been widely accepted that something must be done to help them and, for this reason, a system of special schools, known as *ukeirekō* (reception schools), has been set up.

The *ukeirekō* have been variously described in the Japanese literature, as institutions which offer *kyūsai kyōiku* (relief education) to *kikokushijo* on their return to Japan or as institutions which set out to *sainihonka* (rejapanize) them and *gaikoku o hagashi* (peel off their foreignness). As far as I know, no other country has a comparable system of education to that offered to *kikokushijo* in Japan, although some of the literature about the schools makes them appear similar to Chinese re-education institutions during the Cultural Revolution (see Fyfield, 1982). Yet in all the literature about the *kikokushijo* there are no good descriptions of how the process of educating *kikokushijo* is actually carried out in an *ukeirekō*. This study started as a year's anthropological participant observation fieldwork in one *ukeirekō* in Tsukuba, some 45 miles north of Tokyo. I had already spent a year as a peripatetic teacher in ten junior high schools in Yamaguchi prefecture and I was curious to see how the education offered in the *ukeirekō* differed from the regular state education I already knew.

The description in Chapter 5 of the *ukeirekō* where I undertook my fieldwork shows how different this school turned out to be from the impression I had gained by reading the literature on *kikokushijo*. The significance of the *ukeirekō* depended not so much on the treatment accorded to the *kikokushijo* within it as on the fact that such a school existed at all. The *ukeirekō* proved to be more interested in the education of future leaders of society than in 'decontaminating' *kikokushijo* of their overseas experience. The school modelled itself more on a British public school than on a refugee camp. The teachers sought to instil a combination of 'Japaneseness' and 'internationalness' in their education programmes that seemed to undermine the widely held image of Japan's innate exclusivity, and the problems that such exclusivity caused for *kikokushijo*.

Chapter 6 involves a more detailed examination of some of the theories and material presented in the earlier chapters in the light of data collected during the fieldwork period. It ascertains first that the school where research was carried out is not atypical among *ukeirekō* in Japan. In particular, it was discovered that no teachers in any of the *ukeirekō* are specially trained to deal with *kikokushijo*. Instead, all *ukeirekō* seek their own way of combining international and Japanese values in the education of *kikokushijo*, and differences which occur between schools are only differences of degree. Moreover, there is evidence to suggest that the problems from which *kikokushijo* have been said to suffer have been considerably exaggerated and a case study is taken to show how serious methodological faults may have led to such mistakes. It does not suggest—and for the sake of those *kikokushijo* who told me sad stories of their experiences in Japan this point has to be repeatedly stressed—that *kikokushijo* do not have serious problems in Japan. Many of them clearly do, and these should in no way be ignored or undervalued. Nevertheless, some of the problems from which they suffer are universal problems which result from crossing cultural boundaries; some of them could be the result of simply moving from one school to another within Japan; some of them are suffered by other children in Japanese schools who have never been overseas; some of them may simply be endemic to adolescence. The sum of the problems of *kikokushijo* may not, in fact, be any more than the sum of the problems of regular school students in Japan.

The image of *kikokushijo* as a 'pitiful' group of children in need of special sympathy is also somewhat distorted when they are compared with other minority groups in Japan. Clearly, they fare far better in education and employment than any of these other groups. Indeed, there is even evidence that they are faring better in these fields than the non-*kikokushijo* mainstream Japanese. They are going to the top universities, they are being preferentially employed, they are proclaiming their 'otherness'. They are clearly not behaving as the literature described in Chapters 3 and 4 would lead one to expect. Their status, indeed, appears to have changed dramatically over the past few years.

It is mainly in search of reasons for this change in status that Chapter 7 consists of a historical overview of Japan's relationship with the outside world. It is difficult to summarize such a macrohistorical approach, but, in brief, the picture that emerges is one of a 'history of ambivalence', of swings between xenophobia and xenophilia, of constant debate and divisions over receptiveness to, or exclusion from, the outside world. Similarly striking is the emergence of a recurring pattern of the selection and incorporation of elements from the outside world into Japan without upsetting the nation's sense of its own unique Japaneseness. Occasionally this process has manifested itself in political slogans such as *wakon kansai* ('Japanese spirit and Chinese technology') in the eighth century and *wakon yōsai* ('Japanese spirit and western technology') in the late nineteenth century. Generally, however, it has been a matter of gently shifting trends between open relations and seclusion where, as David Parkin (1978: 290) writes in his discussion of 'internal cultural debates', 'a dominant paradigm must always presuppose an opposite, however shadowy and variable in expression the latter is'. In the case of Japan, however, it is never a question of opposites but rather, as Vincent Brandt (1971: 32) describes in his study of competing ideologies in village Korea, 'the Chinese notion of yin and yang . . . comprising complementary oppositions'. In Japan 'the outside' becomes incorporated into Japanese society so that it can become useful and yet not threatening to the existing social structure.

The study of dynamic political rhetoric has a long history in anthropology, particularly since Edmund Leach's (1954) classic study of the Kachin in Burma, yet it has only recently been applied to Japan (Moeran, 1984; 1985). Moeran (1984: 262–3) shows how the concept of individuality in Japan, generally considered anathema in such a conformist society, has recently been introduced into the society in the guise of a 'Japanese form of individualism'. The term used for this Japanese form, *kosei*, distinguishes it from the egotistical western notion of individuality which is termed *kojinshugi*. The *kikokushijo* are another aspect of Japanized westernism; another example of the process of the west being incorporated into Japanese society, their individualism is also described as *kosei* and thus their ability to act on behalf of Japan after having been through the *ukeirekō* is assured.

The second half of Chapter 7 is a chronological account of how one interest group in Japan—the parents of the *kikokushijo*—made an issue of their children's situation and thereby became involved in the process of effecting change in the national rhetoric. The schools and the special university entrance network, the government grants and the research centres involved in studying *kikokushijo*, did not arise spontaneously out of a sense that something special should be done for these children. They arose because the demands of the parents made such an impression on the establishment in Japan.

That the parents had access to the establishment was due to one factor which differentiates the *kikokushijo* as a group from other minority groups in Japan—their class status. This is something which has been all but ignored in the literature on *kikokushijo*. Although there has been a long and established Marxist tradition in Japan which has studied Japanese society in terms of class interest, this has always been a minority position and appears to have declined, rather than grown, in recent years. As Sugimoto and Mouer (1989: 14), two well-known analysts of the class system in Japan, say: 'The survey finding of the Prime Minister's Office showing that 90 per cent of all Japanese identify with the middle class . . . seems to have become widely accepted as fact, and the number of social scientists seriously probing variation within Japanese society according to income, class, or occupation has markedly declined over time.' In the English-language literature on Japan, discussion of Japan in terms of class has been, until very recently, almost non-existent. Japan is presented and perceived by most western observers as a homogeneous classless society. Yet class is clearly an essential element in understanding how the parents of *kikokushijo* obtained special treatment for them in the Japanese educational system. This is just one of the issues which Chapter 8 attempts to tie together into a single coherent account of why and how the status of *kikokushijo* in the schools studied and in the new evidence uncovered differs so greatly from the image of *kikokushijo* in the accounts described in Chapters 3 and 4. It also seeks to explain why such a small number of children have received so much attention; why all children who have been overseas, regardless of their experience, are treated exactly the same; and why *kikokushijo* themselves are so often excluded from debates about them.

The account in Chapter 8 incorporates a number of different elements that have significance for the understanding of Japan. It emphasizes how different interest groups competing for social advantages undermine the traditional picture of a homogeneous society which acts uniformly and thinks alike. It examines the important debates on the need for educational reform and how to introduce that reform without losing the elements of the system which have been so effective so far. Similarly, it looks at the quandary in which employers find themselves who want both conformist and creative workers and yet see a conflict between the two. It examines the continuing debates over the concept of internationalization in Japan and what it means to be Japanese. It considers the role of the media in disseminating images of what is believed to constitute an 'international Japanese'. It explores the effect of a dramatic demographic swing on the treatment of those Japanese (especially women) who have been overseas.

Through all of this, the point most stressed is that *kikokushijo* as individuals are largely peripheral to the debates about them. This is why quotation marks are used in the title in describing them as 'international youth': they are symbols of 'westernism' and 'internationalism' to which either negative or positive values are ascribed by different groups in Japanese society, regardless of their individual experiences or backgrounds. Some Japanese perceive them as threatening the nation's values; others see them as enhancing. Symbolic analysis explains how such a wide range of children, all labelled as *kikokushijo*, can be considered as a group with the same qualities. Although this type of symbolic approach to understanding the status of different groups in society is relatively new in the analysis of Japan, it is necessary to point out important examples of its use. Yoshida Teigo (1981: 96), for example, has shown how the stranger in Japanese folk beliefs can be given a negative or positive value depending on different circumstances— 'potentially dangerous in ordinary contexts, when there is a release from calamity or unusual good fortune, strangers may be credited for having brought about the happy turn of events'.

Similarly, Emiko Ohnuki-Tierney (1984*b*: 305) has suggested that the status of some of Japan's minority groups has been interpreted very differently at different periods in Japanese history: 'There is massive historical/ethnographic evidence to support the approach that the structurally marginal member of a class, be it a person, a being, or an object, may be assigned the positive role/ power of mediation, the negative meaning of pollution and taboo, or the role of trickster/clown.' The explanation of the changing status of *kikokushijo*—from 'polluted' to 'mediators' in Ohnuki-Tierney's terms—emphasizes the nature of continual change, and potential change, in Japanese society. In particular, it shows how Japan's relationship with the west has evolved so rapidly in recent decades from crushed foe to economic superpartner. Not surprisingly, this rapidly changing relationship has led to tensions and debates in Japan in which *kikokushijo*, as exemplars of this relationship between the west and Japan, play an important symbolic role.

But the changing status of *kikokushijo* also shows how change is managed and manipulated by different interest groups to accommodate demands and initiate new ways of thinking. This is a common process in Japanese society, as Bestor (1989) has shown in his study of the mobilization of 'tradition' by the old middle class in a Tokyo suburb as a means to restate their local power over the new middle class represented by the company 'salaryman'. The significance is that explanations of discrimination against any group in Japanese society in terms of inherent cultural behaviour probably do more to maintain or even exacerbate the problems faced by such groups than to explain them. The low status of most of Japan's minority groups (which will be examined in Chapter 6) can be more closely related to their class marginality than the cultural and ethnic reasons normally cited. The change in the status of *kikokushijo* has, for a number of reasons, been particularly rapid. Nevertheless, it demonstrates the potential for such change in Japanese society. A minority group in terms of numbers is not always a marginal one in terms of access to power. Similarly, explanations of Japanese society in terms of 'culture' tend to reinforce rather than explore stereotypes about the way the society works, unless it is remembered that 'culture' is only shorthand for the confluence of economic, political, and historical forces in an ever-continuing process.

2
Who are the *Kikokushijo*?

Kikokushijo is a recently coined word which, as the anthropologist Sofue Takao (1980: 17) has pointed out, has 'quickly become proper Japanese' (*seishiki no Nihongo*). The word seems to have been invented by the Japanese Ministry of Education (hereinafter referred to by its Japanese name Monbushō) in the late 1960s when the government began to consider policy for returnee children. It is formed from the combination of four Chinese characters which, individually, mean 'return' (*ki*), 'country' (*koku*), 'child' or 'boy' (*shi*), and 'girl' (*jo*), but Monbushō appears never to have defined the term accurately. Sofue (1980: 17) suggests that 'it refers to those students who, because their parents have lived overseas for a long time, have received their education at an overseas school and have then returned to Japan and entered a Japanese school'. Kobayashi Tetsuya (1983: i), the most prolific and, perhaps, most significant Japanese writer on returnees, gives a fuller definition:

Kikokushijo are those who have had the experience of (*a*) being born in Japan and (*b*) brought up in the mainstream of Japanese culture. When they reached a (*c*) certain age, they (*d*) went overseas with their parents. While they were being brought up overseas, they (*e*) received some influence from the local culture. After (*f*) a few years, they (*g*) returned home and were brought up in the mainstream Japanese culture once again [my letters].

Each of the elements of this definition needs to be looked at in more detail.

(*a*) . . . *born in Japan* . . . As Kobayashi himself immediately points out, there is the problem of whether Japanese children who were born overseas and then came with their parents to Japan are *kikokushijo*. On this issue, Suzuki Masayuki (1984: 38) suggests that *kikokushijo* are Japanese children whose parents have gone overseas with the intention of returning at some point (*kikoku o zentei toshite*). Suzuki makes a distinction between these Japanese and Japanese returnee immigrants or their dependants from Latin America, for example, whom he terms *hikiagemono* (repatriates).

(*b*) . . . *brought up in the mainstream of Japanese culture* . . . The significance of this aspect of Kobayashi's definition can be illustrated by two examples. On the one hand, a child born overseas, whose parents are part of the local Japanese community and who is educated, as far as the situation allows, in Japanese customs and language, would be considered *kikokushijo* when his parents returned to Japan and took him with them. On the other hand, a child born in Japan, but not in a totally Japanese environment—for example, where one parent is not Japanese— cannot be *kikokushijo*. Children with only one Japanese parent are generally referred to as *konketsuji* (mixed-blood child) and not included in the category of *kikokushijo*. One of the basic prerequisites of the category of *kikokushijo* is that they are not physically distinguishable from other Japanese children.

Kikokushijo must also have come from the mainstream of Japanese culture: if the few Japanese children who choose to go to international schools in Japan then go overseas, they are unlikely to be classified as *kikokushijo* on their return. Of course, these distinctions are not absolute, but are more a question of degree. In statistics on *kikokushijo*, *konketsuji* are sometimes included, but generally, when the children are taken individually, the fact that they are *konketsuji* or have attended an international school in Japan is likely to be given more weight than the fact that they have lived overseas.

(c) . . . a certain age . . . There appears to be an upper age-limit beyond which a returnee is not classed as *kikokushijo*, but there is no lower limit. Children who lived overseas for only their first year of life will have it marked on their school records and may find themselves included in statistics on *kikokushijo*. Children who were overseas during the year before elementary school, when most Japanese children receive private education to give them a good start in the educational race, will sometimes, when they start school, find themselves in special classes to help them 'catch up'. In one school in Tsukuba, where many foreigners live, such children are taught in a special unit along with foreign children. Returnees who are over the usual age for university entrance do not fall into the category of *kikokushijo*, although some are sometimes mistakenly referred to as such. The special word *shijo* has been coined to denote that these are 'children', and their special significance lies in their relation to the Japanese school system. Officially, Japanese

become adults on the first Coming of Age Day (15 January) after their 20th birthday and, although there are exceptional cases of students retaking their university entrance exams into their early 20s, it would be reasonable to see 20 as the upper age-limit for the category of *kikokushijo*. If the children return before the age of 20, however, and thereby fall into the *kikokushijo* category, they may continue to be called *kikokushijo* well beyond this.

(d) . . . *went overseas with their parents* . . . The overseas experience of *kikokushijo* is perhaps the most important strand of the nexus in which they are discussed, and it is vital to their definition. Indeed, it is common to use the word *kaigai.kikokushijo* (overseas-returnee children), and in Fujiyama Gakuen (the school described in Chapter 5) this idea was so strong that the *kikokushijo* were generally referred to as *kaigaisei* (overseas students). Generally, *kikokushijo* are expected to have been overseas with their parents. One author, indeed, refers to them as *dōhanshijo* (accompanying children) (Satō, 1978: 21). Ohnuki-Tierney (1984a: 43) refers to them as 'children of Japanese parents whose work required the children to be reared in a foreign country'. A large survey by Takahagi (1982: 78) showed that 99 per cent of mothers who went overseas went as housewives, so it would normally be accurate to replace 'parents' with 'fathers'. There are cases, as we shall see, where children sent overseas by themselves also fall into the *kikokushijo* category on their return to Japan.

Another important element of the overseas experience of *kikokushijo* children is that they had no say in where they went, and often none in whether, or for how long, they went. The writer Harumei Osamu (1985) draws an analogy between *kikokushijo* and *hyōryūmin*—Japanese sailors who drifted out of control, caught by currents, to the coasts of Russia and America in the seventeenth and eighteenth centuries. Both groups, Harumei argues, went overseas not by choice but by accident, which left them with the feeling of being victims; both suffered shock from their contact with different cultures, and both faced trouble on their return. This is an analogy to which we will return when we consider the history of returnees in Japan.

(e) . . . *received some influence from the local culture* . . . This is a moot point. In many of the statistics on *kikokushijo*, and in most schools which accept them, a distinction is made between children who went to local schools in foreign countries (*genchikō*), to international schools (*kokusaigakkō*), to supplementary schools that meet either once a week or after school in the evenings (*hoshūkō*), or to full-time Japanese schools (*Nihonjingakkō*). In the official statistics, however, the numbers of children who attended all these different types of schools are invariably added together to form the total number of *kikokushijo*. It is not difficult, for instance, to find children who have spent several years in Japanese schools in South-East Asian countries and hardly know ten words of the local language and yet are still classified as *kikokushijo* on their return to Japan.

(f) . . . *after a few years* . . . Actually, children need to be overseas for much less than this in order to be considered *kikokushijo*. In their mammoth study of Japanese returnees, undertaken in the 1950s, Bennett, Passin, and McKnight (1958: 63) limited themselves to looking at individuals who had spent one year or more overseas. A recent Monbushō survey (1988: 134) of *kikokushijo* also included children who had spent only a year overseas.

Many schools which have a special network for accepting returnees lay down stipulations on how long a child has to have been overseas and how recently he has returned to Japan. The formula at Fujiyama Gakuen was to consider as *kikokushijo* those who had been overseas for two to three years and returned during the past year; for three to four years and returned during the past two years; or for over four years and returned within the past three years. But many other schools were much more relaxed about these regulations. Even in Fujiyama Gakuen, however, children who did not fit into the category for gaining special entry as *kikokushijo* because they had not lived overseas long enough, or had returned too long before, or even both, would find themselves included in the statistics for *kikokushijo*. The school's register of returnee children (*kikokushijo meibo*) included one 15-year-old who had spent the first two years of his life in Canada; one 17-year-old who had spent nine months as a 5-year-old in America; and one 18-year-old who had spent the first two years of her life in America. It is quite common for statistics of overseas children to include the name of any child who has been overseas for three months or more. This is the length of time used in official statistics to define what is termed a 'prolonged' expatriate (*kaigai zairyū hōjin*). Anything less than three months comes under the heading of 'tourism'.

(g) . . . *returned home and were brought up in the mainstream*

Japanese culture . . . A number of *kikokushijo* return to, or end up
in, the international schools in Japan from which entry to Japanese
universities is very difficult. Many of them go overseas again and
those who stay in Japan tend to remain peripheral to the
mainstream society. They come to be primarily identified in wider
society as students of these international schools rather than as
kikokushijo. In contrast to this, one of the important markers of
kikokushijo is the fact that they go through the mainstream
education system.

The above discussion has examined the major elements of the
definition of *kikokushijo*. There is, however, a secondary question.
Why was the word *kikokushijo* chosen to refer to such children?
The last two *kanji* (Chinese characters) of this word are not a new
combination but form a bureaucratic, and somewhat dated, word
for 'child' or 'children'. In part, no doubt, this combination was
chosen for practical reasons. As Stoetzel (1955: 65) pointed out in
his post-war examination of Japanese youth, although there is an
abundance of words for children in the Japanese language, they
tend to be very specific in their scope. *Kodomo* covers the years
from birth to age 6; *shōnen* refers to boys or girls from 6 to about
15, and *seinen* means those from 15 to adulthood, ostensibly at 20
but in some usages not until marriage. Another common word,
jidō, refers to children of elementary-school age (6 to 12), whereas
seito is used for secondary school students (12 to 15). Sometimes
the expression *kikokujidō.seito* is used to cover all returnee
children of compulsory school age but, particularly when the prefix
kaigai (overseas) is added, this is very unwieldy.

Given the number of possible words for children, it may not seem
unreasonable that, for practical purposes, Monbushō decided to
use the already existing generic term *shijo*. Not everybody,
however, is happy with its application. A group of returnee
mothers, who have been campaigning hard to have the special
needs of their children recognized, perceive a discriminatory
element in the use of this word. This group, the Kokusai Jidō Bunko
Kyōkai, conveniently limits its activities to younger returnee
children and can therefore employ the terms *kodomo* or *jidō*.
According to this organization, the juxtaposition of the *kanji* for
child (*shi*) and girl (*jo*) implies, in the context of a society which
equates masculinity with strength, a weak or defective child. The

president of the Kokusai Jidō Bunko Kyōkai maintained, in an interview, that *shijo* has some of the connotations of the English word 'refugee'. This is not a widely held interpretation, however, and attempts by the organization to persuade ministers and others to stop using the word *shijo* have so far met with no success.

The use of the term *kikoku* (to return to one's country) has not escaped censure either. Horoiwa Naomi, founder member of an organization (META) which acts as a support group for returnees in Japanese society, complains that the use of the term *kikoku* categorizes individuals purely on the basis that they have returned to Japanese society. Horoiwa sees it as a definition biased towards the mainstream society, thereby categorizing returnees as different and discriminating against them on the basis that they grew up, or were educated, overseas. As a result she has coined the term *kaigai seichō Nihonjin* (1983*b*: 91) which she translates, rather awkwardly, as 'overseas-bred Japanese' (1985: 11).

It will become clear later why it is so important to look at the problems of defining the term *kikokushijo*, though the broad sweep of the category will be immediately apparent. The vast majority of writers and statisticians on this subject do not give any clear guidelines as to whom they include as *kikokushijo* and whom they do not. To refine Kobayashi's definition quoted earlier, I would suggest that the category of *kikokushijo* includes all Japanese children under the age of 20 who, because of one or both of their parents' jobs, have at some time in their lives spent at least three months overseas, and have returned to continue their education in the mainstream education system. As we shall see, this refers to a very diverse group of children.

JAPANESE OVERSEAS

As we have seen, *kikokushijo* can only be understood in the context of their overseas experience. There are, however, several different categories of overseas Japanese. The Japanese government keeps four major sets of statistics on the number of citizens living, and going, overseas. One of these sets relates to Japanese emigrants and their dependants. The second relates to Japanese tourists. The third refers to Japanese living abroad as permanent residents. The fourth consists of figures on Japanese staying abroad for three months and longer, which will prove the most relevant for this account of *kikokushijo*. It will be useful, however, for understanding the treatment of *kikokushijo*, to look briefly at each particular set of statistics in turn.

EMIGRANTS AND THEIR DEPENDANTS

According to Japanese Foreign Ministry reports, there were around 1.5 million emigrants of Japanese origin and their dependants living outside Japan in 1980 (*DY*, 14 February 1985). The vast majority could be found in the two Americas—800,000 in Brazil and around 600,000 in the United States, of whom almost half were in the State of Hawaii (Wilson and Hosokawa, 1982: 305). The majority of these Japanese emigrated during the Meiji (1868–1912) and post-war periods when Japan was suffering from both poverty and overcrowding. Many of those from the lower echelons of society were encouraged to emigrate by government circles. A few of the dependants of these emigrants returned to Japan for some or all of their education before going back overseas. Those who came from the United States to be educated were known as *kibei*, and Max Templeman (1979) has written a novel that highlights the anomalous position of such individuals in both Japan and the United States, particularly during the Second World War.

As Japan became more prosperous, emigration rates dropped until in 1984 the total number was only 2,446, 60 per cent of whom went to the United States (*DY*, 14 February 1985). Indeed, the phenomenon has recently arisen of 'return migration' of former Japanese citizens, or their dependants, who left Japan in past decades. In part these people are 'pulled' by Japan's new-found wealth and success; in part, especially in relation to Latin America, they are 'pushed' by the massive inflation, foreign debts, growing political unrest, and terrorism in their adopted countries. These 'return migrants' have received little encouragement from the Japanese government, and since the 1960s have been treated the same as any other applicants for immigration to Japan. The problem of overcrowding in Japan persists and, indeed, there are still government initiatives to encourage emigration. Most notice-able of these is a plan for those between the ages of 20 and 35 to spend a three-year period in Central and South America at government expense with a view to long-term emigration (*DY*, 24

October 1984). Similarly, the much publicized 'Silver Columbia' project, sponsored by the Ministry of International Trade and Industry (MITI), encourages elderly Japanese to spend their retirement overseas at the expense of the Japanese government (*JTW*, 14 February 1987).

JAPANESE OVERSEAS TOURISM

If increased wealth in Japan has caused overseas emigration to slow down, it has also encouraged tourism overseas. The Japanese government, moreover, has taken the probably unique step of currently investing heavily in tourism outside Japan as a way of reducing its external trade surpluses. It is aiming for ten million Japanese to be taking annual overseas vacations by 1991. In 1988, the figure had reached 8.4 million—about 7 per cent of the population (*JTW*, 4 March 1989).

A new trend in tourism has been for schools to take trips (*shūgaku ryokō*) to neighbouring countries. Korea, Taiwan, and mainland China are currently the three favourite destinations for such trips (*AS*, 21 November 1983), and Fujiyama Gakuen took its first overseas school trip in 1987 to Taiwan. Despite this growing trend, though, the fact remains that the vast majority of Japanese have never been overseas.

JAPANESE EXPATRIATES: 'PERMANENT' AND 'PROLONGED'

Japanese emigrants can be clearly distinguished from individuals who have retained their Japanese nationality while living abroad. According to the Foreign Ministry, there were 463,680 Japanese residents living abroad as of 1 October 1982 (*JT*, 12 September 1983). Of this total, 53 per cent were in the category of 'permanent' residents (those with the right of permanent residence overseas) and this figure was increasing at the rate of only about 0.7 per cent a year. This category includes most of the Japanese blue-collar workers who go overseas—such as those who work in *sushi* bars or Japanese restaurants—many of whom stay abroad until retirement or longer. Much more substantial has been the increase in the number of 'prolonged' Japanese residents over the past few years. These expatriates form the significant group for research on *kikokushijo*, since *kikokushijo* are the children of 'prolonged' overseas residents. 'Prolonged' or 'long-term' overseas Japanese residents (*kaigai zairyū hōjin*) are those who stay overseas for longer than three months. As Japanese overseas trade has increased, the number of people in this category has risen dramatically. This growth is plotted in Fig. 1.

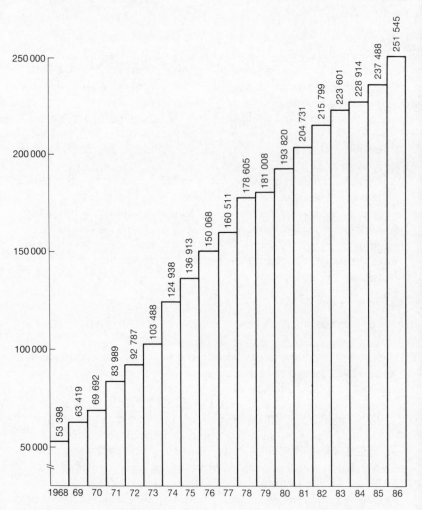

FIG. 1: Increase by Year of 'Prolonged' Overseas Japanese Expatriates
Sources: Kaigai Shijo Kyōiku Shinkō Zaidan, 1980: Monbushō, 1988: 4.

The rapid increase—500 per cent over fifteen years between 1968 and 1983—in the number of 'prolonged' Japanese residents overseas can be most easily explained by looking at the increase in direct Japanese investment overseas during the same period, as shown in Fig. 2.[1] Between 1951 and 1985, Japanese foreign investment totalled $US 83.6 billion, of which 32 per cent went to

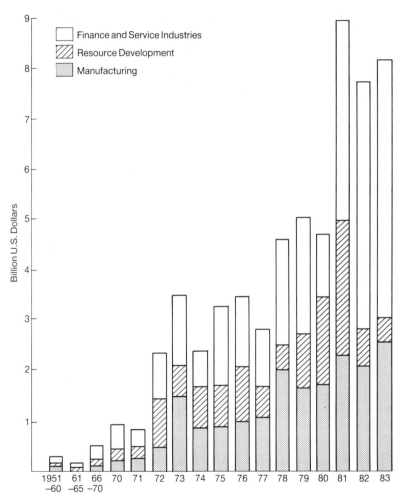

FIG. 2: Increase in Direct Japanese Overseas Investment
Source: Adapted from Economist Rinji Zōkan, 1984: 207.

North America and 23 per cent to Asia (*South*, 1987: 58). Of the 2,659 Japanese industrial establishments overseas in 1982, over 60 per cent were set up in the 1970s (Miyakawa, 1985: 202).

PROFILE OF 'PROLONGED' EXPATRIATES

As the Japanese economy began to take off from the late 1960s, not only did Japanese investment rise dramatically, but so also did the number of Japanese being sent overseas to work.[2] Some of the statistics in Table I, which shows where these expatriates were sent, and how they were employed there, merit further discussion. Almost two-thirds of all 'prolonged' residents overseas are involved in trading, banking, and manufacturing, and this correlates with the growth of overseas investment in these fields shown in Figure 2. In specific regions of the world, however, the percentage is actually considerably higher—in Central and South America about 72 per cent of all Japanese expatriates fall into this category; in Asia almost 77 per cent; and in the Middle East around 86 per cent. On the other hand, while 35 per cent of the entire Japanese overseas population live in Central and South America, Asia, the Middle East, and Africa, only 8 per cent of Japanese students, researchers, and teachers overseas can be found in these areas. In short, there is a tendency for Japanese to go to 'developing' countries for business and 'developed' countries for education.

Not all workers who go overseas take their families with them. The notion of leaving one's family behind when moving to a new work-place is well established in Japan. Indeed, a phrase has been coined for those men who undertake such a move—*tanshin funinzoku* (the bachelor-husband tribe). The majority of these men—somewhere between 130,000 and 150,000—have been sent to outlying districts of Japan to undertake company work. They are generally in the age bracket 30 to 50, and hold jobs at every level of the corporate ladder (*JT*, 14 January 1985). According to Richard Wiltshire (1989: 10), a full one-third of all job transfers now result in *tanshin funin*, with about 175,000 families affected at any one time. In a survey, which allowed multiple answers, to discover the reasons why so many Japanese company employees leave their families behind when moving to distant areas, over 94 per cent cited their children's education, and around 47 per cent cited home-

TABLE I: 'Prolonged' Japanese Expatriates and their Families, by Region and Employment (as of October 1986)

	Asia	North America	Oceania	Central & South America	Europe	Middle East	Africa	Total
Trading Companies, Banks, Manufacturing & Families	40,709	58,588	5,138	8,838	39,331	6,878	4,341	163,823 (65.1%)
News Reporters & Families	389	656	46	50	592	41	79	1,853 (0.7%)
Self-Employed & Families	590	1,056	101	218	3,782	29	125	5,901 (2.4%)
Overseas Students, Teachers, Researchers & Families	3,261	26,711	896	251	14,313	87	122	45,641 (18.2%)
Government Employees & Families	5,341	2,765	606	2,481	4,204	813	1,938	18,148 (7.2%)
Others	2,155	5,694	1,026	413	6,480	160	251	16,179 (6.4%)
TOTAL	52,445 (20.8%)	95,470 (38.0%)	7,813 (3.1%)	12,251 (4.9%)	68,702 (27.3%)	8,008 (3.2%)	6,856 (2.7%)	251,545 (100%)

Source: Monbushō, 1988: 5.

ownership (*JT*, 14 January 1985). The tradition of leaving children behind while going to work away from home also applies to those who go overseas. In 1979, about 19 per cent of children of overseas-assigned Japanese parents remained in Japan (White, *KEJ*, vol. 7: 37). Fukuda Yūsuke (1983) traces this phenomenon back to the Japanese communities in South-East Asia in the seventeenth century. A survey in 1987, however, suggested that Japanese businessmen felt they could stand only two years of a work assignment that forced them to live apart from their families (*JTW*, 22 June 1987).

A number of factors determine whether children are taken overseas or not. Firstly, there are still areas of the world, particularly 'developing' countries, where a significant proportion of workers prefer not to take their children. This is shown in a survey, undertaken in 1979 by the Japan Electrical Workers' Union (*Nihon Denki Sangyō Rōdō Kumiai*), of 2,240 workers from eleven companies (Table II). A second factor is gender. A survey by Onoda Eriko and Tanaka Kazuko (1988: 26–7) shows that parents are more likely to take girls overseas than boys and that they keep them there, on average, one year longer. This, as we shall see, can be related to different socialization pressures on boys and girls in Japan.

A third factor is the age of the child concerned, as shown in Table III. This table illustrates the anxieties of parents about keeping their children overseas beyond a certain age and also the shortage of Japanese senior high schools abroad. (Both points will be examined later.) It also indicates the age-bands of the parents living abroad. In a survey of around 1,000 parents with children in overseas Japanese schools, Kawabata and Suzuki (1981: 31) found that over 80 per cent of the fathers were in the age-band 36 to 45, and very nearly 80 per cent of the mothers were in the age-band 31 to 40.[3] The same survey also showed the high level of education of 'prolonged' Japanese expatriates, which is not surprising when one considers the type of work they undertake overseas. Very nearly 90 per cent of the men had received a university education, while just over 60 per cent of the women had received tertiary education, 35 per cent at university and 25 per cent at two-year junior colleges (1981: 31).[4]

The families of *kikokushijo* can therefore can be categorized as belonging to a well-educated section of Japanese society, where the husband, generally in mid-career, has been sent overseas by the

TABLE II: Overseas Workers by Region: Ratio of those with Family to those without Family

	Asia		North America		Oceania		Central & South America		Europe		Middle East		Africa		Total	
	No.	%	No.	%	No.	%	No.	%	No.	%	No.	%	No.	%	No.	%
With Family	487	71	628	85.7	56	91.8	292	89.3	308	90.9	25	52.1	24	70.6	1,820	81.7
Without Family	199	29	105	14.3	5	8.2	35	10.7	31	9.1	23	47.9	10	29.4	408	18.3

Source: Hirano, 1984: 20. (I have omitted the category of workers in socialist countries, of whom 11 out of 12 took their families.)

TABLE III: Percentage of Children Accompanying Parents Overseas
or Remaining in Japan, by School Level

	Children Accompanying Overseas		Children Remaining in Japan		Total	
	No.	%	No.	%	No.	%
University Students	15	19.7	61	80.3	76	2.2
Senior High School	60	33.7	118	66.3	178	5.1
Junior High School	196	61.4	123	38.6	319	9.17
Elementary School	1,045	83.7	204	16.3	1,249	35.9
Pre-School	1,452	87.7	204	12.3	1,656	47.6
TOTAL	2,768	79.6	710	20.4	3,478	100.0

Source: Hirano, 1984: 20.

organization for which he works. The vast majority of these
families take their children with them, although they appear, as we
have seen, rather more reluctant to take children to developing
countries, or to take children who are further on in their
educational careers. We shall return later to the parents of
kikokushijo and their backgrounds, but we now turn our attention
to the type of education received by these children while overseas.

EDUCATIONAL FACILITIES FOR JAPANESE CHILDREN OVERSEAS

Official statistics divide the educational establishments attended by
Japanese children overseas into three categories: full-time Japanese
schools (*Nihonjingakkō*); supplementary Japanese schools
(*hoshūkō*); and local schools (*genchikō*), including international
schools (*kokusaigakkō*). The earliest figures, dating from 1966,
show that there were then 4,159 children between the ages of 6 and
15 living overseas (Kobayashi, 1978b: 15). Since then, if we look at
Fig. 3, we can see that the percentage of overseas Japanese children

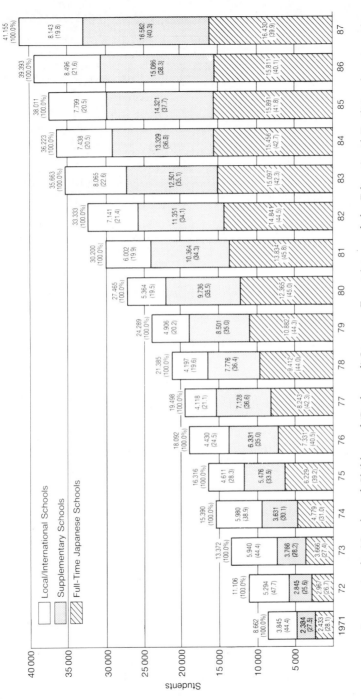

FIG. 3: Increase in the Number of Children of 'Prolonged' Japanese Expatriates and the Educational Facilities they Attend
Sources: Adapted from Ōgiya, 1977: 7; Monbushō, 1985: 4; Monbushō, 1988: 4.

attending full-time and supplementary Japanese schools has steadily increased to around 40 per cent each, while the proportion of children receiving no Japanese education overseas has halved. During the 1970s, the number of children attending full-time *Nihonjingakkō* increased by 500 per cent and *hoshūkō* registers quadrupled. This increase has been paralleled by a large growth in the numbers of these two types of school, as is shown by Table IV.

TABLE IV: Increase in Full-Time and
Supplementary Japanese Schools
Overseas (1971–88)

	Full-Time Japanese Schools	Supplementary Schools
1971	26	22
1972	32	25
1973	37	45
1974	40	55
1975	40	56
1976	45	65
1977	50	67
1978	55	71
1979	62	73
1980	67	78
1981	70	82
1982	72	90
1983	74	95
1984	76	102
1985	78	109
1986	80	112
1987	82	120
1988	83	–

Sources: Monbushō, 1988: 5; Kaigai
Shijo Kyōiku Shinkō Zaidan, 1980:
398–415.

Nihonjingakkō and *hoshūkō*, however, are not evenly distributed around the world: the vast majority of the former are in developing countries, while most of the latter are in developed nations. In developing countries, the majority of children go to full-time Japanese schools: 94 per cent in Asia; 75 per cent in the Middle East; 73 per cent in Central and South America; and 60 per cent in Africa (Fig. 4). These areas together account for two-thirds of all children who go to overseas *Nihonjingakkō*, while accounting for less than one-third of all overseas children.

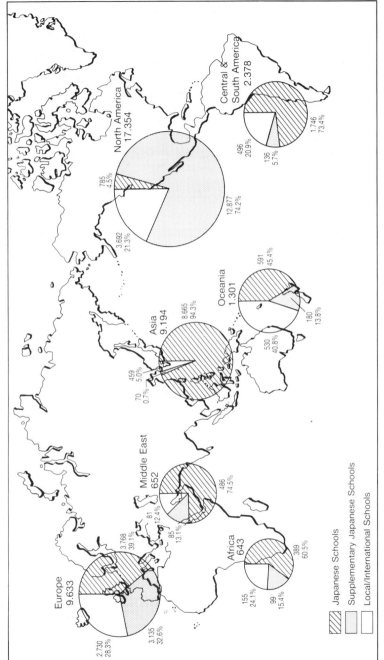

FIG. 4: Educational Facilities Attended by Japanese Children Overseas, by Region (as of 1987)
Source: Adapted from Monbushō, 1988: 6.

Japanese Schools

Supplementary Japanese Schools

Local/International Schools

North America
17.354

785
4.5%

3.692
21.3%

12.877
74.2%

Central &
South America
2.378

496
20.9%

136
5.7%

1.746
73.4%

Asia
9.194

8.665
94.3%

459
5.0%

70
0.7%

Oceania
1.301

591
45.4%

180
13.8%

530
40.8%

Europe
9.633

2.730
28.3%

3.135
32.6%

3.768
39.1%

Middle East
652

81
12.4%

85
13.1%

486
74.5%

Africa
643

155
24.1%

99
15.4%

389
60.5%

Nihonjingakkō *(Full-Time Schools)*

Michael Houser (1982: 16), describing the *Nihonjingakkō* in
London, writes that 'passing through the school's portals is like
stepping into Japan itself'. This was my own impression, not only
of the school in London but also of those in Singapore and Jakarta.
This Japanese atmosphere is one that the schools aim to create in
order to compete with schools back in Japan. It is one indication of
the Japan-centred nature of such schools. In her study of the
Japanese school in New York, Kunieda Mari (1983) found that
only 4 per cent of the children attending it intended to stay
permanently in the United States. Another indication, and one
which distinguishes *Nihonjingakkō* most clearly from the overseas
schools of North American and West European countries, is the
fact that virtually no non-Japanese faces can be seen among the
pupils. Of the 28,785 children in the seventy-six *Nihonjingakkō*
and 102 *hoshūkō* worldwide in 1984, only fifty-eight children were
not Japanese and they all attended the Sydney Japanese School
(Monbushō, 1985: 111). In contrast, of 73,664 children in some
140 American schools overseas in 1975, only 47 per cent were US
citizens, 33 per cent were from the host countries of the schools,
and the remaining 20 per cent were from various other countries
(*KSKK*, No. 9, July 1980: 6–7). Similarly, in the mid 1980s, of
110,000 students in 180 French schools overseas, only 38 per cent
were French; and of 110,000 students in 250 West German schools
overseas, only 18 per cent were German (Monbushō, 1985: 111).[5]

   It is argued by some Japanese that the small number of non-
Japanese children in *Nihonjingakkō* is due to the problems for these
children of being taught in Japanese. The great interest shown by
parents in Sydney, when the first class for Australian children in a
Nihonjingakkō opened there in 1975, would tend to refute this.
Parents in Sydney gave a variety of reasons for wanting to send
their children to the *Nihonjingakkō*, such as: 'I want them to learn
Japanese'; 'I want them to experience the excellent Japanese
education system'; and 'I want them to act as a viaduct [*kakehashi*]
for Australian–Japanese friendship' (Nakabayashi, 1981: 105).
One suspects that the response in developing countries, especially
those in South-East Asia where there is a great interest in Japanese
education, would be more positive still.

   Another, perhaps more reasonable, argument against non-

Japanese attending *Nihonjingakkō* is that there are long waiting-lists even for Japanese children and, as the schools' primary purpose is to provide a Japanese education for Japanese children overseas, they must have priority. In 1984 the Paris *Nihonjingakkō* had a waiting-list of 119 children, and the Rikkyō School in England, a private school and one of the very few overseas institutions at that time catering for children at senior-high-school level, had 227 names on its list (*KSK*, No. 132, 1984: 13).

Nihonjingakkō all over the world follow the curricula of schools back home very closely indeed, so that any child moving from, or returning to, Japan would be unlikely to find himself educationally inconvenienced by the experience. Curriculum changes are kept to a minimum, and are generally limited to those necessitated by the different environment of the school.[6] About 85 per cent of the staff, and all senior teachers, are sent from Japan (Nihon Zaigai Kigyō Kyōkai, 1981: 12). In 1984, this involved sending around 1,000 teachers to teach in *Nihonjingakkō* around the world. Almost all such teachers are on three-year secondments and there is considerable competition among teachers in Japan for these overseas postings. This is no doubt in part due to the attraction of living overseas in the comparatively protected environment offered by *Nihonjingakkō*, but there is also the incentive of a bonus added to the salary which their local education boards continue to pay them while overseas (Monbushō, 1985: 49–51).

Although it is not universal, there is often tension between Japanese employed from the Japanese community already living in the host country, who make up most of the rest of the staff of *Nihonjingakkō*, and those sent from Japan. The locally employed teachers sometimes resent the higher status and salaries of the teachers sent from Japan. They also feel that only they are capable of acting as an interface with the local community and that they have the particular skills needed for teaching in overseas schools.[7]

The remainder of teachers in *Nihonjingakkō* are non-Japanese employed locally to teach foreign languages. Every school has such teachers, and they form one of the very few differences between *Nihonjingakkō* and state schools in Japan, where native language teachers are still few and far between. The native teachers are very much peripheral to the running of the school. They do not generally take part in teachers' meetings and, even if they teach as many lessons as some of the Japanese teachers, they are generally employed on a part-time basis. They hardly ever become form teachers (*tannin no sensei*), and they are not expected to participate in school activities outside their own lessons.

What other elements of children's education in *Nihonjingakkō*, apart from native language teachers, could be said to take account of their residence in a foreign country? A few schools have programmes that are worthy of note. The special programme at the Sydney Japanese school ensures that there are two or three Australian children in each class in the lower part of the school. Joint study, however, is generally limited to music, art, and physical education. The Nichiboku (Japanese-Mexican) School in Mexico City has one campus for *kaigaisei* and another for children of Japanese-Mexican and Mexican parentage (Nakabayashi, 1981: 110–16). The two appear to be quite separate, and although the students come together at lunchtimes, on school buses, and for school festivals, there seems to be little integration.

Most *Nihonjingakkō* have some controlled interaction with the local community, such as open days and school trips, but these are generally limited and tend to decrease with time rather than increase. The principal of one South-East Asian *Nihonjingakkō* told me that the school was wary of approaches from local schools, fearing that it would be taken advantage of owing to its superior facilities. This statement emphasized the isolated nature of this school where the grounds resembled a coach park, with a fleet of twenty-nine buses bought specially to ferry children to and from school and spare them the 'dangers' of the local bus service.

The programme in the Mexico City *Nihonjingakkō* which includes non-Japanese, like that in Sydney, appears to have been set up as much from a growing awareness of the need to pacify local opinion as from a general desire to 'internationalize' the school. There have been several examples of real problems in setting up and maintaining Japanese schools overseas, and only half of the *Nihonjingakkō* actually have the security of licences. The Japanese school in Bangkok, in particular, faced strong opposition in the 1970s in the face of powerful anti-Japanese sentiment (Nakabayashi, 1981: 89–91).

In his book *Sabaku no Nihonjingakkō* ('A Japanese School in the Desert'), Motobayashi Yoshimasa (1977: 105–6) describes the problems faced in setting up a *Nihonjingakkō* in Kuwait and the insistence by the Kuwaiti authorities that they must include some Islamic culture and Arabic language in the curriculum, as well as separating boys and girls in the classroom. The fact that *Nihonjingakkō* are still set up in the face of such opposition is one measure of the importance attached to them by the Japanese. Generally speaking, the host countries give very little or no financial support to the *Nihonjingakkō*. The Japanese schools in England, for example, receive no support from the UK government at any level (Kamijō and McLean, 1983: 7). However, although they are normally set up as private schools, they receive considerable support from Monbushō. The Japanese government meets 65 per cent of the costs of the London *Nihonjingakkō*, the rest coming from students' fees (Kamijō and McLean, 1983: 3), and most *Nihonjingakkō* receive at least 50 per cent of their budget from government sources. Some parents, however, complain that they have to pay more for their children's education overseas than if they had stayed in Japan. Although a Monbushō report (1982: 40) showed that 77 per cent of companies helped their employees with educational expenses while they were overseas, a more detailed breakdown by the Japan Electrical Workers' Union (Hirano, 1984: 114) suggested that only 5.4 per cent of parents were fully supported by their companies, and that 75 per cent of parents with children at *Nihonjingakkō* had to meet the greater share of their overseas education expenses. The average expenditure in 1979 was between ¥25,000 and ¥35,000 a month, depending on the age of the child. However, this figure (which includes all educational costs incurred abroad) was not actually very much higher than for children of the same age remaining in Japan when one included money spent in the informal sector in Japan, which we shall examine later. When compared with parents sending their children to private schools in Japan, it was actually considerably less (see *JEJ*, No. 30, 1986: 1, 12).

It is significant also that the amount of money spent by central government per schoolchild overseas is far beyond that spent per schoolchild in Japan. Shibanuma (1982: 154) has calculated that the Japanese government in 1980 was spending ¥850,000 a year per child at *Nihonjingakkō* as compared to ¥450,000 per elementary-school student, ¥550,000 per middle-school student, and ¥580,000 per senior-high-school student in Japan in 1984 (Tanaka, *MS*, 21 April 1984).

Hoshūkō *(Supplementary Schools)*

As we have seen in Figure 4, *hoshūkō* tend to be found in the more educationally 'advanced' countries of the world. This is in line with the 1976 Japanese government policy statement of support for *Nihonjingakkō* mainly in countries where educational provision was considered poor by Japanese standards (Monbushō, 1985: 98–9). In other countries, parents are officially encouraged to have their children educated in local institutions. The establishment of *hoshūkō* in such countries is another indicator of the worries of Japanese parents overseas about their children's education. Where *hoshūkō* have been set up they have been able to receive only minimal support from Monbushō. This support comes mainly in the form of textbooks, which by law must be sent to all Japanese children of compulsory school-age (6 to 15). Around 4 per cent of teachers in *hoshūkō* are sent from Japan (Nihon Zaigai Kigyō Kyōkai, 1981: 12). These are often retired principals who are sent to organize and run the schools. The other 96 per cent of teachers are recruited from the local Japanese community. The majority of the teachers appear to be women, often with teaching certificates but with very little experience in the classroom. Others, such as students earning a little extra money, may have no qualifications at all.[8]

Of the *hoshūkō*, 80 per cent meet only once a week—generally on a Saturday morning—and concentrate on just a few subjects. Some, however, meet up to six days a week, providing lessons after their students have finished their local school-day. All *hoshūkō* teach Japanese language (*kokugo*), which reflects the biggest worry for overseas parents; 80 per cent of them teach mathematics. Basic mathematics education tends to be considerably more advanced in Japan than in other countries, and children who may be top in their local school overseas will often find themselves struggling in a Japanese school back home. Around 45 five per cent of *hoshūkō* teach social studies to help the children keep up with Japanese history and geography, and about 30 per cent provide some education in science subjects where, as in mathematics, children can easily find themselves behind on their return to Japan.

The impossible hope of a *hoshūkō* is that the children will be able to cram into one morning or a few evenings a whole week's syllabus. They are a compromise between attending the full-time

Nihonjingakkō and having no Japanese education at all. In reality, though, whereas classes in *Nihonjingakkō* are strikingly similar to lessons in Japan, those I observed in *hoshūkō* were very different. The children were restless and inattentive and the teachers made little effort to 'push' them. The parents, waiting next door to take their children home, were unsure about bringing their children to school on a Saturday morning while their non-Japanese school-friends were playing football or shopping in town. Some parents and children felt that perhaps the most important function of the *hoshūkō* was to provide the opportunity to meet other Japanese children and talk Japanese together. Many parents are anxious for their children not to fall behind their peers in Japan, yet at the same time ambivalent about putting them through the pressures of Japanese education while they are overseas.

This same ambivalence can be seen towards the correspondence coursework (*tsūshin kyōiku*) received by almost 60 per cent of Japanese children overseas (Monbushō, 1982: 10). These are special courses, prepared in Japan, for children to work on with their parents or by themselves at home. Many children will spend as much time on this coursework as on the homework for their overseas school, and Farkas (1983) describes the combined load as a great burden. It is questionable, however, whether the load is heavier than the combination of homework and cram school (*juku*) attendance undertaken by their peers in Japan.

Genchikō *(Local Schools) and* Kokusaigakkō *(International Schools)*

All children attending *hoshūkō* should really be included under the category of *genchikō* since the major part of their education is in local schools. Virtually all *genchikō* are schools where the first language is a major western language: English, French, Spanish, Portuguese, Italian, or German. In the vast majority, the main language is English. In areas of the world where one of these major western languages is not the first language, Japanese children will tend to go to international schools. Africa provides an interesting exception to this rule. Kusahara (1984) gives an account of Japanese schools in Africa where the small number of Japanese children, combined with their wide dispersal throughout the continent, meant that only five *Nihonjingakkō* and seven *hoshūkō* had been set up by 1984. Kusahara points out that, in Africa, a higher percentage of Japanese children go to *genchikō* than in Asia, the Middle East, or Latin America. This is because what are termed *genchikō* in Africa are in fact élite schools, dating from the colonial period, with lessons taught in English or French. The other children in the African *genchikō* tend to be European, as are most of the teachers. Kusahara (1984: 24–6) describes how the Japanese have settled in the European parts of African towns and how they have been given 'honorary white' (*meiyo hakujin*) status in South Africa.

In general, Japanese children tend to adapt well to life in local schools overseas. Ono's (1983) analysis of 'Teachers' Verdicts of Japanese Children in US Schools' picks out the following important features: the children are rather shy but eager to learn and generally very intelligent, excelling in mathematics and science; they are meticulous and very neat in all their work; despite initial language problems they tend to adapt quickly to their new environment. Some children seem to agree with this last point: 'I wonder why Japanese people can easily adjust to foreign life, but foreigners can't adjust to the Japanese life?', asks a 15-year-old boy, living in Canada, in a prize-winning essay about life overseas (Asahi Evening News and the Japan Trade Board, 1978: 130).

It would be wrong, however, to suggest, that Japanese children in *genchikō* do not have their problems. They are not used to mixing with children of other nationalities and, when there is a group of Japanese children in a class, it can be difficult to get them to split up. Perhaps most serious are stories told in schools where there is a high proportion of Japanese children, such as a school I visited in North London which had 150 children of thirty nationalities and where the Japanese contingent of thirty-nine was by some way the largest. In this school, the Japanese children tended to stick very much to themselves and were particularly exclusive of children of African origin. A teacher recounted with some shock how occasionally a Japanese child (normally a girl) of 7 or 8 would refuse to touch something an African child had touched, and how the other children would follow suit. On one occasion, this teacher was mixing paints to make a 'face colour' in a 'multi-cultural education' lesson; she started with some white and red, added some yellow, and was picking up the brown when one of the Japanese children struck at her hand saying that one could not have brown in a face colour.

Overseas Educational Careers

Statistics on children attending different types of educational institutions overseas offer only a static picture of their educational careers. In developing countries, in line with Japanese government policy, children tend to have very little contact with the local community. In these countries, *Nihonjingakkō* cover the whole range of Japanese compulsory education and are attended by the majority of Japanese children. Children who do not go to the *Nihonjingakkō* go to élite international schools with the children of other foreign residents, where they normally use English or French as the first language. There may be attempts to supplement this education by attendance at a Saturday *hoshūkō* and, almost certainly, by receiving correspondence coursework from Japan.

In developed countries, Japanese children generally attend local schools until they are 9 or 10, at which age their parents tend to feel it would harm their chances in the Japanese educational system to remain where they are, and, therefore, move them, if possible, to the nearest *Nihonjingakkō*.[9] By the age of 15, however, the vast majority of Japanese children are receiving education back home. Compulsory education in Japan finishes at the age of 15 and the government does not feel compelled to continue supplying an education for children overseas beyond this age. However, 96 per cent of all Japanese children continue their education into senior high school, and, in the case of the type of families from which *kikokushijo* come, the proportion would be closer to a 100 per cent. Many children, especially boys, return to Japan by themselves by the age of 15, either going to boarding-school or staying with relatives while they continue their education. A significant proportion return with their mothers, leaving their fathers to carry on working overseas alone.

Table III, however, illustrates not only the desire of parents for their children to receive a Japanese education after the age of 15 but also the scarcity of Japanese senior high schools overseas. In 1983 Rikkyō School in England had just over 200 children enrolled and more than 200 on its waiting-list, and each year the entrance exam was taken by more than twice as many children as there were places.[10] But this area of educational provision has seen a big increase in recent years. One of the final recommendations of the National Council on Educational Reform (1987: 59) was that more senior high schools should be available overseas, and in 1987–8 four

more were opened, bringing the total to six—all private, and four in
Britain. Reasons for this sudden increase will become clear later.

Not every overseas child, however, follows a typical educational
career. Shibanuma (1982: 155) has enumerated the different views
which inform the decision of parents regarding the education of
their children overseas:

(i) Japan is a homogeneous society so, in order to be successful
in it, children need to be educated in a Japanese way. They need to
be able to adapt to Japan as soon as they return home, so overseas
schools, even in developed countries, should have an entirely
Japanese system.

(ii) Japan should play a major role in international society and
so there should be no need for any Japanese schools overseas, let
alone supplementary schools. Children should go to local schools
overseas.

(iii) Compromise: it is very important to have a Japanese-style
education but it is also important to have internationalistic ideas, so
if there are going to be full-time Japanese schools they should be
open, letting in local children and adapting to the local education
system; or, if there are going to be only local schools, then some
kind of correspondence courses should be set up to provide a
supplementary Japanese education.

It is important to keep in mind these differing viewpoints as we
move on to look at models of Japanese communities overseas.

MODELS OF JAPANESE COMMUNITIES OVERSEAS

Ebuchi Kazukimi (1983: 26–7), an anthropologist who has undertaken considerable research on Japanese communities overseas, has
developed two models which he calls the 'North American Model' (A)
and the 'Asian Model' (B) (Fig. 5). He describes them thus:

The 'North American Model' and the 'Asian Model' represent two
different types of Japanese community overseas each with its own
characteristics. The differences in lifestyle can be explained by the host
country's history and geography and variations in political, social and
economic conditions. At the same time there are differences in attitudes of
Japanese towards societies in which they live, namely a yearning for [*dōkei*]
or an inferiority complex [*rettōkan*] about western culture; and a
superiority complex [*yūetsukan*] about Asian culture.

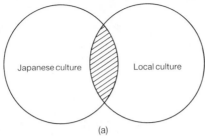

(a)

North American model

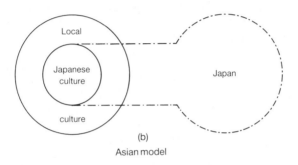

(b)

Asian model

FIG. 5: Ebuchi's Models of Japanese Overseas Communities
Source: Adapted from Ebuchi, 1980: 172–3.

Ebuchi's 'Asian' model is comparable to the 'Ugly Japanese' image (cf. Hidaka, 1984: 38–40; Mouer and Sugimoto, 1986: 53) which is particularly used in the case of Japanese in Asian countries. The proverb *tabi no haji wa kakisute* ('when you leave Japan, leave all shame behind you') is often quoted in the context of Japanese sex tours to Korea and South-East Asia. Hara Kimi (1983: 1–3), having spent two years as a visiting professor in the Philippines and Indonesia, delivered a tirade against the 'ego-centric behavior' of the Japanese living in Asia. She referred to Japanese wives living like 'queens'—knowing nothing of the country they were living in; treating their domestic servants scarcely like human beings; and living in isolated 'island' communities. A large study of the Japanese communities in Singapore and Manila, by a research team from Kyoto University, tends to support this image of a closed community. Over half of the Japanese children interviewed said they had no native friend at all, and over 80 per cent that they had no, or virtually no, contact of any kind with local children (Kobayashi, 1979: 242–3). This image of the 'closed community' is often taken to be general to all developing countries: a report in the *Asahi Shinbun* describes similar scenarios in Brazil, Kenya, and Mexico and *Nihonjinagakkō* are frequently blamed for fostering such attitudes (*AS*, 22 February 1989).

The overall picture, however, is rather more complex than Ebuchi's models suggest. There appear to be contradictory data from both regions of the world examined. In the case of the 'American Model', for example, some have argued that, if one uses indices such as intermarriage, behavioural assimilation, and absence of discrimination, the Japanese appear to be the most integrated of all Asian immigrant groups in the United States (Cheung, 1976; Tsukashima, *JTW*, 4 November 1984). Yet the expatriate community in Los Angeles, described by Minoura (1979), could scarcely have had less contact with the local society. In her analysis of the significant elements in the adaptation of Japanese children to local life overseas, Minoura (1979: 187–90) discovered that, in her sample of sixty mothers, who had lived on average five-and-a-half years in the United States, 62 per cent had very limited or no ability in English and a further 26 per cent had enough only for everyday conversation.

There appears, therefore, to be a clear contrast between sections of the Japanese communities overseas which are totally integrated and those that remain exclusive. This contrast between either almost complete, or virtually no, assimilation also exists among the Japanese in Britain. There is a very closed community of expatriates, centred around north London, with its own shops and restaurants, while, on the other hand, there are also Japanese who have been completely assimilated into the local community.

The same distinction also appears to exist in countries which Ebuchi includes in his 'Asian Model'. Musikasinthorn and Ressler (1980: 16–19), writing about the Japanese community in Bangkok, describe a sharp contrast between the short-term residents, or 'rootless transients', who make up the 5,000-strong Japanese Association, and the much smaller group of 'independent long-term residents': the former take the ashes of their deceased back to their graveyards in Japan, while the latter utilize the services of the Japanese shrine and cinerarium in Bangkok.

Although one must be careful not to over-generalize, it would seem that the lifestyle of Japanese overseas is not determined so much by the host country as by the context in which the individuals left Japan. For a Japanese, one of the most significant aspects of leaving Japan is whether the departure is accompanied by the *intention* to return, since this involves a conscious decision whether to retain Japanese identity. On the one hand those who go overseas not intending to return to Japan (indeed, in some cases, intending to escape from it) appear to assimilate aspects of their host country quickly. Immediate assimilation, when numbers are large, may be impossible, but generally, by the second generation a new 'culture'—Japanese–Brazilian; Japanese–American—has developed (Maeyama, 1984*b*; Connor, 1977). On the other hand the recent advent, and increase in numbers, of 'short-term' Japanese expatriates has led to the growth of 'Japan Towns', in the sense of 'China Towns', around the world over the past ten years. Those living in Japan Towns appear to focus on maintaining their Japanese identity, a mentality which Minoura (1984: 106–9) describes as *kari-zumai ishiki* (awareness of the temporary nature of one's stay).

It is still, however, an oversimplification to suggest that the attitude of Japanese towards their host country is determined only by their intention (or otherwise) of returning to Japan. This is illustrated by the fact that the education received by short-term Japanese residents in Britain is determined as much by their age, their gender, where they live in the country, their parents' views on education, and their financial resources, as on the length of their stay. The result is far from homogeneous: some parents feel it necessary to send their children to the *Nihonjingakkō* in London, others voluntarily keep them at local schools and send them to a *hoshūkō* on Saturdays; some send their senior-high-school-age children back to Japan to a boarding-school or to stay with relatives, others in Japan send children of the same age to Britain to enter an international, or minor public, school. In an important series of surveys, Kawabata and Suzuki (1981, 1982) and Kawabata, Suzuki, and Nagaoka (1982) identified two types of expatriate Japanese parents, both of which intended to return to Japan. Suzuki, in a later article (1984), termed these two groups *genchi shikō no kokusaiha* (an international faction which tends towards the local culture) and *kikokugo no kyōiku jūshi no kokunaiha* (a parochial faction which emphasizes the importance of a Japanese education for children on their return to Japan). As a result of all these different factors, the experiences of Japanese children overseas fall into the different categories described by Furnham and Bochner (1986: 16) as 'monocultural' (i.e. purely Japanese), 'bicultural' (i.e. Japanese and host society), and 'multicultural' (i.e. Japanese, host society, and other national groups resident in the host society).

Such pluralism tends to undermine Ebuchi's rather simplistic models of Japanese communities overseas (Fig. 5). His models do, however, reflect official Japanese government policy towards education abroad, as well as a popular cognitive hierarchy, in Japan, of the value attached to time spent in different countries (see Moeran, 1983: 101). Some *kikokushijo* may feel that they are distinguished on the basis of where they received their overseas experience. As one girl who had spent several years in South Korea writes (*EK*, No. 92, July 1985: 14):

When one hears the word 'overseas' (*gaikoku*), surely the first places that come to mind are America or European countries. When I am asked by my friends, 'What countries have you been to, up to now?', I answer in a small voice, 'I've been to Korea'. This is not because I do not especially like Korea. Indeed during the fifteen years of my life, many of my best memories come from that country. The reason that I use this small voice is because of the image which Korea has among those around me.

However, even if some *kikokushijo* may personally feel that they are treated differently depending on where they spent their time overseas, officially no distinction is generally made between them on any basis—where they went overseas, for how long, or at what age. They are all simply classified as *kikokushijo*.

THE RETURNEE COMMUNITY IN JAPAN

As the number of students going overseas has increased, so proportionally has the number of those returning to Japan. Official statistics on *kikokushijo* have been kept only since 1971, with a gap between 1973 and 1976, but they are worth quoting in full to illustrate this upward trend. As can be seen from Table V, the total number of *kikokushijo* multiplied by five during the 1970s, and increased by a further 40 per cent during the first half of the 1980s. As Table VI shows, the *kikokushijo* are concentrated mainly around Tokyo and Osaka. This reflects the jobs their parents

TABLE V: School Levels to which *Kikokushijo* Return (1971–86)

	Elementary School (ages 6–11)	Middle School (ages 12–15)	Senior School (ages 16–18)	Total
1971	896	435	212	1,543
1972	1,423	515	242	2,180
1973	2,241	685	203	3,129
–				
–				
1976	3,225	1,000	373	4,598
1977	3,963	1,168	628	5,759
1978	4,545	1,301	672	6,518
1979	4,563	1,420	581	6,564
1980	5,137	1,500	867	7,504
1981	5,723	1,874	873	8,740
1982	6,215	2,275	1,073	9,563
1983	6,302	2,258	1,224	9,784
1984	6,207	2,291	1,280	9,778
1985	6,325	2,564	1,288	10,177
1986	6,466[a]	2,531[b]	1,501[c]	10,498

Source: Monbushō, 1988; 57.
[a] 61.6 per cent.   [b] 24.1 per cent.   [c] 14.3 per cent.

TABLE VI: *Kikokushijo* by Region of Japan to which they Returned between April 1986 and March 1987

Region	Number of *kikokushijo*	Percentage
Tokyo (Kantō) Area	7,211	68.7
Osaka/Kyoto (Kinki) Area	1,659	15.8
Kyushu	308	2.9
Hokkaido	101	1.0
Shikoku	55	0.5
Other	1,164	11.1
TOTAL	10,498	100.0

Source: Monbushō, 1988: 58.

undertake overseas, since most major government, business, and academic institutions are based in these two areas. This concentration in two of the major Japanese cities has led, in part, to the highlighting of the situation of the *kikokushijo*. These urban areas are also significantly the areas with the best educational facilities in Japan.

RETURNEE SCHOOLS (*UKEIREKŌ*) AND THE SPECIAL UNIVERSITY ENTRANCE NETWORK (*TOKUBETSU WAKU*)

What happens to *kikokushijo* when they return to Japan? Although it is not clear how they reached such figures, Murase (1980: 47) and Katō (1986: 62), respectively, suggest that about 20 per cent of *kikokushijo* in the late 1970s and 50 per cent in the mid 1980s attended schools which were part of the special education system for returnee schoolchildren. These schools are known by a variety of different names, but one generic term is *ukeirekō*, which literally means 'reception school'. One of these schools has been in operation since the 1930s, another was set up in 1964, but the vast majority, even if they already existed as educational institutions, have only become part of the *kikokushijo* education network since the late 1960s.

The type of education offered by *ukeirekō*, however, varies greatly. The schools can be categorized first by their status (i.e. national, public, or private) and then by level (i.e. elementary, middle, and senior). They can also be categorized according to their principal method of treating returnees: in particular, whether they have separate *kikokushijo* streams or whether *kikokushijo* are mixed in with other children.

Over and above the central government system of education for *kikokushijo*, several prefectural education authorities have set up their own schemes, such as the 'centre' schools of Tokyo's twenty-three wards which take a high proportion of *kikokushijo* (*DY*, 15 January 1984). By 1986, fourteen of Japan's forty-seven prefectural boards of education gave *kikokushijo* special consideration in application procedures, screening, and other matters, while a further twenty-one planned to introduce a similar system in the near future. Only three did not allow *kikokushijo* with language problems to attend classes in a lower grade for a short time while they caught up (*JTW*, 22 February 1986). As a result of these policies, 640 schools were specially designated by local education authorities to accept *kikokushijo* in 1988.

Those who return to Japan at senior-high-school level, or even later, may be interested not so much in which schools they can apply to, but in which universities. A very striking phenomenon has been the setting up of a special quota (*tokubetsu waku*) for *kikokushijo* in certain departments of more than half of the national universities—including the top ones such as Tokyo, Kyoto, Keiō, Waseda—as well as many private and public universities.[11] *Kikokushijo*, who meet the necessary criteria, may gain entrance either through a special entrance examination, as a result of their overseas qualifications and reports, or through an interview. In the case of Tsukuba University, a student who has studied for two or more years overseas may be admitted on the basis of a recommendation from his high school, an interview, and the composition of a short essay (Katō, *KEJ*, Vol. 2, 1983: 182). Statistics from 1985 suggest that over 90 per cent of *kikokushijo* who entered Japanese universities did so through this special system (Monbushō, 1988: 87). The significance of this will become clear in Chapter 4 when we take a look at the Japanese educational system.

GOVERNMENT FINANCE

There are three main aspects to a discussion of government financial aid for returnee children: firstly, the proportional increase in the amount of aid over recent decades; secondly, the change in policy as to which government ministry supplies the aid; and thirdly, the total amount of aid currently being granted.

If, like Hirano (1984: 27), we take 1969 as our base line, the overall expenditure on overseas and returnee education had increased some seventy-fold by 1985. The Foreign Ministry contribution, however, which in 1967 accounted for 97.6 per cent of all government expenditure, had multiplied only 6.8 times by 1985, while Monbushō expenditure went up 2566.4 times in the same period to account for 90 per cent of the total contribution by 1985. This trend is illustrated in Fig. 6.[12]

A breakdown of government expenditure on *kikokushijo* education shows that, of the ¥16 billion spent in 1987, by far the greatest proportion—over 85 per cent—was spent on sending teachers overseas and paying their salaries (Monbushō, 1988: 25).

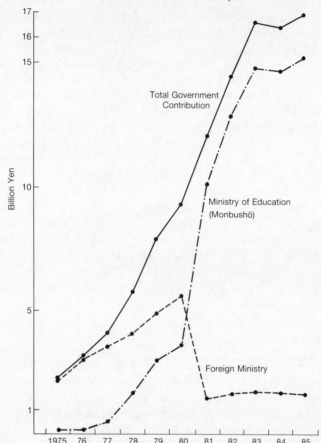

FIG. 6: Increase in Government Aid for Overseas Children's Education (1975–85)
Source: Adapted from Monbushō, 1985: 23.

COMMERCIAL AND VOLUNTARY SUPPORT ORGANIZATIONS FOR *KIKOKUSHIJO*

Along with the growth of returnee schools, a special body, the Kaigai Shijo Kyōiku Shinkō Zaidan (known in English as Japan Overseas Educational Services), was set up in 1971 to advise on overseas education and supervise the establishment of Japanese schools abroad. It also prepares correspondence courses, publishes a monthly magazine (*Kaigai Shijo Kyōiku*), and offers advice to departing and returning children. To this last end, it has three advice centres (*sōdan shitsu*), which operate full-time in Tokyo and Osaka and part-time in Nagoya. Between them the *sōdan shitsu* received some 8,000 enquiries in 1984 (Hasebe, 1985: 169). Kobayashi (1978*b*: 16) describes the Kaigai Shijo Kyōiku Shinkō Zaidan as 'a good example of the voluntarism characterizing overseas education'. It is supported by some 600 companies with overseas operations (Monbushō, 1985: 123), but 55 per cent of its funding now actually comes from Monbushō. We shall see later how it managed to secure this government support.

Companies with a large number of workers overseas (such as JAL, Marubeni, Tokyo Bank, Mitsukoshi Shōji, Mitsui Bussan) also have their own small offices concerned with the welfare of these employees and their families. They keep employees informed of the latest news concerning overseas and returnee education through regular newsletters and may even offer direct advice. JAL has has even set up a school to help *kikokushijo* on their return. Other organizations, both voluntary and commercial, have also seen a need to provide for *kikokushijo*. Many *kikokushijo*, for example, attend special conversation classes in the language schools run by foreign native speakers, in all big Japanese towns and cities. The commercial sector also offers more specialist services, as illustrated by the large number of advertisements carried in *Kaigai Shijo Kyōiku*, the most widely distributed magazine for overseas and returnee children. This magazine carries advertisements for textbooks, reference books, cassette tapes, video machines, schools with dormitories, and institutions which run individual guidance courses for *kikokushijo*, such as the Fukushi Kokusai Kyōiku Academy (Fukushi International Education Academy) which offers 'Quick Adaptation, Supplementary Teaching, and Advice on Educational Careers'.

The voluntary sector is best represented by an organization called the Kokusai Jidō Bunko Kyōkai. This was set up by a group of high-powered returnee mothers, based around the diplomatic corps, with the aid of a British writer of children's books. It has branches all over Japan, and runs weekly evening meetings to which children who have lived abroad are taken by their mothers and where they are made to speak the language they learnt overseas. (This is generally English, although there are also branches specializing in French and German.) The Kokusai Jidō Bunko Kyōkai has also proved an effective lobbying group for better government provision for *kikokushijo*.

LITERATURE

Another voluntary organization is a support group for *kikokushijo* called META, which was started by a bilingual returnee. One of the main aims in setting up META was to challenge the mainstream perception of *kikokushijo* in Japan—a perception widely disseminated through the large amount of literature on the subject. Official statistics suggest that Japan is the most literate nation in the world, with one of the highest publication rates for all forms of literature. This is one reason why certain bookshops in areas of Tokyo and Osaka, where the head offices of Japan's government departments and biggest companies are located, include special sections marked Kaigai Kikokushijo Mondai ('The Returnee Children Problem').

The literature on *kikokushijo* can be divided into several distinct categories. Firstly, there are essays by overseas and returnee children about their personal experiences. Most of these are compilations of prize-winning essays sponsored either by the Kaigai Shijo Kyōiku Shinkō Zaidan or by various overseas regional organizations such as the Ō-Nichi Kyōkai (European–Japanese Association). They contain polished, well-constructed essays or poems; two popular categories are *haiku* and *tanka*, the indigenous and rather esoteric Japanese poetic forms. Such compositions appear to be judged as much for their style as for their content and can be seen partly as an attempt to maintain Japanese language ability overseas. These works, however, provide interesting insights into the children's own perceptions of their position, which are so often missing from the debate.

A second category of literature on *kikokushijo* is composed of accounts by adults of their time overseas: some of them about their own experiences, some of them reflections on their children's experiences. Konishi Sayaka (1983), for example, for twelve years brought up her children in Washington, where her husband worked as a journalist, and she uses her experience to describe the benefits and disadvantages of the Japanese and American educational systems and to offer her prescription for successful adaptation from one to the other. A similar account is presented by Hatano Kanji (1973) from an analysis of the published diaries of Japanese parents who have lived in the United States, West Germany, China, France, England, and the Soviet Union.

A third category consists of advice manuals on Japanese schools and universities for overseas and returnee children. Almost all of these are published under the auspices of the Kaigai Shijo Kyōiku Shinkō Zaidan, although earlier guides were sponsored by national newspapers, the *Asahi Shinbun* and, particularly, the *Nikkei Shinbun*. These manuals present a good source of information on official attitudes towards overseas and returnee children.

A fourth category is comprised of more popular discussions of the whole phenomenon of *kikokushijo*. Some of these books are written from personal experience by educators and teachers (e.g. Inui and Sono, 1977). In general, however, they are accounts, aimed at a wider public, of serious research undertaken on *kikokushijo* education. Japan has a tradition of producing such popular books out of serious research, a genre known as *keimōsho*, which Hata and Smith (1983: 362) describe as 'attractively bound, popular paperbacks of a semi-academic and highly readable nature'. These constitute 'an important "second income" for Japanese academics who, up until recently, were underpaid by Western standards' (ibid. 385). The works of Kobayashi (1981), Kondō Hiroshi (1984), Nakane Chie (1972), and Tsunoda Tadanobu (1985) can be included in this genre. We shall examine the ideas put across in these books in the next chapter.

The major source of views and information on *kikokushijo*, however, is the mass media. A cursory search through three of the major newspapers—*Mainichi*, *Yomiuri*, and *Nihon Keizai*, which have a combined daily circulation of over twenty-three million copies (Keizai Kōhō Center, 1985: 94)—during a four-week period in mid-1984, turned up seven articles directly concerned with *kikokushijo*. I would estimate that, from the mid-1970s, there may have been as many as one item a week on *kikokushijo* reaching a national audience through newspapers, popular magazines, and television programmes.

The media have therefore provided a very important platform for those concerned with *kikokushijo* to present their case to the widest possible audience. The issue of *kikokushijo* has also, on the other hand, provided the media, particularly the newspapers, with material to pursue their own causes. Japanese newspapers have the highest *per capita* readership in the world (Foreign Press Center, 1982: 12) and although all major newspapers in Japan profess political neutrality, as Reischauer (1983: 199) says, 'most of them tend to lean slightly to the left of center and to be critical of the government'. The so-called *intelli* (intellectuals) who write for the papers have often seen the treatment of *kikokushijo* as a good basis on which to attack the conservatism of the Japanese government.

RESEARCHERS

There are several different ways of assessing the amount of research carried out in Japan on *kikokushijo*: the number of researchers who claim to be undertaking research on the subject; the amount of work they produce; the number of seminars they support; the amount of money they spend. Since, as we shall see, I became almost as interested in the community of researchers as in the children themselves, I shall give some width to all these dimensions.

The Ibunkakan Kyōiku Gakkai (Cross-Cultural Education Study Association) is the largest association in Japan of individuals interested in overseas and returnee education. Its three-day 1984 conference in Fukuoka was entirely given over to discussion of *kikokushijo* education. In 1982, it had 170 members of whom one-third stated *kikokushijo* as their specific research interest. But this association is centred on only one of the major research institutes (Kyoto University) and is very much the creation of one individual (Kobayashi Tetsuya). There are other major research initiatives into *kikokushijo* education and adaptation: at Tokyo University (under Azuma Hiroshi); at the International Christian University (under Hoshino Akira); at Tsukuba University (bilingualism under Matsubara Tatsuya and psychiatric adjustment under Inamura Hiroshi); at Kobe University (under Kawabata Matsundo); and also at Sophia (Jōchi) University (under Anne Murase).

Since the nature of the Japanese university system means that graduate students tend to stick closely to the fields of interest of their supervisors and professors, there is also a large core of post-graduate research into the *kikokushijo* phenomenon. The study of *kikokushijo* also seems to have become popular among Japanese students taking degrees overseas.[13]

Apart from these academic researchers, there are two major centres of practical research on *kikokushijo*. One is the Kaigai Shijo Kyōiku Shitsu (Overseas Children's Education Office) at Monbushō, which collects data on overseas and returnee children, publishes up-to-date statistics, carries out surveys, and oversees the Ministry's financial intervention. The second is Tokyo Gakugei Daigaku Kaigai Shijo Kyōiku Centre (The Tokyo Gakugei University Overseas Children's Education Centre), which was set up as a twin institute to Japan Overseas Educational Services to carry out research on overseas educational projects, bilingual education, adaptation problems, and the teaching of overseas and returnee children. It is based on the Tokyo Gakugei Campus which is the site of the first national—and, until the late 1970s, the best-known and most researched—school for *kikokushijo*. Its senior staff are university professors and retired returnee schoolteachers, and altogether it boasts a staff of around thirty members.

Among them, these researchers, both academic and otherwise, produce a huge amount of literature on *kikokushijo*. Much of that produced by the larger research units is highly quantitative and often carried out for reasons of expediency. Much of the work of individual researchers tends to concentrate on case studies of particular children. We shall look in the next chapter at the assumptions inherent in both these categories of work.

Not only do all the different research units produce a massive amount of literature, they also sponsor and organize an impressive array of seminars and conferences. Schools, companies, ministries, universities, and private organizations convene their own seminars, often annually, and frequently with the same speakers and similar audiences. In the twelve months from June 1984 to May 1985, I attended three two- or three-day seminars on returnee children in Japan with around 200, 60, and 100 participants respectively.[14] Most of those attending the first two of these seminars were teachers of *kikokushijo* and those at the third were researchers, but in all three seminars there was an interesting mix of both these groups.

It is less easy to give an indication of the amount of money spent on *kikokushijo* research. In part this is because much is undertaken in the course of normal duties and covered by normal salaries. Monbushō, however, supports not only its own office, the Kaigai Shijo Kyōiku Shitsu, but also the Tokyo Gakugei Research Centre and the Kyoto University unit. The Gakugei Centre receives over

¥35 million a year to support its activities (Monbushō, 1988: 25), and the Kyoto University unit was granted very substantial funds to produce its work in the mid-to-late 1970s.

In this chapter the main 'actors' involved in discussions about, and treatment of, *kikokushijo*—the parents, the government, the schools, the mass media, the support groups, the researchers, and the children themselves—have been briefly introduced. Two points, in particular, need to be stressed: the vast amount of attention which the subject of *kikokushijo* has received, and the wide range of children who are treated as *kikokushijo* on their return to Japan. Next, we need to examine the dominant image of *kikokushijo* in Japan.

3

The Cultural 'Problems' of *Kikokushijo*

In 1984, one of Japan's most respected academic publishers, Hyōronsha, produced the twenty-first volume in its Education Titles (*Kyōiku Sensho*) Series. This book, entitled *Sāsha no Funtōki* ('The Chronicle of Sāsha's Hard Struggle') and subtitled, rather more revealingly, *Yattsu no Kuni no Gakkō de Manande* ('Learning in the Schools of Eight Different Countries'), made quite an impact when it appeared. Its author wrote under the *nom-de-plume* Asai Satoru and the tale he had to tell was an extraordinary one.

Satoru was born in Japan but, when he was 6, as he was about to enter elementary school, his father, a railway engineer, was instructed by his employer to go overseas and decided to take young Satoru along with him. Thus began Satoru's adventures since, even by Japanese businessmen's standards, his father was excessively peripatetic. In eight years he went to no fewer than seven foreign countries—West Germany, Holland, Austria, the Soviet Union, Egypt, Israel, and the United States—and in each, Satoru attended a local school. As a result, he found himself participating in military training in Israel and, in New York, becoming involved with a gang of juvenile delinquents.

Despite these potentially difficult experiences, Satoru flourished. Indeed, he writes of the great benefits he derived from having attended this succession of schools overseas. Life took a sharp downward turn, however, when he returned to a Japanese state junior high school. His years abroad meant that he had almost completely lost his Japanese language and this made him an object of ridicule. He was teased mercilessly about his 'funny' Japanese until one day he turned on his tormentors and beat them up so seriously that he was placed under the supervision of a probation officer (*hogoku*).

At this point, though, life took a turn for the better as Satoru was given automatic entry to a good senior high school through the special system for *kikokushijo*. When it came to university entrance examinations his overseas experience again paid off in his favour. He applied to the foreign-language department of Tokyo University

(Tōdai) and, since he had managed to retain his German so well, was accepted at the first attempt.

It was during Satoru's third year at Tōdai that his book came to be written. He had taken a course in comparative education and met a professor in that department who, impressed by Satoru's experiences, suggested that he write a book. This professor had then persuaded Hyōronsha to publish the book both for its comparative accounts of foreign education systems and also for its good examples of the 'problems' faced by returnee children. The book sold well and Hyōronsha were soon receiving letters of appreciation from readers, particularly schoolteachers. As one teacher wrote: 'There are many children in my class coming from and going overseas, and I definitely want to use this book as an inspiration to them.' The *Mainichi Shinbun* also picked the book up and, on 14 December 1984, gave it an excellent review, complete with photographs of the author and one of his overseas schools, and revealed his real name. The review was headed *Shōichi kara Chū-san made Ten-ten-ten-ten-ten-ten-ten-tenkō Hakka Koku* ('Eight Changes of School and Country between the Ages of 6 and 15') and down the middle ran the large banner headline *Nihon ga Ichiban Warukatta* ('Japan was the Worst'). The main sub-heading read simply *Ijime* ('Bullying').

As a case history of a returnee child in Japan, *Sāsha no Funtōki* would be an excellent example but for one little difficulty—the author had never been outside Japan in his life. Two long-term acquaintances of Satoru saw the *Mainichi Shinbun* article, recognized his face and name, and informed the newspaper's editor that the author had in fact received all his schooling in Saitama Prefecture just outside Tokyo. Informed of this, Hyōronsha moved swiftly and, in a nice example of publishing pragmatism, offered a refund to anyone who had already bought a copy of the book, and reclassified remaining copies as fiction.[1]

The above story could simply be put down to the fantasy life of one individual. Indeed, the *Shūkan Asahi*, from which the above account is drawn (Kubota, 1985: 24–7), did run an investigative piece on Satoru's background by interviewing old schoolmates and neighbours, but discovered only that Satoru was excellent at foreign languages and had been something of a loner. More interesting, though, than the individual perspective is the fact that Satoru's account managed to convince not only the professor of comparative education who recommended it, and the publishers of a specialist series of books on education, but even teachers of returnee children themselves. Satoru himself apologized profusely for having embarrassed both his professor and the publishers, but insisted that he had simply missed the chance to tell the truth, that the book was based on careful research and was accurate. This story therefore provides an excellent illustration of the massive media interest in, and the readiness of the Japanese (even specialists) to accept the popular perception of, the education of Japanese children overseas and their 'problems' on their return.

PERCEPTIONS OF THE OVERSEAS EXPERIENCE OF JAPANESE CHILDREN

We have seen, in the previous chapter, the great variety of ways in which Japanese children may experience life overseas. However, just as any child who returns from overseas is labelled *kikokushijo*, so any child receiving education overseas is called *kaigaishijo* (overseas child). Such overseas experience is generally viewed as exciting and interesting, yet problematic. Children who live overseas are considered different from those who have never left Japan, and, importantly, they often come to accept this image, as illustrated in the following essay (Kaigai Shijo Kyōiku Shinkō Zaidan, 1984: 124–5) by a 14-year-old boy, who at the time of writing was attending a local school in Houston and a supplementary Japanese school once a week. The title, *Wareware Kaigaishijo* ('We Overseas Children'), suggests that he perceived a common thread in the experience of all such children.

On a certain fierce sultry midsummer's day . . . I was pondering to myself such questions as: . . . what did it mean to be a *kaigaishijo*, what sort of a person was it? I stood up and went to fetch a Japanese dictionary. This is what was written: *kaigai*—'countries across the sea'; *shijo*—'child or children'. How commonplace; surely *kaigaishijo* has a deeper meaning than that. A *kaigaishijo* is a Japanese who, when he first goes abroad, can't speak the local language. Then, over a period of two or three years he begins gradually to become unlike normal Japanese. This is not a process of adaptation to the local culture [*genchika*] but the development of the unique personality of the *kaigaishijo*.

In my case, I came to the United States six years ago. Last year, when I went back to Japan for a while, the thing which struck me most forcibly was the sheer number of people. That is exactly the impression that Americans receive when they go to Japan. I have been in America so long now, that I have become almost completely Americanized [*Americajinka*]. But not totally. When I went back to Japan, when I arrived in Tokyo, tears began to trickle down my cheeks. Then, when I was walking along the streets of Osaka too, I really had the feeling that I had returned to my home town [*furusato*]. It is as if I am at the same time both Americanized and Japanese . . . . However much I become assimilated to American culture, there are some things which it is important for me to do as a Japanese. It is a real tragedy [*hijō ni kanashii tachiba ni aru*], but *kaigaishijo* must learn to live by finding a fine balance between Japanese society and the local society. This is what makes *kaigaishijo* unique. This balance, however, between Japanese society and the local society cannot be obtained so easily. For example, if I receive a good report at my American school, if I am praised by an American, I accept the compliment and simply say, 'Thank you'. However, if the same thing was said to me by a Japanese, I would have to say, 'It's nothing, it's nothing'. That's not such an easy thing to do.

. . . The way of thinking of *kaigaishijo* is also unique since, although they are Japanese, their way of thinking is a little different from that of most Japanese. For example, there is the *kaigaishijo* way of thinking about foreigners and foreign languages. *Kaigaishijo* gradually come to like the local people [*genchijin*], to speak the language, and try as hard as possible to get on cordially with the people of that country . . . . However, most Japanese junior-high-school children, since they hate English, say that it is sufficient for Japanese to speak Japanese. This is something which we *kaigaishijo* cannot believe. Only in Japan do people think like this.

Kaigaishijo render service to the world, not just to Japan, not just to one single country anywhere. They think in terms of the whole world; that is to say, of becoming 'People of the World' [*sekaijin*] . . . . Thus it is that *kaigaishijo* are not just 'children across the sea', but people with unique, un-Japanese personalities and ways of thinking.

In another article in a daily newspaper (*DY*, 4 January 1985), a returnee describes herself as an 'Earthman', and such self-applied soubriquets referring to their 'international status' are common among *kikokushijo*. These examples illustrate how Japanese children overseas tend to define, or accept a definition of, themselves not only as different from other Japanese but also as belonging to a group which shares important characteristics. But the enthusiasm and idealism of *kaigaishijo*, apparent in the above essay, are marred by the constant worry as to what will happen on their return to Japan. As a Monbushō survey (1982: 14) shows, this constitutes a major fear for all overseas Japanese.

EXTREME VIEWS OF RETURNEE 'PROBLEMS'

When we look at a few of the admittedly more extreme popular images of the reactions of *kikokushijo* on their return to Japan, it is easier to understand the source of *kaigaishijo* worries. In December 1982, most of the Japanese-language newspapers reported the story of a 19-year-old who had murdered his uncle and aunt with a baseball bat. In Japan's tight-knit families, murder of kin is not rare, but what was picked up by the media was that this particular boy had lived for eleven years in the United States, and that his Japanese was not perfect. According to police reports, his uncle had mocked him for his poor Japanese and, in a rage, the boy had committed the crime. The newspaper headlines read 'Returned Boy', 'Japanese Language Complex', and 'Despised for his Poor Japanese', and almost all the articles added, in parenthesis, that there were, at the time, more than 30,000 young Japanese in schools abroad (see *AS*, 12 December 1982; *JT*, 19 January 1983).

In March 1985, a similar case occurred when another 19-year-old suddenly declared that his mother was the devil and threw her from the window of their second-floor flat in Osaka (see Satō, 1985). The reasons for this extreme behaviour were declared to be slightly more complicated than in the earlier case. This time the headlines ran 'Migration Overseas, Change of School, Father Living Away for Work . . . . The "Composite Causes" for a First-Year Exam Retake Student who Killed his Mother'. This young man's father had been posted to Fukuoka the year before and had taken a flat there, leaving the family in Osaka—an example of the *tanshin funin* phenomenon which we have already discussed. The boy had also had to change school in Japan; the negative public perception of which is well summed up by Yokoshima (1977: 142), who writes that 'according to children, nothing is more unpleasant than changing schools'. In the article, however, Satō gives greatest prominence to the subject of the young man's experience overseas. The coverage of the murder included a photograph of the

Nihonjingakkō in Brazil which the young man had attended for four years, the comments of a friend from elementary school in Japan who remembered him as very bright and active before he had gone overseas, and an interview with a professor of psychiatry, Inamura Hiroshi, who has gained a reputation for his expertise in such cases. Inamura is reported (Satō, 1985: 201) as saying:

The children in the overseas Japanese schools are all about the same level, they are all well behaved. They constitute a kind of 'pure strain' [*junsui baiyō*], right? Therefore, when they return to a Japanese school, to a completely different set of circumstances with bullying all around them, there appear to be some children who cannot adapt.

If the experience of returnees does not drive them to homicide, then there is always the opposite extreme. An account of the suicide of a 20-year-old high school student, who had returned from Los Angeles all of five years earlier, was headlined 'Repatriate Student Leaps From High Rise' (*DY*, 13 December 1983). The fact that he was a returnee was deemed to be significant although he left no note and any discussion of his motives could only be based on supposition.

What is thought to cause these extreme actions? Essentially, the problem is seen to be the inability of returnee children to readapt to Japanese culture and language, which leaves them marked as 'different', makes them the subject of bullying and ridicule, and, in turn, leads them either to hit out against their tormentors or else to turn their frustration in on themselves. We have seen a good illustration of this theory in Satoru's fictional 'life-story'. It is not difficult to find other popular articles to support this view since there is no doubt that some returnees are bullied. The victims of bullying are often said by their persecutors to be too presumptuous (*namaiki*), opinionated (*shittakaburi*), or meddlesome (*deshabari*). These are all characteristics popularly associated with *kikokushijo*. An article in the *Mainichi Shinbun* in July 1985, entitled *Kikokushijo no Namida: Ijime no Senrei* ('The Tears of Returnee Children: A Baptism by Bullying') tells of the experiences of a returnee who, after having stones thrown at her, her clothes hidden, and her *futon* (bedding) stripped off, was forced to move to another school. More often, though, the ill-treatment of returnees is manifested through ostracism and rejection or, alternatively, cruel taunting about their overseas experiences (Nakatsu, 1979; Muro,

JTW, 2 April 1983; Ōsawa, 1986). As one *kaigaishijo* wrote (Ō-Nichi Kyōkai, 1984: 100):

I have come from a school in Osaka, but my memories of that school are not particularly good . . . because I spoke Japanese just like a foreigner, knowing only about two words. Since I wrote all of my composition in English, I was taunted [*baka ni sareru*]. Moreover, because I was born in America, I had few friends and often things were said like, 'You dropped the atom bomb' or 'You American idiot'.

An hour-long documentary screened on 1 June 1986 on the commercial television channel TBS put forward a strongly negative image of the experience of *kikokushijo*. Called *Boku wa Nanijin Desu Ka?* ('What Country Am I From?'), the programme began by discussing the problems of non-adaptation for *kikokushijo* on their return to Japan, using as an example the case of one girl who was unable to make friends, was punished by her angry teachers by having to kneel in the corridor (*seiza*), and ended up suffering from *tōkōkyohi* (school withdrawal syndrome) (see also Dōmoto, 1987). (This 'disease' has gained increasing attention in Japan and will be examined in more detail later.) Such negative accounts of *kikokushijo* experience can be found even in school textbooks (see Wakabayashi *et al.* (n.d.): 296–8).

This perception of the experience of *kikokushijo* as seriously problematical has also been disseminated to audiences outside Japan. The following syndicated Kyōdo Press Agency report offers a typical example: 'On returning to Japan, the children (and their parents) undergo what can only be called "reverse culture shock". Although not unusual for anyone returning home after a long absence, in Japan the effects can be particularly severe, resulting in outright alienation, murder and suicide' (Robbins, *DY*, 18 March 1984). Similarly, in an article entitled 'Sadistic Bullying Causes School Suicides in Japan', the journalist Robert Whymant writes that 'Children of Japanese who have worked overseas . . . are frequently singled out for bullying' (*Guardian*, 30 September 1985). Indeed, the same story can be found in major organs of print all over the world—the *New York Times* (19 October 1980), *Far Eastern Economic Review* (Willis, 19 January 1984), *Newsweek* (Reiss, 27 February 1984), *Wall Street Journal* (Browning, 9 May 1986), *Le Nouvel Observateur* (Muller, July 1986), *Times Educational Supplement* (Greenlees, 20 May 1988)—as well as in

many of the recent bestsellers on Japan in the English language
(Ozaki, 1980: 210; Christopher, 1983: 165–6; Reischauer, 1983:
421; Vogel, 1983: 243; Woronoff, 1983: 332–3; Taylor, 1985:
237–40).

THE 'SPECIAL NATURE' OF JAPANESE SOCIETY

The problems faced by overseas Japanese children on their return to
Japan underlie most people's perception of why it was necessary to
set up special schools and a special university entrance network for
these children. Nakanishi (1985: 17) has broken down these
problems into two main types: the negative reaction (*iwakan*) of
kikokushijo to the special quality (*tokushitsu*) of Japanese culture
and the differences between the Japanese educational system and
other educational systems outside Japan. This chapter will examine
the cultural side of the argument; the next will examine the
educational one.

At its most simple the cultural argument goes something like this:
as a homogeneous island people with a long period of seclusion
(*sakoku jidai*) from the outside world in their past; a unique
language and set of cultural values which require constant attention
from birth in order to be mastered; and an intrinsic propensity to
form introverted groups of like-minded souls, it is only natural that
the Japanese have an innate sense of suspicion towards anything
coming from without. The Japanese expression *deru kugi wa
utareru* ('the nail that sticks up, gets knocked down') is often cited
in this context (Brockman, *JTW*, 14 February 1987; Robbins, *DY*,
18 March 1984; Willis, 1984). The fact that overseas Japanese are
different, or are perceived as different, is important. The word for
'different' (*chigau*) also means 'wrong'. The conformist, homogeneous nature of Japanese society can be seen to militate against
minority groups and overseas Japanese are also, of course,
statistically, in a minority category—the 250,000 Japanese 'long-
term expatriates' constitute a mere 0.2 per cent of the total
Japanese population and even the total number of those who have,
at any time, belonged in the 'expatriate' category is probably less
than 1 per cent.

The assumptions inherent in the cultural explanation of returnee
'problems' are, firstly, that Japanese culture consists of a cluster of

values (what Minoura [1979] calls a 'cultural complex'), and secondly, that by living outside Japan even for a short period of time individuals either lose, or never fully learn, the skills thought necessary to adhere to these values. The argument continues that through not learning, or not fully expressing, these skills, returnees are not 'real' or 'complete' Japanese. Hence it is that terms of derision for *kikokushijo* include *han-Japa* (half-Japanese), *henna-Nihonjin* (strange Japanese), and *chūtohanpa Nihonjin* (half-baked Japanese) (see Horoiwa, 1983*b*: 92).

An understanding of the values of Japanese society has therefore been seen as essential in explaining the 'problems' of returnees. Equally, a study of these 'problems' has been considered a means to examine what it is to be Japanese. Theories of 'Japaneseness' have therefore been employed in a circular manner to explain the 'problems' of *kikokushijo*. This is not surprising, since the search for, and examination of, specifically 'Japanese' values is practically a national pastime in Japan and many such ideas are so widely disseminated that they are taken for granted by a broad cross-section of the Japanese public. As a genre, these theories are referred to as *Nihonjinron* (theories of Japaneseness).

It would be difficult to exaggerate the extent to which *Nihon-jinron* beliefs are held in Japan,[2] although it is only comparatively recently that, as a phenomenon, they have come to be examined critically. Peter Dale (1986: p. ii) graphically illustrates their influence:

Just imagine the situation which might ensue had English letters over the past hundred years been singularly preoccupied with the clarification of 'Englishness', not only as an essayistic form but as a major subject of austere academic research. Imagine then dozens if not hundreds of works pouring from the presses of Oxford and Cambridge, in which the Hare Professor of Moral Philosophy discussed the uniqueness of the English ethical tradition, or Wittgensteinians examined at book length hundreds of terms in the Oxford English Dictionary to derive concepts of Englishness in such terms as 'fair play', 'good form', 'gentlemen', 'guv'ner' etc., or wrote books on the influence of bad weather on parliamentary institutions and democracy, of cricket on the outlook of the British people, of matriarchy as a constant element underlying British institutions from the times of Boadicea through to Mrs Thatcher; treating everything under the English sun as consequences of some peculiar mentality unchanged since one's ancestors first donned woad and did battle with Caesar; imagine this as something which is filtered down through newspapers and regional media to everyday life, and you have something of the picture of what has taken placé in Japan.

Here Dale has picked out some of the most important elements of the *Nihonjinron* genre. Although much of this work is produced by respected academics from respected institutions, it is often produced in the form of popular accounts, the *keimōsho* already discussed in Chapter 2. The high status both of the individuals who produce the work and of the publishers confers authority on the findings. (We shall return to this point in Chapter 8.) Essentially, the message of the *Nihonjinron* genre is that Japan, the Japanese, and Japanese society are unique in the world—topographically, linguistically, structurally, culturally, even anatomically. In the study of *kikokushijo*, then, this is used to explain why they have problems adapting first to foreign cultures and then to Japanese culture on their return.

An interesting example of the use of *Nihonjinron* theories in the context of Japanese going, and returning from, overseas is Kondō Hiroshi's popular book *Culture Shock no Shinri: Ibunka to Tsukiau tame ni* ('The Psychology of Culture Shock: How to Get On in Different Cultures'). Kondō (1984: p. iv) is a psychologist who spent fifteen years in the USA and (like many *Nihonjinron* authors) admits quite readily to writing from his own experience. He also uses many of the major *Nihonjinron* sources in his own account of how Japanese society works and how this causes culture shock for anyone entering the society from outside (1984: esp. 119–60). Under the heading of ethnocentricism (*jibunkachūshinshugi*), he emphasizes the 'deep-rooted island mentality' of the Japanese and discusses the significance of being an island country (*shimaguni*) inhabited by one race (*tan'itsu minzoku*) with a long period of isolation from the outside world (*sakoku jidai*). He shows (1984: 130) how these historical features have a psychological legacy which affects Japanese when they go to live overseas:

. . . once Japanese find themselves in an environment where everything is different—including the way people look and the way they speak—from what they are accustomed to, then they, instinctively or unconsciously, retreat into the shell of their own culture and become autistic [*jiheishō*]. In the search for psychological security, they come to despise foreign culture and foreigners and become ethnocentric.

The theme of the homogeneous nature of the Japanese people can be found in almost all *Nihonjinron* accounts of Japanese society. Indeed, Reischauer (1983) and Vogel (1983), two of the most influential admirers of contemporary Japan in the west, isolate Japan's cultural homogeneity as one of the country's principal strengths.

Kondō has also isolated other 'unique' features of Japanese culture, the development of which, he believes, has been aided by the homogeneous nature of the society. Among these, one of the most important is the concept of harmony (*wa*) which embodies the idea that relations between people should be based on a philosophy of peace and that conflict should be avoided at all costs. An understanding of *wa* is considered by most *Nihonjinron* authors to be central to an understanding of Japanese society. Minoura (1984: 49), in her discussion of Japan's 'cultural complex', invokes Lebra's concept of *omoiyari* (empathy with others' feelings) in this context. Kondō explains *wa* in terms of the *ringi seido*—a system of gaining the total consent of a group before a decision is finally reached—which usually goes hand-in-glove with the idea of *nemawashi* by which support is ensured before a new idea is instituted or even publicly floated. In English, the idea of *wa* is usually discussed in terms of consensus.

The belief, widely held by Japanese, that they live in a consensus society is commonly explained in terms of the fact that, if people did not subjugate their individual desires, and were not sensitive to each other's feelings, life would be intolerable in such a small country with such a large population. A second popular explanation is that Japan is traditionally a society based on rice-growing agriculture, which requires co-operation among its members, whereas western societies are based on the structure of hunting communities which encourage the development of individualist mentalities (see Ishida, 1971: 39). According to this theory, the basic social unit in Japan is not the individual but the group—individuals realize themselves through social groups, of which they may belong to several but one is generally dominant. The idea of a group-oriented Japan as opposed to an individual-oriented west is one of the most common themes in works on Japan and has probably received its grandest exposition in the work of the anthropologist Nakane Chie. Indeed, her book *Japanese Society* (1970) was felt to explain the way Japanese society worked so clearly that in the early 1970s free copies were distributed from Japanese embassies around the world.

Nakane's thesis, which both Kondō and Minoura include in their models of Japanese society, is that social position in Japan is decided by an individual's 'frame' (*ba*). This 'frame' is more important than the individual's personal attributes: to use Nakane's (1970: 2–3) own examples, the fact that he works for Mitsubishi is more important than whether he holds a doctorate or is a filing-clerk. As a group provides an individual with his identity, so it must have a strong sense of its own group identity and this leads to its exclusive nature and the development of a strong distinction between inside and outside. Taylor is among those who feel that Japanese exclusivity towards foreigners is simply the same procedure writ large: depending on the context, Japanese see themselves in terms of larger and larger groups. This does not, however, he says (1985: 90), extend beyond the shores of Japan to embrace mankind as a whole. According to Nakane, within the group and between groups, relationships in Japan are essentially hierarchical. This is the source of the phrase most commonly associated with her work, *tate shakai* (vertical society). According to this theory, in a one-to-one situation no two individuals are exactly equal and their relationship is ordered according to strict principles of hierarchy. An individual's 'frame' determines his position in society, and it is on this basis that he can communicate with others. On the other hand, an individual without a 'frame' is marginalized in Japanese society, is essentially without a social identity, and may find himself ostracized (*murahachibu sareru*).

According to some *Nihonjinron* authors, being Japanese also presupposes an ability to practise a specifically Japanese means of communication. Miller (1982) has given a thorough (if occasionally intolerant) account of many of the more popular contemporary theories of 'unique' Japanese communication processes. A particularly popular theory, however, which he does not discuss is that of *haragei*, literally 'the art of the belly', which proposes that by virtue of their common racial origins any two Japanese have the potential for silent communication—through the centre of their bodies. A sense of special communication not only is applied to the human universe in Japan, but is also central to the idea of an 'unique' relationship between the Japanese and their natural world. Kondō (1984: 123–5) describes this as the Japanese 'sense of aesthetic appreciation', an idea which has perhaps found its ultimate application in the work of the neurophysiologist Tsunoda Tadanobu

(1985), who suggests that Japanese have a different feeling for nature from others owing to their unique brain structure.

The above cultural values—homogeneity, harmony, consensus, groupism, exclusivity, hierarchy, ostracism, and 'unique' forms of communication—constitute only some of the major elements of Kondō and Minoura's Japanese 'cultural complex'. They are ideas readily recognizable to the majority of Japanese. Alan Booth's (1985) account of his walk the length of Japan is replete with examples taken from conversations with Japanese along the way. These elements form a generally taken-for-granted definition of 'Japaneseness' which explains why the experience of being *kaigaishijo* and *kikokushijo* is seen as inherently problematic.

Kikokushijo AND JAPANESE CULTURE

Nakane Chie has applied her model of Japanese society to the explanation of why Japanese have trouble adjusting to life overseas and why those who do adjust to it have trouble readjusting to Japanese society.[3] Like most of her work on Japanese society, much of the book is anecdotal, and she begins with a story that has become one of the myths of the literature on overseas Japanese (see Kanazawa, 1984: 117). Nakane (1972: 14) recounts the experiences in London of a Tibetan village chief and a Japanese, neither of whom had been outside their own country before. Told simply, while the Tibetan was amazed by what he saw in terms of material goods, he had little trouble adapting culturally to his new environment and soon settled in. For the Japanese, of course, there was no problem coping with the new environment materially, but he was totally unable to adapt culturally and as a result suffered the most terrible culture shock. Nakane's thesis implies that members of a 'vertical society' cannot live in any society where relationships are not hierarchically ordered and, since there is no other society with a vertical system like that of Japan, they will always have serious problems when they go to live overseas (see Hata and Smith, 1983: 374).

Nan Sussman essentially supports Nakane's thesis in her research on the *kikoku salaryman*, the fathers of the *kikokushijo*. Problems for these repatriate salarymen, according to Sussman (*JTW*, 12 October 1985), include the fact that they are too forward in expressing their ideas and too individualistic for work in the context of Japanese corporations. Moreover, they have lost their place in the corporate structure and, as Nakane (1970: 109–12) has suggested, they may have to compensate for this loss by deliberately recreating, if possible, the links and chains that formed their social hierarchies before they went overseas. As with *kikokushijo*, adults too may be teased and bullied on their return. According to Kondō (1984: 231), 'There are many cases where those residents and workers who return from overseas are criticized as "smelling of butter" (*butterkusai*),[4] "demented from living overseas" (*gaikoku-boke*), or "big mouths about their overseas experiences" (*kaigai seikatsu o hana ni kakeru*)'. Not only have they lost their place in the social hierarchy, but in terms of *Nihonjinron* theories of groupism, they have also lost their group identity and become too individualistic.

Inamura Hiroshi, the Japanese psychiatrist, in his book *Nihonjin no Kaigai Futekiō* ('The Non-Adaptation of Japanese Overseas'), presents a series of case studies from around the world to illustrate graphically the psychological and physical dangers of being an overseas Japanese. He suggests not that all Japanese are incapable of adjusting to life overseas, but that those who can do so are often those who are unacceptable in Japanese society. He describes (1982: 174–5) the case of one Japanese man, aggressively individualistic and temperamentally unable to associate with those around him in Japan, who went to the Middle East as an engineer and adapted to the local community extremely successfully. In general, Inamura's definition of Japanese values and his explanation of why these raise problems for those going overseas draw uncritically on the ideas previously discussed under the generic heading of *Nihonjinron*. He does, however, also include more practical issues which he believes could have a psychological effect on Japanese overseas, among them the absence of Japanese food. He gives one example (1982: 180–2) of a Japanese in the United States who developed neurotic symptoms and recovered only after being counselled to eat Japanese food and speak Japanese.

After cross-referencing the problems suffered by Japanese overseas with their age and sex, however, Inamura expresses particular concern for children—not only in their adaptation to their host society overseas, but also in their readjustment to Japanese society on their return. As a demonstration of how negatively he views the whole experience, in a later, more prescriptive paper (with Araki Hitoshi), he writes (1983: 157) that 'children had better not be moved around from one country to another' and that 'it can be said for children, the provisional limit of overseas life is about two years' (1983: 158). In a paper in 1987 (with Tamura Takeshi), he catalogues a frightening series of problems recounted by *kikokushijo* who had been sent for psychiatric treatment.

One of the more specific applications of *Nihonjinron* theories can be found in the work of Minoura (1979), who proposes the theory that in Japan the 'other' constitutes the major point of reference, while in the United States it is the 'self'.[5] Her major objective is to discover both the factors which determine how these points of reference (what she terms 'cultural grammars') become fixed, and the factors which effect individuals who move from one 'grammar' to another. Her highly quantitative analysis leads her to the conclusion that age-linked factors play the primary role in the acquisition of 'cultural grammars', and that acquisition is also more influenced by extra- than by intra-familial factors. She sees the age of 9 as a crucial turning-point, what she terms 'the 9-year-old wall' (*kyūsai no kabe*), in the acquisition of a 'cultural grammar' (1984: 271). Before this age, she believes that what has been culturally and socially learnt can easily be unlearnt. But, during the period between the ages of 9 and 15, 'cultural grammars' become permanent.[6]

Minoura's work falls into the category of work termed culture-and-personality studies where culture is seen to determine personality. This is a common belief in Japan. Bruce La Brack neatly summarizes this view in his comment that to whatever extent a second non-Japanese culture is learnt, there is an equivalent loss of Japaneseness in the eyes of stay-at-home Japanese (*JTW*, 13 August 1983). Befu Harumi (1983: 246) describes this phenomenon as a 'zero-sum game'.

The idea of a 'zero-sum game' is particularly seen to pertain to the use of Japanese language. Both Hatano (1973: 44–5) and Nomoto (1985) suggest that learning more than one language may have debilitating effects on the individuals involved.[7] In a conference on returnee children in 1985, Nomoto suggested that it could leave the individual involved unable to function properly in any language and thereby intellectually impaired. At the same conference, Ebuchi (1985) posited that 'Japaneseness' was generally defined by the formula: Japanese blood plus Japanese cultural skills plus Japanese language. In similar vein, in a chapter on 'Race and Language: Language and Race', Roy Andrew Miller (1982: 144) quotes the eminent linguist Suzuki Takao as saying, 'To be a Japanese, at the same time that it means being a member of the Japanese race, also means speaking the Japanese language.' Miller (1982: 283) goes on to suggest that '. . . the Japanese language has gradually been elevated to the position of one of the major ideological forces sustaining Japanese society, at the same time that it helps that society to close its ranks against all possible intrusions by outsiders'. It is, perhaps, this connection between race and language which explains the great significance given to the maintenance of Japanese language skills overseas.

Part of Miller's critique—and certainly much of his, and also Dale's (1986) scepticism—is reserved for the work of Tsunoda Tadanobu, whom we have already mentioned. Tsunoda (1985: p. vi) claims that owing to the structure of the Japanese language the functions of the two cerebral hemispheres in the Japanese brain become the inverse of those of any other people, except Polynesians who share a vowel-based language with the Japanese: 'The Japanese language shapes the Japanese brain function pattern, which in turn serves as a basis for the formation of the Japanese culture.' By virtue of their language, therefore, Tsunoda avers that the Japanese are culturally distinct from other people.

In support of his thesis, Tsunoda undertook considerable research on *kikokushijo* in the Hatano Family School in Tokyo. This is a short-stay school, supported by the Kaigai Shijo Kyōiku Shinkō Zaidan, the aim of which is to facilitate the adaptation of returnee children. As a result of tests carried out at the Hatano School, Tsunoda declared that the functioning of the brain of Japanese (which is determined by the use of the Japanese language) suffers severely from interference by foreign languages. More serious is his assertion that this functional pattern is finalized by the age of 8. He argues, therefore, that damage could result if Japanese attempt to learn foreign languages (except presumably Polynesian) before that age. Furthermore, he points out (1985: 103–8) that any Japanese child who lives overseas before the age of 8 will never be able to acquire a Japanese pattern of cerebral functioning, and that those who go overseas after that age will be seriously impaired in their ability to think in a Japanese fashion.[8]

Not many of those who study the problems of *kikokushijo* in relation to the Japanese language go as far as Tsunoda. Nevertheless, even those who ostensibly support bilingual education concentrate on the language problems of *kikokushijo*. Kamijō Masako (1983), for example, insists that insufficient acquisition of the Japanese language is the major difficulty faced by *kikokushijo*; while Kusanagi Hiroshi (1980: 142), working as part of Tsukuba University's bicultural education study group, believes that, because of their language 'problems', *kikokushijo* should be treated differently from other Japanese children:

> It is difficult to treat returnees like ordinary children at Japanese schools . . . particularly because of the lower level of their Japanese language due to living overseas. . . . It is true that on the surface they soon have no problem understanding Japanese. . . . But actually there remain weaknesses in their Japanese which affect their school performance.

Kusanagi concludes that the apparent ability of *kikokushijo* to speak Japanese should not be taken at face value. He describes their vocabularies as crude (*yōchi*) when compared with regular students and says (1980: 158) that although *kikokushijo* 'can cope well with words learnt at school, those who have been to an elementary school overseas have problems making their own sentences, choosing an exact word or using idiomatic expressions in Japanese'.

As we shall see in Chapter 6, there is some debate about the extent of *kikokushijo* language problems. But there tends to be an inherent assumption that because they lived overseas these problems must be severe. It is not only a question of vocabulary. There is no doubt, for example, that some returnees are, through lack of practice, weak in their knowledge of more formal Japanese. As Goldstein and Tamura (1975: 68–95) point out, learning the Japanese language is largely a question of memorizing ritualized phrases and expressions.

According to Nakatsu (1979), it is the whole socio-linguistic structure surrounding the Japanese language which causes *kikokushijo* the most problems. *Kikokushijo* do not recognize the fact that everything in Japanese should be stated in an indirect way. Hence, some returnees may have problems because their Japanese is, in a sense, too correct: for example, they may use too many personal pronouns (Sukita, 1984; Kondō, 1984: 136). It can even be considered a problem if *kikokushijo* complete their sentences in too final a manner. According to Nagashima (1973: 92 ff.), in Japan the responsibility for comprehending a message rests with the receiver, not with the sender. Precision in completing a sentence may therefore imply that the receiver is not sufficiently sophisticated to pick up its meaning without having it spelt out.

Whether they are weak or just 'too good' at Japanese language, it is assumed that *kikokushijo* have linguistic problems. As in other areas, not only has there been considerable research to explain the 'problems' of *kikokushijo*, but also a great deal of work, quantitative and qualitative, which has set out to 'measure', and thereby propose remedial measures for, such 'problems'. Indeed, the major criticism (see Saitō, 1986: 255) of a large project undertaken by Takahagi *et al.* (1982) which seriously questioned the extent to which *kikokushijo* really did suffer from problems was that it did not offer any practical advice to these children. The most influential work in the area of measuring *kikokushijo* problems has been supervised by Kobayashi Tetsuya at Kyoto University. Since it first appeared in 1978, Kobayashi's work has been cited and utilized uncritically by many other writers on *kikokushijo* (see Ōta, 1983; Furuhashi, 1984).

Kobayashi's project was set up in the early 1970s under the auspices of, and funded by, Monbushō. His research was based on questionnaires and clinical psychological tests which looked at the adaptation patterns of about 650 children both overseas and on their return to Japan. Kobayashi (1982*b*: 86) began from the premiss that such experience was inherently problematic:

When children who are brought up within Japanese cultural boundaries are suddenly put into a different cultural environment, they at first experience culture shock owing to the cultural gap between the two environments, and to overcome this shock they practise cultural learning [*bunka gakushū*]. This is the normal process by which adaptation takes place within children, and if it is not thoroughly mastered, non-adaptation symptoms [*futekiō shōjō*] appear. This condition can be seen both on going to and returning from foreign countries.

Kobayashi then set up six models to 'measure' patterns of adaptation from one society to another (Fig. 7) which can be summarized thus:

A   Fast Adaptation Pattern (*sokushin-gata*): adapt to new environment in a rather short period after return.

A: *Fast Adaptation Pattern*

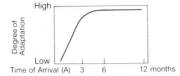

B: *Intermediate-Speed Adaptation Pattern*

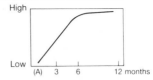

C: *Slow Adaptation Pattern*

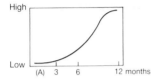

D: *Half-Way Frustration Pattern*

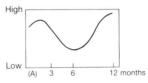

E: *Stable Pattern*

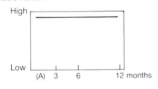

F: *Non-Adaptation Pattern*

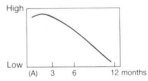

FIG. 7: Kobayashi's Patterns of *Kikokushijo* Adaptation
Source: Adapted from Kobayashi, 1982*b*: 93.

B   Intermediate-Speed Adaptation Pattern (*chūshin-gata*): require 3 to 6 months.

C   Slow Adaptation Pattern (*chishin-gata*): difficulty at first and then need 6 to 12 months for complete adaptation.

D   Halfway Frustration Pattern (*chūkan zasetsu-gata*): experience frustration while in process of adaptation.

E   Stable Pattern (*muhendō-gata*): adapt immediately to new environment and experience no difficulty.

F   Non-Adaptation Pattern (*futekiō-gata*).

Adaptation (*tekiō*) was determined through using a computer to cross-reference four major variables: catching up with school work; health and physical condition; life at school; and relationships with friends. These were measured using questionnaires and psychological and scholastic ability tests. Kobayashi's results can be seen in Table VII.

TABLE VII: Kobayashi's Figures for
Adaptation Patterns of 655 *Kikokushijo*

	While Abroad %	On Return %
A	41.4	41.8
B	32.8	23.4
C	8.7	16.5
D	1.2	2.4
E	5.8	6.4
F	0.2	0.8
TOTAL	89.7	91.3
Others	4.7	2.3
Unknown	5.2	6.4

Note: Kobayashi does not distinguish between *kikokushijo* on the basis of where they went overseas nor for how long nor in what type of school, but, as in our definition in Chapter 2, classifies them as one homogeneous group.

Source: Kobayashi, 1982*b*: 94.

From these figures Kobayashi inferred, by adding groups A, B, and E (which adapted quickly), that it was significantly easier to adapt to a new environment overseas after six months (80 per cent) than back into the Japanese environment (71.6 per cent). He concluded that there were several reasons why it was more difficult to adapt back into Japan. Partly it was because there were expectations that it would be the other way round but 'it can also be said that foreign cultures are generally generous to foreigners and alien elements... while Japanese society is exclusive (*haitateki*), thus making the adaptation of returnees very difficult' (1982*b*: 97).

Kobayashi then goes on (1982*b*: 99–100) to suggest the significance of various factors in the process of adaptation:

Those who resided in a foreign country for less than two years adapt back into a Japanese environment within six months, those who stay any longer

overseas tend to show signs of non-adaptation. . . . However, those who
spent their time overseas in upper elementary school and junior high school
have more trouble than those who were educated overseas during
kindergarten and lower elementary years. . . . Children who have mothers
who adapt well into the local life are also quick in adapting into the local
community, however they tend to take longer adapting back into the
Japanese environment. . . . Those who attended the full-time Japanese
schools were naturally (*tōzen*) fastest in adapting back to the Japanese
environment. . . . Looking at the relationship between adaptation and the
means to facilitate and hasten adaptation to Japan, it is helped when
parents make their children attend *juku* [cram schools] or encourage them
to make friends so that they are able to adapt to the surrounding
environment.

Kobayashi himself carefully avoided making value judgements
about the effects of overseas education, never implying whether
quick adaptation back to Japan was good or bad. His work,
however, was quickly taken to show that *kikokushijo* suffered from
severe adaptation 'problems' on their return to Japan, and that
special care was needed to ensure that they avoided the worst of
these 'problems' or were able to overcome them. In particular, he
coined the term *futekiō byōjō* (non-adaptation syndrome)—often
shortened to *futekiō byō* (non-adaptation disease)—and thereby
introduced a medical model that became an increasingly common
element in the discussion about *kikokushijo*.

According to one *kikokushijo* informant, this medical model had
been used by a counsellor at an advice centre (*sōdan shitsu*) to
which she and her brother had been taken on their return to Japan
in the mid 1970s. The counsellor had said that the purpose of the
visit was to form a diagnosis (*shindan*) of the seriousness of their
'non-adaptation symptoms' (*futekiō byōjō*) based upon the length
of time they had spent overseas, the types of school they had
attended, and their current language ability. The resulting conclusion—that she was suffering from a slight case (*keishō*) while her
brother was more serious (*jūshō*)—led to the latter being advised to
attend a private school with a large returnee population and the
former being recommended to go to any state school with an
integrated system for *kikokushijo*.

We can see this medical model in more detail in an essay by
Kubota Morihiro (1983), a teacher in a special unit for *kikokushijo*, who presents a detailed case study of one of his students, a
boy who had been in New York for ten years and began to show

signs of what Kubota terms 'identity confusion' and 'neurosis' after his return to Japan. Kubota believes the child suffered from a 'double-layered' (*nijū kōzō*) identity which caused psychological disturbance. In the case of this particular boy, the result was so severe that he stopped attending school. Kubota summarizes this process as in Fig. 8. In the spirit of offering practical advice, he concludes (1983: 64) with a warning to other teachers that even when *kikokushijo* do not seem to be having adaptation 'problems', their apparently successful adjustment should not be taken at face value.

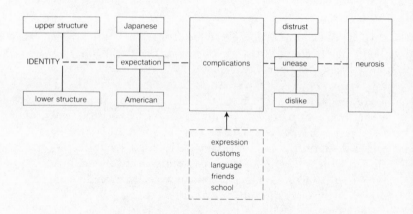

FIG. 8: Kubota's Model of the Double Structure of Identity Leading to Neurosis
Source: Adapted from Kubota, 1983: 64.

A rather more intriguing source for this type of argument on returnee adaptation problems is META, a support group for returnees. The founder of META, Horoiwa Naomi, takes a stance based both on her own experience as a returnee to Japan and on the research she undertook for her Master's thesis. Whereas Kubota looked at the idea of adaptation from the viewpoint of the teacher, Horoiwa searched for a definition of successful adaptation from the viewpoint of the individual returnee. Their basic models, however, are remarkably similar. Horoiwa (1983*a*) proposes two patterns of returnee adaptation, both of which she regards as somewhat pathological. She says that returnees are looked upon as either incomplete foreigners or incomplete Japanese because there is no concept of something in between. As a result, returnees respond to Japan in two different ways. There are those she labels as belonging to the 'subtraction model' (*kezuritorigata*), who give up something in order to be able to re-enter Japanese society, and there are those whom she describes as belonging to the 'addition model' (*tsuketashigata*), who add their overseas experience on to their 'Japaneseness' and thereby challenge society as a new type of Japanese (1983*b*: 96–7). 'Subtraction modellers', according to Horoiwa, tend to criticize 'addition modellers' because they themselves have had to give something up, whereas the 'addition modellers' find themselves considered as not 'real' Japanese, and thus excluded from mainstream society. According to Horoiwa, therefore, returnees always find themselves either bowing to, or opposing, social pressure. Both types of returnee may suffer severe identity problems, as their views of themselves clash with those of society.

The foregoing has included only a few examples of work— popular, personal, academic— supporting and disseminating the idea that *kikokushijo* experience is inherently problematic, and underlying the dominant perception and acceptance that something needs to be done for such children. The sphere in which most help has been deemed necessary is the educational system. The next chapter will explain why this has been so, as well as providing a context for understanding the significance of a school with returnees which is examined in Chapter 5.

4

The Educational 'Problems' of
Kikokushijo

In his study of overseas businessmen, Ishida Hideo (1983: 74–5; (n.d.): 35–6) has clearly shown that the biggest personal worries of this group concern not their own careers but the education of their children. In order to understand this finding, a basic knowledge of the history and structure of education in Japan is essential.

The history of education in Japan is well covered in English language literature on Japan (Passin, 1965; Kobayashi, 1976; Cummings, 1980; Rohlen, 1983; Dore, 1984) and, not surprisingly, has left an important legacy for future Japanese generations.[1] The most important aspect is that education, as a concept, has been given great respect in Japan at least since the introduction of Chinese writing in about the fourth century AD. As Merry White (1987: 187) says: 'Elsewhere regarded as a "soft" issue, education in Japan is a concern which even the most macho political leader sees as critical.' A primary reason for this consensus of opinion on the importance of education is what White describes (1987: 187) as a 'traditional, deep-seated national preoccupation with resource scarcity'. Human beings are Japan's most important resource.

By the eighteenth century, Japan had what can only be described, in a global context, as a very well established education system. Dore (1984) offers a particularly graphic description of the different systems of education which existed for the different social classes in the Tokugawa period. Education in the schools for the higher classes, in particular, in this period had many of the features of the contemporary system, such as the standardization of curricula (1984: 74); the lack of intellectual excitement (1984: 83); the automatic promotion of slow students (1984: 87); the belief in the equal potential of every child (1984: 103); the teacher-centred nature of the lessons and the lack of opportunity for students to ask questions (1984: 140–1); as well as the potential for social mobility through education (1984: 293). These will all be studied in more detail.

It has been estimated that in the first half of the nineteenth century more than 40 per cent of boys and 10 per cent of girls in Japan had obtained schooling outside the home (Dore, 1984: 254). This comparatively high rate of education provided an excellent basis for the rapid economic, social, and political reforms during the Meiji period. Building on this foundation, the Meiji oligarchs set up a system of mass education, believing that education was a key, if not *the* key, to successful modernization. Without totally abandoning the system that already existed, they adapted it and added to it by borrowing selectively from several western sources. From France they took the idea of a centralized authority and a strong emphasis on state-run normal schools; from Germany, a system of higher education built around a few élite public universities; from England, a belief in spartan character-building through athletics and moral discipline; and from the United States, many practical pedagogical techniques and an interest in vocational education (Hurst, 1984: 3). In 1875, around 35 per cent of children were receiving elementary education. By 1905, thirty years later, it was over 95 per cent.

With 1945 and Japan's defeat in the war, the Americans attempted to dismantle the Japanese education system—which they considered to have been a vital element in propagating pre-war and wartime ultranationalism—and completely reconstruct it along American lines. There has been a great deal of debate as to how much change was actually effected by the occupation reforms (see Trainor, 1983; Nagai, 1985), but the opinion of many critics is that while the structure of the education system was radically altered, neither the content nor beliefs in the purpose of education were much changed: it remained an essentially 'Japanese' system with western elements added to it.

EDUCATION FOR THE CREATION OF A WORKFORCE

A legacy of the Meiji period is the very strong belief remaining in Japan that the primary purpose of education is to provide the nation with a workforce. This idea that the purpose of education is to serve the nation is what Karabel and Halsey (1977: 8–12) term the 'functionalist' theory of education. To outline this theory very briefly, raw material in the shape of uneducated schoolchildren is fed into a national educational system in order to produce what the nation demands. In the case of Japan, because of the lack of natural resources, the demands of industry are believed to represent those of the nation. In particular, it is the big companies—because of the security they can provide for their workers in terms of higher salaries,[2] life-time employment, and fringe benefits—which provide the model for the ideal workplace, and from their workers they demand the ideal qualities shown in Fig. 9.

FIG. 9: Images of the Ideal Japanese Male and Female Worker

Ideal (Male) Worker =	a worker who will conform to the company ideology and not cause trouble;
	a worker who will work hard and put the company before his personal well-being;
	a worker who will persevere and always try his hardest and
	a worker who is literate, numerate, and has generally proved his ability in being able to understand and apply new ideas quickly when they are put to him.
Ideal (Female) Worker =	a worker who will cheer up the workplace by her presence (the 'office flower'—*shokuba no hana*);
	a worker who will leave when she gets married and become:
	(*a*) a wife who provides a comfortable home for a husband to relax in after work and
	(*b*) a mother who will ensure that her children become the ideal (male or female) workers of the next generation.

These ideal images are important for understanding not only the education system in Japan but also the treatment of returnees. They are generalized images, but at the same time present a Weberian 'ideal type' that is accepted by the majority of Japanese.[3] Even Kamata Satoshi's (1984) clandestine entry into the Toyota car plant and his vehement written attack on it attest to the strength of these images of the 'ideal' Japanese worker. Essentially, the Japanese company worker—blue- or white-collar—is seen to owe his first allegiance to his employer.[4] The ideal male worker is one who is prepared to sublimate his individual desires and ideas to the whole company ethic. Thus, the company is more interested in 'generalists' than 'specialists': it will inculcate into the generalist its own specialist ideology and skills. This means that the worker may often be tied to one company, since his skills are limited to the conditions of the company where they were learnt and are not easily transferable. One of the favourite sources of new recruits in big companies is said to be graduates in physical education from top universities. Such students are seen to have proved their worth and dedication by entering top universities but have not imbibed ideas that may prove difficult to change or eradicate.[5] Hidaka Rokurō (1984: 113) offers a common left-wing explanation of this situation: 'To a regulated society [like Japan], an independent awareness of freedom and a clear commitment to freedom spell trouble. It would be a disrupting element in the contemporary social order if so many students with critical minds sprang out of the universities into the outside world.'

The strength of the image of the ideal worker is reflected to some degree in the worries of overseas Japanese. It is commonly feared, for example, that those who go (or remain) overseas at the undergraduate or postgraduate level may find that the specialist skills they learned overseas are more of a hindrance than a help when it comes to looking for jobs in Japanese companies. As Minoura (1984: 109) writes: 'There is a strong belief among both parents and children interviewed that, if one wants to get on in Japanese society, one has to graduate from a good Japanese university.' White (1980) and Ishida (1983), among others, have shown in graphic detail how even established company members who are sent overseas fear the charge, when they return, that they are too individualistic, lack sufficient perseverance, and pay too much attention to their home life. Women who go overseas worry that they may be seen as too ambitious in their own careers, and hence unfeminine. More importantly, they are regarded as unable to give their full attention to the care of their children and their home.[6]

There is little doubt that the image of the ideal Japanese worker as illustrated in Fig. 9 is generally accepted in Japan. However, employers recognize that not all the products of such an educational system will be equally good and they need to differentiate between them. In theory, they could provide their own tests, interviews, and examinations, but in Japan this is not necessary: they allow the educational system itself to sort out the best potential workers. The educational system in Japan judges students on the basis of their ability to conform, work hard, and persevere, as well as on their literacy, numeracy, and ability to apply ideas quickly, and it sorts them into different streams accordingly.

The higher the status of the company, the bigger its attraction is and therefore the better able it is to take individuals from the top streams of the educational system. In theory, big companies are not interested in who one's father is or how much money he earns, but simply in whether one had the ability to get into a top university. People are judged, therefore, not so much on their social background as on their educational history. This accounts for the popular description of Japan as a *gakureki shakai* (educational background society).[7] To put it more attractively: in Japan one is born twice—once to one's natural parents, once to the educational system. Such a system, therefore, demands that there be equality of opportunity: everyone must have the same chance of getting into a top university and thereby of being selected for a high-status job in a top company.

As we have seen, most Japanese will insist not only that they belong to a homogeneous group in terms of race, language, and culture, but also that they are members of a virtually single-class, or classless, society. Surveys every year show that around 90 per cent of all Japanese consider themselves to be members of an amorphous 'middle class' (*DY*, 17 January 1985). The idea that everyone has the same chance, if they work hard enough, of getting into the top universities, ensures that those who get there are considered to have done so on merit.

INDIVIDUAL SELF-INVESTMENT IN EDUCATION

The weakness of the 'functionalist' model of education is that it does not account for the individual's ability to think for himself and decide courses of action based on past experiences and future possibilities. The 'human capital theory of education' (Karabel and Halsey, 1977: 12–16) expresses this idea very well. By investing in themselves through education, people are able to sell their skills more profitably in the labour market. This can be seen very clearly in the Japanese case, and can be explained by using Fig. 10.

Schooling in Japan is compulsory between the ages of 6 and 15.

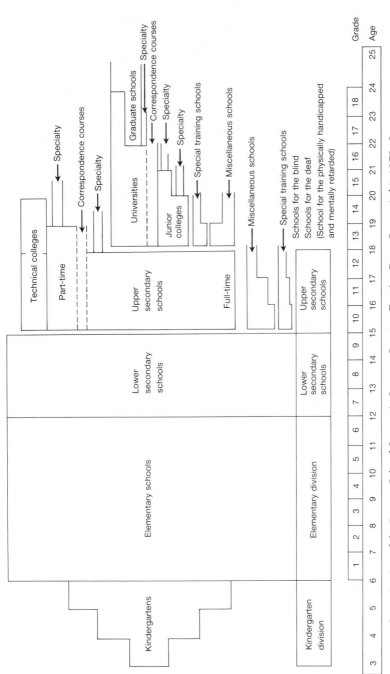

FIG. 10: Organization of the Present School System in Japan   *Source:* Foreign Press Center (ed.), 1978: 5.

Even before the age of 6, however, there is considerable investment in education in the form of kindergartens: 94 per cent of all children entering elementary school have been to kindergarten (Ohki, *JTW*, 14 December 1985).[8] These are not babysitting facilities but are used for educational purposes. Indeed, babysitting and nannying facilities are rare in Japan where society expects a mother to devote twenty-four hours a day to looking after her young children (see Hendry, 1986).

Around 99.5 per cent of all schoolchildren are awarded a certificate for completion of compulsory education up to the age of 15. This certificate is supposed to attest to their numeracy and literacy and it forms the basis of the official assertion that Japan has one of the highest literacy rates in the world. Of these 'certificated' students, around 94 per cent continue to non-compulsory senior high school and almost all of these complete their education up to the age of 18. Beyond that, a large proportion continue to some form of higher education. To cater for these students in 1988, Japan had no less than 488 universities offering four-year courses and 571 colleges offering two-year courses. Even this large a number of institutions for a population of 120 million, however, is insufficient for the demand, and every year it is calculated that about 25 per cent of all those seeking places in establishments of higher education fail to obtain them (Rohlen, 1983: 84). Thirty-seven per cent of the age group currently continue to tertiary education, and if one includes the 2,622 special training schools in the equation, then the figure is over 52 per cent (*J*, No. 469, 2 March 1989). This enormous demand for higher education is largely due to the belief in the principle that to achieve his highest worth in the labour market the individual must proceed as far as possible in the educational system. The question, however, is not only how far he goes in the system, but also at which particular institution he finishes. The 488 universities are far from having equal merit in Japanese eyes, so it is not just a matter of gaining entry to the university itself, but of entry to a good university. There is a pronounced hierarchy of universities in Japan, at the peak of which stands Tokyo University: to graduate from Tokyo University is practically to ensure a prestigious job, a high salary, and excellent status for oneself and one's family.

So how do people in Japan go about ensuring good social status for themselves? As we shall see, though the ideal is of a system in which everyone has an equal chance, there are methods by which some people can make their chances more equal than others. One way is through private education. Schools in Japan are divided into three categories. The most élite are the national schools, which constitute less than 0.5 per cent of all schools. (These will be discussed in more detail later.) During the compulsory education stage, the great majority of children attend state schools which are supported by a mixture of local and central government. At the senior-high-school level, however, as Table VIII illustrates, almost 30 per cent of all students attend a private school.

TABLE VIII: Percentages of Private/State School Students, by School Level (1981)

	Elementary	Middle	Senior	Universities
National	0.4	0.7	0.2	22.8
Local	99.1	96.5	71.7	2.9
Private	0.5	2.9	28.1	74.3

Source: Ministry of Education, Science and Culture, Research and Statistics Division, 1982: 22.

Despite the fact that private education can be very expensive and state education is available, some parents feel that the former may provide their children with better educational chances and are therefore prepared to invest substantial sums of money to this end. A few private senior high schools—such as Nada, described by Rohlen (1983: 18–28)—have for thirty years or more been counted among the best senior high schools in Japan for university entrance purposes. Traditionally, however, the best senior high schools have been the top local schools in each area. Generally speaking, there is a four-layered hierarchy with a few private schools at the top, followed by the bulk of the state schools, below which lie the rest of the private institutions. At the bottom of the pile are the remaining state establishments, often night or vocational schools, which mop up those who are unable either academically to enter a better state school or financially to pay for a private education. As Mouer and Sugimoto (1986: 207–8) point out, however, some parents support private education not only for academic reasons, but also because of a feeling that 'their child will receive more individual attention, will have more opportunity to develop his or her own personality [*kojinsei*], and will be more refined [e.g. not exposed to mass culture]' Almost three-quarters of all students in tertiary education go to private universities and colleges—often very expensive institutions with poor academic reputations—sometimes in the belief that any university is better than none at all.

A second route to a good university is through one of the élite channels that exist in Japan. This so-called 'escalator system' exists in relation to many national universities as well as some of the top private institutions, such as Waseda or Keiō. To enter university via this channel, children normally have to succeed in entering the kindergarten at the very bottom of the 'escalator' and to do this they must take an entrance examination which can be very competitive: for instance the entrance examination for the kinder-garten attached to Gakushūin University—where the Imperial family receive their education—accepts only one out of every five or six of the 3-year-old applicants (Ohki, *JTW*, 14 December 1985). Some kindergartens, however, think that 3-year-olds are a little too young for examinations, and hence are reported to give the tests to their mothers instead (Dore, 1982: 49). The idea here is not to test for genetically inherited ability in the children—an idea that has little potency in a system that aims to give every child a fair chance—but to find children who will be provided with a good and supportive environment for study at home. For those children who have to take the examinations themselves, however, there are even pre-kindergarten establishments to prepare them for this test (see *TS*, 4 May 1984).

Other forms of self-investment consist of parents sending their children to live with relations or friends, or moving themselves in order to fall within the catchment areas of state schools with particularly good reputations (Glazer, 1976: 828). Much more common efforts at self-investment, however, can be seen in the institutions known as *juku* and *yobikō*. The first of these, *juku*, are best thought of as cram schools. Most schoolboys, and a considerable proportion of schoolgirls, will attend *juku* normally after, but sometimes before, school, three times a week on average, from the age of 12 onwards. There they will either prepare for, or revise, their school work in the hope that they will always be a little ahead of, and certainly not behind, their peers. The quality of *juku* the child can attend depends, of course, on how much the parents are prepared to pay. The second of these institutions, *yobikō*, are a special type of cram school for students who either failed to get into any university the first time round, or failed to get into the university of their choice. At a good senior high school with a reputation for getting its graduates into top universities, up to 70 per cent of students may first attend *yobikō* for a year or more.[9] Students who go to *yobikō*, or who retake entrance examinations for university by themselves, are known as *rōnin*. This means literally 'wave man' and was the term given to *samurai* warriors of the feudal period (1603–1868) who had lost their masters. There is some stigma attached to being a *rōnin*—rather like the idea that it was careless for a *samurai* to lose his master[10]—but there is rather more condemnation of the system that allows such a situation to exist. *Juku* and *yobikō* together, therefore, provide what can be called an informal education network which runs alongside the formal system.

An even more 'informal' system of education is provided by the Japanese mother (Vogel, 1963: 251–2). A mother in Japan is judged socially on the success of her children, and also, since public careers for women are still generally disapproved of in Japanese society, the best way for her to realize herself as a person is through her offspring. Mothers therefore pressurize their children to work hard; they attend endless Parent–Teacher Association meetings, sometimes go to special classes to be able to keep up with their children and help them in their homework, and stand outside the halls where their children are taking examinations. They are even said to have sat in on lessons when their children are sick. Such mothers are known as *kyōiku mama* (education-crazy mums). A mother whose child is successful in the educational system is praised as a good mother even if she has done little or nothing to help. A mother whose child fails, however, is severely censured, especially if it is thought that she sacrificed her own children's (and particularly her son's) career for her own. As Befu (1986: 25) says, 'Neglect of one's responsibility as a mother is inexcusable under any circumstances.' Motherhood *per se* has high status in Japan, a working woman often has much less. When one talks about a child's parents in an educational context, therefore, one is generally talking about his mother.

The result of this extra investment in education is that it clearly creates inequalities in the system. As Nishimura (*AS*, 27 May 1984) says:

Although there is a principle of equality in education, actually the state of the family finances can affect students' chances. However good a student is, much depends on whether his or her parents can support the burden of paying for extra tuition and other educational expenses . . . so that the principle of educational equality is on the verge of collapse.

Rohlen (1983) has clearly shown how the senior-high-school destinations of students—the stage at which schools are streamed into different status categories on the basis of entrance examinations—reflect their family background. Children from the poorest families are significantly more likely to end up in the lower-level night senior high schools while those from the richest families attend the top state and private institutions. In these latter families, the parents can afford the extra tuition to help their children pass the entrance examinations and mothers can afford to stay at home to aid their offspring.

There is clear evidence that financial investment has particularly good returns by the stage of university education. In 1974, the average family income of students at Tokyo University was four million yen; the average for students at all state universities was around three million yen; while the average income for the rest of the population was only 2.4 million yen (James and Benjamin, 1988: 136). This tendency, according to Sakakibara (1988:27), is on the increase, leading her to argue that, in effect, 'a monied class . . . passes on its powers through inheritance'.

THE EGALITARIAN NATURE OF JAPANESE EDUCATION

Evidence concerning the effect of family background does not completely invalidate the argument of Cummings (1980) who sees equality as the key to the Japanese educational system. There is no doubt that the system is still generally *perceived* as egalitarian and great efforts are expended within the formal sector of education to maintain this impression. This is effected through a number of measures. All state schools in Japan, for example, are built to the same design so that no parents can complain that their children are being unfairly disadvantaged in any particular institution. The centralization of the system also ensures that, rather as in France, almost all schoolchildren in Japan follow basically the same curriculum. Monbushō decides which textbooks can be used in schools; each prefectural board of education decides which of these can be used in their prefecture; and then each school district will decide which of these can be used in their schools. Generally speaking, all the schools in a given area will be using the same textbooks, and throughout the country there will be very little variation. Although in theory each prefecture has educational autonomy, in practice Monbushō is able to ensure strict uniformity between schools.[11]

The system of examining all students by means of multiple-choice questions, considered in Japan to be the most objective method, has resulted in a situation where virtually all examinations are reduced to a formula which can be answered by filling in a computer card with a pencil. This is not just the case for sciences but also for humanities and languages. English, for example, is one of the most important examinations for university entrance and almost all students will study it for three or four lessons a week between the ages of 12 and 18. Yet most of them, after six years, will be unable to hold a conversation with a native English speaker since English is taught not for communication but for examination purposes, rather as Latin or ancient Greek are (or were) taught in Europe. Below are two sample questions from the entrance examination to a private university in Tokyo: only one of the four choices given is considered correct (Gill, *JTW*, 7 September 1985).

If you'd like some ice, I (   ) some from the refrigerator.
(*a*) get   (*b*) will get   (*c*) would get   (*d*) should get

The ratio of men (   ) women in the class was seven to one.
(*a*) to   (*b*) and   (*c*) against   (*d*) for

A similar concept applies even in art lessons: teachers mark drawings and paintings by very strict criteria concerning which skills should have been learnt by which grade. This system leaves little room for the notion of the naturally 'artistic' and 'unartistic' individual. Perseverance is seen as the main route to success in art as in all other subjects. In a survey undertaken by Lebra (1982: 84, 269) on the reasons for individual success in Japan, over 70 per cent attributed it to diligence, endurance, and effort rather than natural ability. Hardship is, and always has been, integral to the learning process in Japan.

A final way of maintaining the perception of the equality of the educational system in Japan can be found in the way students are treated at school. There is no streaming by ability in Japanese schools. Indeed, efforts are made to ensure that each class in a grade has an equal range of student scores so as to avoid the charge of unfair discrimination. Similarly, the teacher treats the class as a whole and not each student as an individual. Lessons therefore tend to be totally teacher-centred. The teacher teaches and the student listens and learns. In such a system it is possible to teach very large classes and, on average, junior- and senior-high-school classes in Japan consist of around forty-eight students. Education is also school-centred; the purpose of the school is to pass on information to the students and hence students must adapt to the school as the school will not adapt to them. Strict rules and guidelines are laid down on every aspect of school life from curriculum to hairstyle, and a refusal by any student to follow these may, as we shall see in the next chapter, lead to expulsion.

One of the apparent contradictions of the Japanese educational system is that while demanding competition among individuals, it also instils into those individuals the ideas of conformity which are so important to employers in Japan. Essentially this can be explained by the fact that competition occurs when students move *between* one stage of the system and another, which may be from as early as the age of 3, while *within* each establishment they will find the emphasis on conformity. As Vogel (1963: 66) says: 'Once a child is admitted to a school, grades are not given great importance, and there is a strong feeling of group solidarity which serves to inhibit competitiveness between the students.' This can be seen in the example of group education described in the next chapter. Within any given institution the individual is always seen in the context of a wider group. This is a theme which perhaps reaches its apogee on sports day when it is common for the whole school to be divided into just two teams, the Red Team and the White Team (denoted by the colour of reversible caps) and when individual successes receive no prize but count towards the whole team's score (see *DY*, 12 October 1984; Hendry, 1986: 142–3).

THE ROLE OF TEACHERS IN JAPANESE EDUCATION

Teachers clearly play a very important part in a system where they must, on the one hand, pass on a body of knowledge and, on the other, try to create well-rounded students. Many teachers see the second of these tasks as the more important. Subject-teaching often consists of no more than reading the teacher's copy of the school textbook and setting and marking endless examinations to ensure that students are keeping up to standard. Lessons are not exciting and students are not encouraged to ask questions. If they do, then they risk being labelled disruptive. Although he may enter the profession with great idealism, the teacher is not normally expected to engender any intellectual curiosity in his students, but rather to provide them with the facts and techniques they need in order to pass the examinations. Outside the lesson, though, he will generally feel responsible for creating the right moral attitude in his students. The teacher is the model of behaviour and the students follow his example: the root of the Japanese verb *manabu* (to learn) is the verb *maneru* (to imitate) (Seward, 1984: 30). The teacher in Japan is therefore treated with very great respect and has high status, the word *sensei* having something of the ring 'Doctor' has in Europe. This status is reflected in the high proportion of teachers who are university-trained, as well as in the number of men who enter the profession, especially in high schools (Glazer, 1976: 836–7, 846).

Even if it does not require much lesson preparation, being a teacher in Japan requires considerable dedication and responsibility. It is a twenty-four-hour job since a teacher cannot be seen behaving inappropriately or immorally at any time, and, should a child get into trouble outside school, the authorities are at least as likely to contact his form teacher as his parents. Not surprisingly, many teachers complain that they are little less than mothers and fathers to the fifty children in their care. Rohlen (1983: 190), however, talks of a new trend among younger teachers to see their work less in terms of a 'vocation', as has been traditionally the case, and more as a job in return for a salary—' "*salariiman* teachers"— teachers who work for salaries, as in business, rather than out of devotion'.

Teaching as a whole is a reasonably static and secure profession in Japan. The vast majority of teachers enter the profession as soon as they leave college (in their early 20s) and remain in it until retirement. Moreover, teachers tend to remain in the same teaching district for the simple reason that special qualifying exams have to be taken to teach in state schools in a new area and few experienced teachers are able to compete well enough, in their non-specialist subjects, with recent graduates. There is also the suggestion—

rather as we have seen with the big companies—that boards of education, certainly in more conservative areas, find younger teachers more attractive, both because they are cheaper and because they are potentially less troublesome. A desire to move in mid-career tends to be stigmatized in Japan as an indication of either disloyalty or lack of perseverance. This type of thinking also determines the appointment of principals. Naturally there are many exceptions, but essentially the prerequisite for becoming a school principal is never to have 'rocked the boat' to the extent of coming into conflict with the local board of education. Principals in state schools are generally given little freedom within their own schools and are perceived largely as implementors of local education policy.

Severe restrictions are placed on the right of local education boards (*kyōikuiinkai*) to employ foreigners. In 1984, a celebrated case involving a young Korean woman who had been born and raised in Japan, and who was hired by the board of education in Japan's Nagano prefecture to teach in an elementary school, was widely reported in the media. This teacher had not only passed the prefectural certification examination but had also acquired more than five years' experience as a supply teacher, yet, because of her Korean nationality, Monbushō persisted in denying her full accreditation, stating that the employment of foreign nationals as public servants was against the law. The case received much publicity, not least because, in theory, the right to appoint teachers belongs to the local education board. In this case, after much argument, Nagano prefecture conceded and the woman was finally appointed as a permanent instructor with duties equivalent to those of a teacher but with a much lower salary and limitations that ruled out the possibility of promotion to a supervisory position. Monbushō remained unmoved by protests, insisting that because public servants took part in the exercise of public authority and the shaping of public policy, they must be Japanese citizens (see *AS*, 8 April 1985).

THE EDUCATIONAL 'PROBLEMS' OF *KIKOKUSHIJO*

How does the Japanese educational system affect returnee children? Some argue that it militates against them in almost every way because education in Japan consists of accumulating facts in a carefully structured sequence, and therefore to be absent from the system for even a short period of time is to miss out on an essential part of this body of knowledge. Moreover, in Japanese schools great emphasis is placed not only on what the student does, but on the way in which he does it. There is a correct way of doing almost everything from holding a pen to holding a tennis racquet. Matsubara Tatsuya lists almost all the subjects taught in schools and suggests how returnee children are discriminated against in each of them. The biggest problems, he suggests (1980:48), are in Japanese-language lessons which can have potentially disastrous effects on *kikokushijo*:

Regarding the Japanese language they cannot read *kanji* [Chinese characters] and their vocabulary is behind that of their peers. They are poorer in composition and comprehension. . . . Their poor comprehension and expression makes them dislike playing with friends, they become withdrawn [*mukuchi*], and teachers frequently misunderstand or mistreat the child as if he were suffering from a speech defect [*gengo-shōgaiji*] or were mentally retarded [*seishin hakujakuji*].

Matsubara suggests that sometimes *kikokushijo* lack the vocabulary even to understand mathematics lessons. In geography they have problems because they do not know the names of Japanese places; in social studies they lack the background knowledge of Japanese history; they do not understand the idea that the Japanese educational system is based on memorization, not report-writing; in music they cannot play the harmonica or the recorder, nor can they read music—all skills which every Japanese child learns in elementary school; in draftsmanship (*zukō*) they do not know how to draw in the correct manner; in gymnastics they may not have learnt how to use the parallel bar. Even in English, Matsubara (1980: 48–9) argues, though there are generally fewer problems than in other subjects, some *kikokushijo* are weak at grammar and poor at translating simply because they cannot express themselves well enough in Japanese. Inui and Sono have tried to measure the difference between *kikokushijo* and other students in their performance in the basic school subjects of Japanese language, social studies, mathematics, and science. They concluded (1977: 137) that four terms after the children returned to Japan, they scored, on average, around 10 per cent lower than their peers in these subjects.

Kikokushijo are considered to have such serious educational problems in Japanese schools that teachers, employers, and their own parents have argued they have 'special educational needs'. Indeed, having a returnee child in a regular school may be considered so problematic that teachers and parents of other pupils may insist on his being moved to a *ukeirekō*. It is, perhaps, not difficult to understand why some teachers believe that *kikokushijo* need specialist education. Japanese teachers are poorly trained to cope with such children. Not only do they have up to fifty students in a class but their teaching practice will generally have lasted only two weeks, the first devoted to observation and the second consisting of a mere eight practice lessons. According to a comparative survey by Yanagi (1983), Japanese teachers are considerably more critical of their pupils' self-motivated behaviour and assertion of their uniqueness than their American counterparts. In this sense, Japanese teachers may see the *kikokushijo* as a threat. Returnee students, particularly those who have been in schools in the west, do not accept that the teacher is always right; they know that the Japanese style of teacher-centred lesson is not the only way of learning; and their foreign-language ability is sometimes far superior to that of many Japanese foreign-language teachers. The following description by Matsubara Tatsuya (1984: 20), from one of the most popular English-language teachers' magazines, must have struck a painful chord with many readers:

There are some teachers of English who do not like to teach classes with children who have returned from English-speaking countries. These children have really acquired a grasp of the English language, and have a good accent and superior skills in composition. Having themselves only received a Japanese English education, there are some among those who hold a licence to teach the English language whose accent and conversation skills are uncertain [*fuseikaku*]. Therefore, they find their lessons are difficult to conduct if there are *kikokushijo* present and they dislike this to such an extent that they try to avoid lessons [*keien shitari*] with *kikokushijo*. Some teachers even develop neuroses and lose confidence in their ability to teach.

Even in such traditional Japanese academic strengths as science and mathematics, though returnees are sometimes poorer at application, one informant believed that they might understand the theory better than some of their teachers. Since teachers are generally not accustomed to having either their knowledge or their judgement questioned, and especially not in class in front of others, it is not surprising that they are apt to label returnees who indulge in such practices as disruptive and in need of help to adapt to the Japanese educational system (Kobayashi, 1981: 163–4). In extreme cases, they may even resort to physical punishment.[12]

As with the teacher, the traditional role of the mother in Japanese society may also lead the *kikokushijo* to be branded as in need of help. As we have seen, mothers are expected to sacrifice their own interests to those of their children. White (1980) has demonstrated how the parents of *kikokushijo* have to face the pressure of ensuring that their children have not suffered from their overseas experience. There may also be strong pressure, however, from the mothers of classmates of *kikokushijo* to have the latter sent to special schools. Such mothers worry that having returnees in the class may slow down all the other students or that the teacher may devote too much individual attention to the *kikokushijo*.

Finally, one can easily see how, in the context of the Japanese educational system outlined above, employers may also feel that *kikokushijo* need to go to special schools. Japanese schools are expected to produce individuals able to adapt quickly to company ideologies and pick up new skills; individuals prepared to remain with the company for life; individuals able to concentrate for long periods of time on a single subject; individuals who do not insist on the question 'why?'. In such a context, returnee experience, or at least the commonly held perception of returnee experience, appears to stand in direct opposition to industries' needs: the alleged individualism of *kikokushijo* clashes with Japanese group values; their supposed free-thinking with Japanese harmony; their perceived dilettantism with Japanese diligence and single-mindedness. Some employers may believe that *kikokushijo* not only slow down their non-*kikokushijo* classmates, but also introduce them to non-conformist and disruptive ways of thinking.

CALLS FOR EDUCATIONAL REFORM

Despite the obvious role of education in Japan's post-war 'economic miracle', there have, in recent years, been calls for educational reform. A three-year council appointed by the then prime minister, Nakasone Yasuhiro, was in session from mid 1984 to consider what direction Japanese education should take into the next century. The pressure for this reform has come from several sides.

Some from the political right wing feel that the Americans imposed educational reform on Japan after the War, and that as a result Japan's youth have lost pride in their country and lack a sense of identity. This faction advocates a return to traditional educational values, yet, although it has been very vocal, it does not appear to have been one of the main pressure groups.

Another, more powerful, group demanding reform is, perhaps rather surprisingly, the employers. More than any other group, they recognize the significance of education for economic success, and more than anybody else they recognize that change is necessary if Japan is to retain its place in the world as an economic superpower. In part, employers object to a system that allows high-school leavers to spend several years in a kind of limbo as *rōnin* before they enter university, during which time they add to the country's economy only through the informal sector of education. In part, also, they complain that university is a waste of time—for most students an enjoyable four-year moratorium between the rigours of high-school and company life. It is very difficult to fail a university degree in Japan, hence university students often place more importance on their social lives than on their academic work (see Zeugner, 1984).

More important in the minds of some employers, however, is the belief that more emphasis needs to be placed on creativity in the educational system. Until recently, Japan could rely on a conforming, well disciplined, literate, and numerate workforce to take ideas originating in the west and adapt and perfect them.[13] Employers are now, however, beginning to fear that there are no longer enough ideas originating in other countries, and Japan's workforce must begin to produce ideas of their own. The educational system must therefore become more flexible and individualistic. Morita Akio (1987: 164), the co-founder and chairman of the Sony Corporation, sums up this viewpoint clearly:

There is growing discontent in Japan today with the current educational system, which forces students to spend much of their time learning how to pass examinations in order to get into good schools. The system does not leave them enough time for experimentation and original thinking. The system has served us well up to now, but ways are being explored to make the system more efficient and relevant to the new times we are living in. . . . From a management standpoint, it is very important to know how to unleash people's inborn creativity. My concept is that anybody has creative ability, but very few people know how to use it.

Another important pressure group demanding education reform consists of the parents of children who have just been, are currently going, or are about to go through the Japanese educational system. The importance attached to education in Japan places great social and economic pressures on the individual and the family, and the expansion of tertiary education has not been able to keep up with the demand. As the system becomes more competitive, the work becomes more difficult and more children fall behind and cannot catch up. Some of these children, labelled as 'failures' by the system, or simply mentally exhausted, relieve their frustration on those around them or on themselves. As a result, bullying and school violence, though still uncommon by western standards, are on the rise in Japan, and schoolchild suicides and murder of close kin are not such unusual events. Parents are therefore demanding the liberalization of the educational system, more freedom of choice over courses, and less uniformity in the treatment of students as ways of relieving the pressure on their children.

While there is great interest in those who survive and prosper in spite of the rigours of the education system—there are sometimes newspaper articles about students who have passed into Tokyo University at the fourth, fifth, or even sixth attempt—the idea of a more liberal educational system remains something of a dream for most Japanese. The massive success of Kuroyanagi Tetsuko's autobiography, *Madogiwa no Tottochan* (1982), can be explained not only by the national interest in this, by Japanese standards, most unconventional woman (a major television personality) but also by its depiction of a school which could allow a girl, labelled 'overactive' as she was at an early age, to develop fully as an individual.[14] The open acceptance of the second-generation Japanese boy, who arrived at the school from the USA during the War with virtually no Japanese language ability and taught the other children English, presupposes the type of educational environment demanded by Ōsawa Chikako (1986) in her book, *Tatta Hitotsu no Aoi Sora* ('Under the One Blue Sky'). To place one's child in such an institution, however, remains in the realms of fantasy for most Japanese parents. Attempts at educational reform have continually failed to produce major changes in the system. Len Schoppa (1988) suggests that the recent council for reform—attacked by a strange alliance of the left-wing unions and the conservative Monbushō—was also stymied by an inability to produce genuine plans for change. Moreover, while there is considerable support throughout

Japan for radical changes in the educational system, it is equally obvious that very few parents are prepared to jeopardize their own child's future by opting out of the current system. Rohlen (1983: 108) expresses this point succinctly:

A division arises . . . between public values and private interests, between idealism and reality. The public, idealistic goals remain central to the rhetoric of politicians, officials, teachers, parents, and students. And they are all sincere in their desire that education further the development of democracy and promote individual growth. Yet, when the chips are down, most parents want success for their own children more than anything else.

Despite all the rhetoric, the advice that parents seek is not how to change the educational system but how to ensure that their own children succeed in it. Rather than withdraw their children from the potential dangers of the 'examination hell', they seek advice on how to minimize its effects.

There has been one area, however, in which demands for reform of the educational system do seem to have met with genuine proposals. This is the area of the 'internationalization' of Japanese education. As we shall see, 'internationalization' is a term with a large number of meanings in Japan, but in the context of education it has generally been defined as the inclusion of more foreign, generally western, language teaching and education for 'international understanding' (*kokusai rikai kyōiku*) in the curriculum, the exchange of students and teachers from abroad, and, significantly, provision for overseas and returnee Japanese children (see Kobayashi, 1980: 244). The significance for *kikokushijo* of the 'internationalization' of education in Japan will become clearer later.

Sanuki Kazuie (1984) sums up the reasons why *kikokushijo* are generally perceived as being in need of special education. Firstly, he suggests that *kikokushijo* suffer culture shock on their return to Japan and require special help if they are to adapt to life in Japan. In many cases, they may suffer problems such as *tōkōkyohi* (school refusal syndrome) and become *ochikobore* (school drop-outs). Secondly, extra special care is needed in dealing with the language problems of these children. Thirdly, because of the nature of the education system in Japan and the fact that they are generally poor at Japanese, mathematics, and other subjects, *kikokushijo* generally do badly in examinations and therefore need a special system to get them into schools and universities.

The last two chapters of this book have covered many of the main reasons why the need to set up special schools in Japan for *kikokushijo* was accepted. The fact that such schools exist can be understood only in relation to the general belief in the special nature of the Japanese 'cultural complex' and the Japanese educational system. In this context these special schools are seen as helping the *kikokushijo* readapt to Japanese society. Their experiences overseas are believed to have created problems for them. At its worst, the individual *kikokushijo* may be seen as suffering from some underlying, often pathological, problem that needs treatment in the form of adaptation education (*tekiō kyōiku*). According to Nishimura Yoshihiro (*JT*, 9 November 1984), head of the Kaigai Shijo Kyōiku Shinkō Zaidan, schools for *kikokushijo* work on the basis of having 'successfully educated' a certain number of children, while those involved in such education should be seen as 'courageous people tackling this issue'. A number of expressions have been used to describe the education of *kikokushijo* in the *ukeirekō*: Inui and Sono (1977: 143) call it 'Japanizing' (*Nihonka*) and 're-dying' (*somenaoshi*), and, even more graphically, Befu (1983: 247) uses the phrase 'peeling off foreignness' (*gaikoku hagashi*). During my fieldwork in one of these *ukeirekō* for *kikokushijo*, however, I discovered that the picture was in fact very different from the images these expressions suggest.

5

Case Study of a School with *Kikokushijo*

From April 1984, I undertook one year's participant fieldwork at a school which I shall call Fujiyama Gakuen, in Ibaraki Prefecture, just north of Tokyo.[1] The fact that the school was called a *gakuen* (literally, 'academic campus') identifies it immediately as a private institution: all national and local schools, and indeed most private schools, are referred to as *gakkō*. Fujiyama Gakuen is unusual in being a six-year institution covering both the junior- and the senior-high-school years. As we have seen (Table VIII), only around 3 per cent of Japanese schoolchildren attend private junior high schools, while almost 30 per cent attend private senior high schools. These figures, however, are for the whole country and the percentage is much higher in urban and richer prefectures (James and Benjamin, 1988: 149). It is therefore partly a reflection of the concentration of returnees in urban areas that, according to Murase (1980: 47), over 60 per cent of all *kikokushijo* probably attend private schools.

Although it was opened only in 1979, Fujiyama Gakuen is a well-known school for research on *kikokushijo*. Roughly 25 per cent of the students at Fujiyama were classified as *kaigaisei*, the school's term for returnees. No less than four of the studies discussed in Chapters 3 and 4 included research undertaken at the school, in the form of questionnaires or very short interviews with *kikokushijo*. My own project was, however, the first anthropological fieldwork based on the participant observation approach.

I entered Fujiyama Gakuen at the beginning of the Japanese school year as a part-time English teacher. I taught special classes given for returnee students in the first three grades (ages 12 to 15) which consisted of eight, sixteen, and nine children respectively, whereas the average class size in the school was over forty. Throughout the year I lived in a small room (known as a *dokushinshitsu*, or bachelor pad) at the end of one of the school dormitories. I attended all the staff-meetings for full-time teachers as well as their parties and extracurricular activities, and was generally considered the same as the full-time foreign teachers. This meant that I was treated as much like a Japanese member of staff as possible. One of the cornerstones of the school principal's educational philosophy was that the foreign staff were on the same salary structure, assigned the same duties, and expected to fulfil the same roles—including the co-ordination of meetings when their turn came on the rota—as their Japanese colleagues. This experience as a teacher in Fujiyama led me to ask very different questions about *kikokushijo* experience from those asked by previous researchers.

THE GEOGRAPHY AND HISTORY OF FUJIYAMA GAKUEN

Fujiyama Gakuen is situated in Tsukuba Gakuen Toshi (Tsukuba Academic City) which, as I was told prior to my arrival, 'is not typical of Japan'. The word 'Gakuen'—the same as in Fujiyama Gakuen—is used to distinguish Tsukuba from the industrial cities and agricultural towns of most of Japan. Concentrated in 27 square kilometres, there are now two universities (Tsukuba University and a small institute of library and information science), thirty-one government research institutes, thirteen government-related facilities, and seven private institutes. This makes Tsukuba home to about 45 per cent of the total government research workforce in Japan, and probably the largest city in the world devoted to the development of science and technology—larger than Novosibirsk in the Soviet Union, the Île de France, or the Chapel Hill Research Triangle in North Carolina (*DY*, 13 September 1984).

The plan for Tsukuba was conceived during the early 1960s when the Japanese economy was growing at a rate of more than 10 per cent a year and there was concern to create a more balanced regional distribution of resources. By the mid-1960s, there was an added incentive to resettle government research institutes outside the overcrowded metropolis of Tokyo (Houser, 1984: 12). Tsukuba, a largely unsettled area of flat land in the Mito plain only 45 miles to the north-east of Tokyo, appeared an ideal site for such a plan and as a result the outline of a city, with wide roads and public utilities, was drawn up. The first research centre was built in 1968 and, at about this time, as a reaction to the massive campus unrest of the late 1960s, the idea of building a new type of university at Tsukuba, to be directly under government control, was floated. The university and the research institutes now form the basis of the city. In the whole Tsukuba area, there are some 3,500 academics, 7,000 researchers, and 8,500 students, giving it the obvious nickname of 'The City of Brains' (Houser, *THES*, 29 July 1983).

Despite more than ¥1.3 trillion having been spent on the creation of Tsukuba by the early 1980s, even its most ardent supporters could not call it a fully functional city. One Japanese academic living in Tokyo described it as *Nihon no Siberia* ('Japan's Siberia'). Tsukuba retains a 'frontier-town' image largely as a result of the high proportion of *tanshin funin* who commute to the area on a weekly basis: only 50 per cent of the university staff live on, or near, the campus (Houser, *THES*, 29 July 1983). The institutes and buildings which have been built are widely spaced out, and it has been estimated that a 40-per-cent increase in the present population would be needed fully to populate the city. The problem of underpopulation is exacerbated by the poor transport facilities to the site: few people use the current system because of its poor service, and Japan Railways refuse to expand services until there are more passengers. The local bus service is also poor and Fujiyama Gakuen has to make special arrangements for its commuting students. This isolated setting, however, is not an altogether unattractive feature to Japanese. About 70 per cent of Japan's land area is uninhabitable owing to the mountainous terrain and the remainder is therefore extremely crowded. The possibility of giving their children an education in a pleasant countryside environment is very attractive to many parents and Fujiyama makes full use of this in its advertising.

It was partly in an effort to encourage migration to the Tsukuba area that the government gave substantial financial support to the 1985 World Exposition—a forum for the demonstration of the latest technological developments from around the world—which was held in the area. During the six months of the Exposition there were some twenty million visitors, which did much to confirm Tsukuba's standing, both at home and abroad, as the Japanese city of the future.

TSUKUBA UNIVERSITY AND THE FUJIYAMAKAI

The University of Tsukuba has a reputation for being 'international' owing to its comparatively open policy on accepting foreign researchers and students and, more recently, because it has been appointed by the government as one of the major new centres for training native teachers of Japanese as a foreign language. This latter is a first step towards the goal of increasing the number of foreign students studying in Japan to 100,000 by the beginning of the twenty-first century. The fact that Monbushō could 'appoint' a national university to such a role is the legacy of a crucial factor in the creation of Tsukuba University.

The initial impetus for reform of the universities came as a reaction to the massive campus unrest of the late 1960s. Throughout this period, the universities were pressurized into considering various programmes of self-reform. In July of 1969, Tokyo Kyōiku Daigaku (Tokyo University of Education) produced a radical new plan for a university at Tsukuba. The radical aspects of the plan included multidisciplinary schools (*gakugun*); 'outsiders' on the university governing board; multiple appointments for teaching staff so as not to restrict them to one subject; and finally an administrative structure that would give considerably greater power to the university's president than was previously the case in national universities.

Tokyo University of Education itself had only been founded in the period immediately after the Second World War, and was formed from an amalgamation of the prestigious Tokyo Arts and Sciences University (Tokyo Bunrika Daigaku) established in 1929 and the Tokyo Higher Normal School (Tokyo Kōtō Shihan Gakkō) founded in 1877. According to Cummings (1978: 322), this amalgamation was not completely successful as the original factions continued their rivalry in the new institution. There were also severe political cleavages between faculties exacerbated by the fact that the institution was divided among several sites. From the mid 1950s, there was talk of moving to a new integrated site as a way of solving these internal problems. In 1963, as plans for Tsukuba Academic City began to get underway, Monbushō approached the new president of Tokyo University of Education and asked him if he would be interested in moving there. This proposal created even greater rifts between the faculties and only the generally conservative faculties of science, physical education, and agriculture were positively in favour of the move. In spite of this, in 1973, the university opened on its new campus.

Cummings (1978: 325) describes Tsukuba as a 'conservative symbol' since its reforms were so in line with the wishes of Monbushō from which it had full support. The conservative reputation of the university remains. It has been purposely designed with no large meeting place in which students can gather to organize or demonstrate. Indeed, the students must receive university approval for any assembly. In 1984, the university authorities forbade the students to hold their annual fair because they claimed the students had violated university rules by staging a political event the previous year. A group of 150 students staged a sit-in before the university called in the police to remove them from the campus (*JT*, 27 October 1984). When, in 1983, several universities, including Sapporo and Waseda, refused to take an American army captain as a student in deference to left-wing protests, Tsukuba was happy to offer him a place.

In academic terms, Tsukuba has achieved an enviably good reputation in a very short time, and has risen high in the hierarchy of Japanese universities. Entrance to Tsukuba University is highly competitive. As a result of this, Fujiyama Gakuen's connection with the university is of considerable significance. Since the school does not bear the name of the university, however, most Japanese are unaware that there is any connection between the two. Fujiyama Gakuen was founded by the Fujiyamakai (Fujiyama Association), the old-boy network of Tsukuba University and its predecessor institutions. The Fujiyamakai has some 30,000 members, many of them in the educational world, and, as one of the projects to mark its centenary in 1977, it decided to set up a school in the Tsukuba area.

It is the political background to the founding of Tsukuba University and Fujiyama Gakuen's relation to the university which explains the following anonymous attack on the school in 1985 in the 'tabloid' newspaper *Tokyo Sports*, well known for its gossip and anti-establishment views. The story carried several provocative and prominent banners: *Kyōiku ni Na o Karita Riken Shūdan* ('An Interest Group which has Borrowed the Name of Education'); *Kanryō Ōkoku o Hadaka ni Suru* ('Exposure of a Bureaucratic Kingdom'); *Monbushō: Sangaku Kyōdō no Inbō* ('Monbushō's

Plot with Industry–University Co-operation'). The article describes Tsukuba University as an institution created to destroy the power of the so-called 'red teachers' in Tokyo and to wrest control from students in the universities. It then claims:

One of the leaders of the former Tokyo University of Education's right-wing group is presently head of Tsukuba University. . . . He set up an old-boy network called the Fujiyamakai of those intellectually leaning to the right [*migiyori*] who supported his viewpoint. From funds which the old-boy network collected . . . a new high school for boys and girls was opened. . . . This school can be called a mini-Tsukuba University. All of Tsukuba University's schools are strictly controlled and most of them have a complete dormitory system. This is a system to produce an uncontamin-ated strain [*junsui baiyō*], and turn out individuals who are useful citizens for the State [*kokka*] and its political leaders [*iseisha*]. What is their aim? The Fujiyamakai have not forgotten the pre-war system. . . . They support nationalist education and consider the current democratic education a nuisance. . . . In order to promote their beliefs, they recreate interest in the imperial education system. That is why they impose the severe dormitory system.

Much of the article is nonsense. The Fujiyamakai was in existence for almost a hundred years before Tsukuba University was built and has always been highly respected for its varied ideas on education. Its linking of the history of the founding of Tsukuba University and Fujiyama Gakuen is therefore decidedly specious. The newspaper was clearly looking for a way to attack both the type of educational reform being pursued by Prime Minister Nakasone, and the right wing who were demanding a return to traditional educational values. Nevertheless, the article does highlight the controversy underlying the creation not only of the university but of any school offering a different educational system from that of the norm. The suggestion of anything less than total equality among schools is clearly anathema to certain sectors of the Japanese press and public. It is with this theme in mind that we can turn to a more detailed examination of the organization of, and philosophy behind, Fujiyama Gakuen.

PROFILE OF FUJIYAMA GAKUEN

The Principal

When the general assembly of the Fujiyamakai decided, in May 1977, to found a school, a search committee was set up to find a suitable principal. According to the history produced for the association's centenary, it was only by chance that the committee heard about Sakamoto Minoru, who had graduated from Tokyo University of Education in 1954, but once they had, they 'selected him like a shot' (*shiraha no ya o tateta*). In Japanese terms, he was an unconventional choice. Certainly by the criteria outlined in Chapter 4 for selecting Japanese principals, it would have been nearly impossible for him to be appointed as principal of a state school. For a start, he was only 48 years old, while most Japanese principals are appointed in their late 50s. Even more unusual was the fact that he had not worked continuously in high-school education, a feature which is often taken in Japan to be a sign of either too much individuality or an inability to persevere. He had changed jobs every eight years, starting his career as a high-school teacher in biology, then moving to the Tokyo municipal board of education, before working for the Tokyo Denki Kagaku (TDK) company in their Taiwan branch where he was generally responsible for employees' education.

But the most important distinction between Sakamoto and most Japanese principals was that he ran the school very much according to his own ideas. He had a strong personality and held tight rein not only over the school but even over the school governors. He was greatly respected by his teaching staff and had considerable charisma. Several teachers, describing how they came to the school, would tell how he had inspired them with his vision of a new type of education and then, in mock disbelief, shake their heads at how easily impressed they had been. When the school governors (*rijikai*), finding him immovable on several issues—which included increasing average class sizes from forty-eight to fifty students— tried to appeal over his head directly to the staff, the latter, some with great emotion, all fell in line behind the principal. The principal had designed the school in terms of both its physical layout and its academic structure, and those of the staff who spoke at the meeting with the governors described it as a school with which they were proud to be associated. One senior teacher explained: 'I have been here from the very start of this school. If the school was not to survive, then neither I, nor my wife, nor my family would have anything left.'

Few teachers would have suggested, though, that the principal's idealism was not grounded in hard reality. Indeed, some said that he was not a teacher but a businessman. In part, this was a legacy of his work with TDK, one of Japan's biggest companies; in part, it was due to the length of time since he had actually taught, although he had taken it upon himself, as we shall see, to deliver the 'moral education' element of the curriculum for all Fujiyama students. Mainly, though, his reputation as a businessman was due to his recognition that, as a private school, Fujiyama was fully involved in the marketplace, and that the school was under heavy pressure from the governors to provide evidence of healthy finances. Indeed, the school's financial situation—in particular the large amounts still owed to the local municipality for the land on which the school stood—was the main reason given by the governors for calling a meeting to encourage the teachers to take more students in their classes.[2]

The Governors

The governors of the school were all senior and respected members of the Fujiyamakai. Apart from the one meeting with the teachers mentioned above and the beginning- and end-of-year school ceremonies, they had little direct contact with the school. They were generally seen as figures of the establishment: at important school ceremonies the head of the governors would always bow to the 'national' flag and once commented how proud he was to speak before it.[3] Many teachers thought that the governors would have preferred Fujiyama to be a traditional type of school, a *shingakkō* (examination-based school) concentrating solely on preparing students to pass the examinations into the top universities.

The Fujiyamakai had invested heavily in the school. They had collected around ¥900 million in donations, using their contacts throughout the business world, to set up the school. Their reputation as an educational organization rested largely on the success of the school. The success of the school rested totally on the reputation it built up as an educational establishment. It was a sign not only of the strength of the principal's character but also of the governors' trust in him, that they allowed him to implement his own ideas on education in the school. Two highly complimentary articles about Fujiyama, one in the *Nihon Keizai Shinbun*, Japan's most respected financial newspaper, and the other in the semi-academic journal *Chūō Kōron*, did much to reinforce their confidence.

The Teachers

Most of the teachers had been introduced to the school by pre-existing staff members, a common recruitment method in Japan which serves to bind new members into a ready-made network of human relations, providing added surety for the school. Some of the first teachers were recruited by the principal himself. These included the head of the senior school, who had been a former pupil of the principal, and the head of student affairs, who had been his son's form teacher in a small school in the north of Japan. Similarly, a significant proportion of the teachers had been to the universities of the Fujiyamakai and had learnt about the school through other members (normally professors) of the association, or had been recommended by them.

The teachers at Fujiyama came from all over Japan, ranging from Hokkaido in the far north to one of the small Goto islands off Kyushu in the south. Mostly, they had had good, though generally not outstanding, academic careers proceeding through the state high-school system to a variety of universities, including Tokyo, Kyoto, Sophia, Tokyo Kyōiku Daigaku, Tsukuba, and even (in the case of one retired principal who had returned to teaching) the pre-war Tokyo Higher Normal School.

The teaching staff at Fujiyama differed in a number of important aspects from the staff groups of most Japanese schools. The principal, who played the major part in the recruitment of all teachers, insisted in an interview with *Chūō Kōron* that, since it was so hard to be a teacher in a school like Fujiyama—with its dormitory duties and the need for a teacher to be with students virtually all the time—he was only interested in those with certain qualities: 'We restrict ourselves to "people with real-life experience" [*jisshakai keiken no aru mono*].'

Many of the younger teachers had come straight to the school from university, although several had continued as postgraduates and completed Master's degrees. This is relatively uncommon in Japan—only 5 per cent of university students become post-graduates—where graduates are generally expected to join a company immediately on completing their first degree. Many of the older teachers in Fujiyama had had varied careers: they included a former Olympic gymnastics candidate who had been teaching in Thailand for five years; his wife, also a gymnast; a former editor of an English-language magazine; a student of European baroque music who had spent seven years in Switzerland; a caster of metal art objects (*bijutsu chūzō*); employees of two different publishing companies; two former members of the Japanese equivalent of the Peace Corps (Japan Overseas Co-operation Volunteers), one of whom had been in Costa Rica for over two years and the other in El Salvador for some four years; and a teacher who had gone of his own initiative to Wales where he had gained a teaching certificate in physical education.

All the teachers, of course, were properly qualified: indeed, the school employed a former member of an electrical company in the school office for a year while he undertook the necessary examinations for teaching at high school. Even those few teachers who had experience of teaching before coming to Fujiyama, however, were atypical of the majority of teachers in Japan: two were senior members of an organization called the Seito Seikatsu Shidō Kenkyūkai (one of the more influential educational organizations in Japan, which we shall discuss in more detail later), one of whom has some fourteen books to his name and is among the best-known educational philosophers in contemporary Japan.

One of the more noticeable features of the teaching staff at Fujiyama as a whole was their experience overseas. Apart from those individuals already mentioned, at least two other teachers had spent a year studying overseas and the vast majority had travelled abroad. Unlike most teachers in English-language departments in Japanese schools, most of the English teachers were confident not only in reading but also in speaking English, and several could manage other languages as well. In addition to this, unlike the normal reluctance discussed in Chapter 4 to employ foreign staff on the same terms as Japanese colleagues, Fujiyama had two full-time foreign teachers of English—one American, one

Canadian—as well as three part-time foreign teachers, and weekly visits by native teachers of German, French, Spanish, and Chinese. In 1986 an Afghani teacher, whose visa was about to expire and who was unable to return home for political reasons, joined the English department.

About 40 per cent of the total staff of 105 at Fujiyama were classified as *hijōkin* (part-time) as opposed to *sennin* (full-time). This distinction was not based simply on the number of hours taught, and indeed, many part-time teachers taught as many hours as full-time teachers. Instead, the important distinction was that the part-time teachers were not expected to participate in extra-curricular activities, such as formroom periods and dormitory and lunchtime duties. This made them peripheral to the real running of the school. The full-time kitchen and office staff were invited to attend school meetings and parties, such as *bōnenkai* (end-of-year) and *shinnenkai* (start-of-year) parties, but the part-time teachers were not. This created a sense of an élite centre and an expendable periphery such as that found in Japanese companies (Dore, 1973: 38–9), the periphery being eligible for few of the benefits, a much lower salary (about half), and none of the security of the centre.

Again, as in Japanese companies, the division between the categories of full- and part-time workers was largely determined by gender: women accounted for less than one-third of the full-time, but over half of the part-time, teachers. Moreover, no woman held a senior job such as head of grade or department, and there was only one female form teacher in the whole school. This was partly due to difficulties in persuading older women with families to move to the school dormitory, but it largely reflects the wider sexual discrimination in Japanese society. Moreover, according to Elizabeth Mouer (1976: 172), women teachers in the 1970s in Japan generally faced greater discrimination in terms of pay and status in private schools than in state schools.

Among the part-time teachers at Fujiyama there were a retired principal and vice-principal who had been hired specifically for the purpose of giving advice to the young and inexperienced teachers in their departments. According to James and Benjamin (1988: 101) the use of underemployed educated workers (such as young women and retired men) is common in the private education sector as a means to keep down wage costs. Indeed, finance was certainly an important factor behind the recruitment of a large proportion of young teachers at Fujiyama. Salary scales in Japan are closely linked to age, and the hiring of young staff meant that the school could keep its wage bill down while establishing its financial security.[4] There is no doubt, also, that it was easier for the principal to educate young and inexperienced teachers in the school philosophy, and some junior members of the staff occasionally complained that he treated them as scarcely different from the students.

The dormitory was the central focus for most of the full-time teachers. Some of the older teachers could afford to build houses away from the school to which, as they saw it, 'escape' was occasionally possible, but generally speaking, they were tied to the housemasters' flats at the end of 'their' corridors. Fujiyama has the third largest number of dormitory beds—550—among Japanese schools. The principal claimed to have visited many other boarding-schools, as well as reading accounts of boarding systems in institutions such as British public schools, in his search for the ideal dormitory set-up. One of the main purposes of the boarding system at Fujiyama was to create a 'family atmosphere' thought conducive to a good educational environment. This was made easier by the distance of the school from any large town, the minimal contact with the local community, and the gathering together of a large group of teachers from all over Japan who could not easily return home. Indeed, within six years of the school's foundation, the staff had manifested an extraordinarily high rate of preferential endo-gamy with no less than six marriages taking place between teachers. As with many marriages in Japan, these were privately initiated but were then given public recognition by the principal who not only gave his approval but also acted as the symbolic go-between (*nakōdo*) at the actual wedding ceremony (see Hendry, 1981: 140–7). Indeed, the principal several times expressed regret that there had not been more marriages between staff, and occasionally he jokingly castigated the younger male teachers for not having had the nerve to propose to a young British woman who had taught at the school previously.

The encouragement of married couples teaching in the same school is interesting in view of the fact that it is forbidden in most state schools in Japan. It was an endless source of humour at Fujiyama—particularly when couples took opposite sides in debates—and the real or potential relationships between teachers was a major source of gossip not only among students but also among the teaching staff. Staff marriages normally took place during the traditional spring-wedding season which falls between the end of one academic year and the start of the next. In retrospect, it is perhaps not surprising, then, that I made my initial greetings and final farewells to the staff at the wedding celebrations of two pairs of teachers from the school. At staff meetings throughout the year, the principal would also present teachers with traditional envelopes of money on the birth of a child, the construction of a house, or even the acquisition of a new car. This all added to the feeling of being 'one family'.

The Parents

I undertook a survey of 166 students at Fujiyama, of whom just over half—51 per cent—had been overseas. The sample was taken across the school grades with a slight under-representation of replies from students in the first and fifth years. The main purpose of the survey was to gain a clearer picture of the family backgrounds of the students.

Over two-thirds of those who responded said that their mothers were housewives. Of the working mothers, twelve were school teachers, one of the few high-status occupations for women in Japan outside the home; nine were receptionists, usually in their husbands' medical or dental practices; a further nine were teachers of various traditional skills or hobbies (*o-keiko*); four were researchers in the Tsukuba area; and three were self-employed.

A list of fathers' occupations is given in Table IX. The category of 'salaryman' (white-collar company employee) is complex since it covers employees from the lowest levels of the company to the top. According to Nakane (1970), a Japanese company worker's identification comes primarily from the company to which he belongs rather than from his actual role within the company, and several students in fact simply gave the name of their father's company in place of his occupation. A number of factors would suggest that these 'salarymen' were closer to the top ranks of their companies than the bottom. Firstly, Fujiyama's fees were, in 1984, among the most expensive in the country;[5] secondly, about 30 per cent of the children polled had at least one sibling in the school (for

TABLE IX: Father's Occupation of a
Sample of Fujiyama Gakuen Students

Salaryman	49[a]
Company Head	4
Doctor	16
Dentist	3
Professor	16
Researcher	13
Teacher	5
Craftsman	7
Diplomat	6
Banking	12
Airlines	5
Salesman (car/insurance)	5
Architect	4
Self-employed	4
Engineer	3
Journalist	3
Administrator	3
Farmer, post office head, artist, ship's captain, estate agent, translator, tax inspector, legal writer	1 each
No answer	1
TOTAL	166

[a] This represents 29.5 per cent.
Companies named included Mitsui
Bussan, 4; Mitsubishi, 3; Hitachi, 2; and
Toshiba, NEC, IBM, Marubeni, 1 each.

which there was no reduction in fees);[6] and, thirdly, the school did not offer any scholarships for poorer students.[7] Even setting aside the category of 'salaryman', however, an examination of the rest of the fathers' occupations reveals the generally high-status nature of the families of Fujiyama students: 16 per cent were doctors or dentists, and a further 29 per cent combined to form the similarly respected category of professors, researchers, and teachers.

The types of school the 166 students had attended immediately before entering Fujiyama are given in Table X. Very few of the children (6 per cent) compared to the total number of children classified as *kikokushijo* in the school (25 per cent) had returned directly from overseas. Some of them had been in Japan for several years before entering Fujiyama. Although only 8 per cent of the students polled went to private schools before entering Fujiyama, this is significantly higher—ten times higher in the case of

TABLE x: Type of School
Attended by a Sample of
Students immediately before
entering Fujiyama Gakuen

	No.	%
Private	14	8.4
National	4	2.4
Overseas	10[a]	6
Public	138	83.3
TOTAL	166	100.0

[a] 4 *genchikō*, 6 *Nihonjingakkō*.

elementary schools—than the national average. Parents who invest
in private education at the elementary and junior-high-school levels
have to pay considerable sums for the higher teacher-pupil ratio
which they offer.

One question in the survey concerned the religious background
of the children. According to James and Benjamin (1988: 62), over
30 per cent of private schools in Japan are founded by religious
organizations, of which about 70 per cent are Christian. Fujiyama,
however, was not a Christian foundation, although seventeen of the
children polled said that their families were Christian, and a further
three said that one parent was Christian—a total of 12 per cent—
while another four expressed a personal interest in Christianity.
This is significantly higher than the less-than-1 per cent of the total
Japanese population estimated to be Christian. Significantly,
although they represent such a small proportion of the population,
Christians tend to hold important positions within Japanese
society. They also tend to be more committed to their religion than
most other Japanese religionists and hence Christianity is seen by
some to be a sign of individuality (Suzuki, 1974: 71–87; Caldarola,
1979). Moreover, the influence of Christian thought in Japan has
far exceeded the actual number of practising Christians, particularly in the areas of social welfare, hospital, prison, and educational
reform, and especially the education of women. It is interesting,
therefore, that the schools in Japan with the three largest
populations of *kikokushijo* (ICU, Dōshisha, and Gyōsei), as well as
many of the other private instititutions for *kikokushijo* (such as
Keimei and Nanzan), are Christian foundations.

The only time that pupils' family backgrounds were specifically mentioned at Fujiyama was at the meetings to select new students. Unusually for a Japanese school, entrance involved not just an examination, but an exceptionally elaborate procedure including writing an essay (about their family, for example), a personal interview with each child by a panel of three to five teachers, and an interview with the child and at least one parent or guardian by the principal. Moreover, every year thirty students were accepted through what was known as a *suisen seido* (recommendation system) on the basis of their elementary school reports and their performance in a group discussion observed by Fujiyama teachers. These procedures, the school felt, ensured the acceptance of only those who were the 'right kind' of student from the 'right sort' of family. At the final selection meetings, which would go on into the early hours, teachers could effectively veto certain students or offer to take responsibility for others. The principal always had the final say. He supported the acceptance of siblings and there was always a small category of students, euphemistically described as 'from the school office' (*jimushitsu kara*), who, the principal clearly thought, constituted special cases. It was assumed that these were children of important school benefactors. He made it quite clear, however, that even if there were a strong obligation on him to accept a certain child, he would not do so if he felt the child's performance was really too far below par.

The result of the selection procedure at Fujiyama was that the students tended to come from a well-to-do, high-status stratum of Japanese society. As we shall see, this background was not played down in the school by encouraging the students to think of themselves as being like all other Japanese children, but was generally emphasized to make them aware of their social position and how they should develop the attitudes appropriate to this position. This is just one part of the school philosophy which we need to examine.

FUJIYAMA GAKUEN'S EDUCATIONAL PHILOSOPHY

In the summer of 1984 the following front-page editorial appeared in the *Nihon Keizai Shinbun (Nikkei)*:

In one corner of Tsukuba Academic City stands the private Fujiyama High School. It has a separate recruitment [*betsuwaku boshū*] for the education of the children of the many researchers in the area who go or return from overseas. It also has many overseas teachers and teachers with overseas experience, and further it has a dormitory. . . . It is in its sixth year now and, if it can maintain its unique educational content, then it will bring a breath of fresh air to our troubled high-school education. If I can give just one example, it is of the individual research projects which all second-year senior-high-school students must produce. Students can choose their theme according to their own interests . . . and some of the final reports are better than ordinary university graduates could write. This 'thinking for oneself, making one's own decisions, expressing oneself' type of education is also employed for career guidance. It is not just down to choosing a university within a certain range based on one's grade in the practice examinations [*mogi shiken*]. In the careers room one can see lined up many course outlines [*rishū annai*] for university students' use and students can choose their professors, departments and subjects freely from what they learnt from their individual study projects and so on. . . . Just doing school work is avoided in this school. Besides the individual research reports, sports and club activities are strongly emphasized. I hope this type of education takes root and is successful. That is to say that while throughout the country the majority of schools are competing to get their students into the best universities, this school's teachers, parents, and students are not afraid to stand alone.

The fact that this article was published in the *Nikkei* is not in itself surprising. As long ago as 1978, Murase (1978: 12–13) pointed out that the great interest expressed by the *Nikkei* in *kikokushijo* educational matters was likely to be for the simple reason that its readership included many families who lived, or had lived, overseas. Rather more surprising is the fact that the piece was written and researched in the middle of the school's summer vacation when the only children around were those practising for various club events. In fact, the piece was based entirely on an interview with the school principal. It is a statement of the school's essential philosophy, or what is known in Japan as its *tatemae* (public policy).

During the period of my fieldwork, the principal elaborated on the school's philosophy in a couple of other lengthy published interviews and at the four *setsumeikai* (explanation meetings) held during the autumn term for the parents of prospective students. In one interview, he selected what he described as the 'hidden curriculum'—he used the term *ura bangumi* (literally, the 'prog-ramme on the other channel')—as one of the keys to understanding the Fujiyama system. By 'hidden curriculum' the principal was referring to a 'whole-person education' which paralleled the academic curriculum. As we have seen in Chapter 4, schools in Japan generally do not see their purpose as solely academic. Few, however, have as clear a notion as Fujiyama of how to give such a 'whole-person' education. This 'hidden curriculum' at Fujiyama, according to the principal, rests on a number of 'pillars' (*hashira*). In the first four grades of the school, these are mainly programmes such as 'exploring Japanese culture' (*Nihon bunka o saguru*) and 'the practice of group activities' (*group katsudō no jissen*). In the last two grades—when students are 17 or 18—the emphasis changes to 'understanding different cultures' (*ibunka o rikai suru*), 'thinking about a future life' (*shōrai no ikikata o kangaeru*), and 'seeking individuality' (*kosei o motomeru*).

In his interview for *Chūō Kōron*, the principal chose the various school trips as examples of the content of the 'hidden curriculum'. In most schools, these occasions consist of little more than sightseeing tours to various famous places in Japan and provide little of educational interest. They are normally known as *shūgaku ryokō* (school trips). To distinguish Fujiyama's school trips from this tradition, the principal has coined the term *kenshū ryokō* (study trips) and given them very clearly defined educational objectives. First-year students go on a camp, some 30 miles from the school, for two nights. Here they are divided into groups of eight with individuals being given different responsibilities. These groups do everything 'by themselves', from cooking three meals a day, to orienteering, plant observation, and studying geological strata. In the second-year students' camp of three nights, they have to put up their own tents and, while covering up to 60 to 70 kilometres on foot in groups of four or five, collect data for a research report. Even when it rains they must continue because, as the principal explained in the interview, 'there is such a prevailing tendency [*fūchō*] towards over-protection [*kahogo*] in our society that children can't even experience boiling rice in the rain'. This comment, like most of the principal's examples, related to an actual incident. After twenty-four hours of incessant rain during their camp, the second-year teachers requested permission to bring the students back to school early. The principal refused, and, when they returned, publicly berated the teachers concerned for not having previously worked out an alternative course of action, until one of the female teachers broke down in tears. As so often, when he was unhappy with some of the staff, he would ask rhetorically whether they were really 'Fujiyama-type' teachers, thereby differentiating between them and teachers in other Japanese schools.

The third-year students' topic on 'seeking Japanese culture' included a week in Kyoto. Teams of seven or eight children worked independently on their own projects, free to go anywhere they desired in the city as long as they remained in their groups. Before they set off, the principal told them that if there was an accident they had to use their heads. The purpose of the exercise was to make them 'think by themselves'. If they could not do that, then they were not real *Fujiyamasei* (Fujiyama students). This was a common motif of the principal's speeches and, as with the teachers, *Fujiyamasei* were encouraged to regard themselves as different from other schoolchildren. The idea of appealing to Japanese students to perform or behave well, so as not to bring shame on their schools, is very common, but, as we shall see later, the creation of a specifically 'Fujiyama-type' student involved the mobilization of different symbols and language from those normally used.

As for the international dimension of the school which the *Nikkei* so applauded, we have already seen that Fujiyama taught extra foreign languages and employed foreign teachers. The fact that I was undertaking research in the school was also on occasion advertised as an indicator of the school's international outlook. Every year a few foreign students came to the school: normally, one stayed for the whole academic year and others for just a few days. At any one time, there were always five or six Fujiyama students overseas on exchange schemes organized by Youth For Understanding, American Field Services, Rotary Club, and United World Colleges among others. These exchange programmes are all highly competitive and are presented in the Japanese media as a rather glamorous escape from the Japanese educational system. Some teachers expressed reservations about the effect these exchanges had, feeling that they tended to leave the children with rather unrealistic views of the country they visited (normally America), a superficial fluency in English, and a negative attitude towards Japan and Japanese ways. Nevertheless, Fujiyama's success in the competition for these exchange schemes was widely advertised by the principal in interviews and meetings. This was further emphasized when, in two consecutive years, three out of the seven Japanese students awarded two-year scholarships to the United World Colleges were from Fujiyama.

Japanese children are generally so busy cramming for examinations that they rarely have the chance to develop their own specialist interests. For this reason the year-long fifth-year individual research projects (*kojin kadai kenkyū*) were one of the most unusual examples of Fujiyama's educational programme. These projects were compulsory; the school insisted that a student could not graduate until he had submitted his work. As both the *Nikkei Shinbun* and the *Chūō Kōron* articles stated, some of these projects were excellent: they were all kept on file in the library, and a volume of summaries and reports from supervising teachers was produced annually. Each year, the summaries of the best projects were delivered orally at the school festival or, if they were works of art, put on show. Many of the projects produced by *kikokushijo* were examinations of foreign cultures or languages, or comparisons between Japan and other countries. Interestingly, however, in five years, there had been only one project on *kikokushijo* themselves. This was carried out in 1980 and called *Kaigai.kikokushijo no Kikokugo no Mondai* ('The Problems of *Kikokushijo* after they Return'). The author used Satō Hirotake's (1978) book as a model and distributed a questionnaire to students in the first and fourth years to find out what was thought to make life most difficult for *kikokushijo*.

The individual research projects of the fifth year tied in with another important element of the school's philosophy—preparing students for a future career in which they were personally interested. This idea was enshrined in the school brochure thus: 'Through the medium of a six-year dormitory programme, the school wants to discover the strengths, interests, and aptitudes of each student so that it can provide career guidance which will eventually lead each individual into the most suitable occupation.' Hence, students were encouraged to strive for entrance to the university courses they were interested in rather than simply aiming for the best-ranked university regardless of their interests. In this context, the principal gave the example of a student who could have gone to a university in Tokyo but, because he was interested in fisheries, went instead to a much less prestigious, but more appropriate, institute on the island of Okinawa. In similar vein, he would stress at the *setsumeikai* that the school encouraged the children to develop all-round skills throughout their time there. The six-year curriculum means that children do not have to concentrate on senior-high-school entrance examinations for the last two years of their junior high school, but instead can develop their extra-curricular club activities. Much emphasis is placed on these club activities, and students who fail to participate are watched with considerable concern.

The dormitory, as we have already seen, was a further unusual element in the school's structure. Only one-third of all the students lived in the dormitory throughout the year, but every year commuting students were also required to spend a few weeks in the dormitory on what was known as *tanki nyūryō* (short-term dormitory experience). These sessions were held separately for each grade, and special events were organized to coincide with them and, according to the school brochure, work towards 'the aim of strengthening understanding and friendship through communal living'.

Despite the dormitory system at Fujiyama, there were virtually no ancillary staff. Most Japanese schools do without ancillary staff as a way to encourage children to take responsibility for their own actions. In Fujiyama, however, this idea was extended to encourage them to take a positive interest in their environment. The principal himself was a keen gardener and groups of dormitory students were detailed to get up at six o'clock in the morning on a rota basis to clean up the school grounds and gardens. Special emphasis was also placed on gardening activities in home economics lessons (*kateika*).

The above description presents some of the major elements of Fujiyama Gakuen's public face. Few teachers in the school, the principal included, were unaware of how idealistic a programme it appeared. Indeed, soon after the appearance of the *Nikkei Shinbun* and *Chūō Kōron* articles, it was felt necessary to prepare a short appendix to the school brochure informing all parents of prospective students how much hard work and dedication was required of children and to ensure that they had realistic expectations. It is therefore important to examine how the school policy was created and discussed by the teachers in the school.

DEBATE AND FACTIONS AMONG TEACHERS

During the meeting with the board of governors which was described earlier, one of the governors remarked that Fujiyama had two contrasting reputations: one which was genuinely complimentary and another which suggested that if the school retained its current educational system then it would end up as a third-rate institution. The governor stressed that he wanted to judge the school not merely on the basis of its entrance examination results but also on how the students fared when they left university and entered society. But as the school had only been in existence for five years, he said, this latter aim was not yet possible and the school could only be judged at the present time on the examination results.

The comments of the governor reflected a common fear of those concerned with private education in Japan. Even if such schools are not under any immediate financial threat, they face an uncertain longer-term future (Nishimura, 1987). As the end of the second baby boom draws near, the demographic trend shows that the number of high-school students in the early 1990s will be some 20 per cent lower than in the mid 1980s.[8] Some private schools will certainly founder and only those with the best reputations will survive. The crucial question is how best to build such a reputation. This issue was the most important point of discussion between the teachers, the principal, and the governors throughout the year of my fieldwork at Fujiyama. It was a debate that had doubtless raged since the school was founded, but one that acquired particular significance during the academic year 1984/5. This was the sixth year of a six-year school, and thus Fujiyama was about to produce the first graduates who could be said to be entirely the product of the school's educational philosophy.

At the first meeting of the 1984/5 school year, one of the most senior teachers stood up and asked the principal whether he would make a statement on Fujiyama's educational policy. Was Fujiyama really an experimental school or was emphasis going to be placed that year on getting students through the university entrance examinations? After much vacillation, the principal seemed to opt for the former aim as the school's priority while also emphasizing the importance of the latter. Afterwards, there was talk among some teachers that the idea of an experimental school was only the principal's *tatemae* (public policy), and that his *honne* (true motive) was for good entrance results to the top universities. Certainly, the relief when at the end of the year one student was accepted by Tokyo University and others by Kyoto, Keiō, and Waseda—the top four universities in Japan—was evident throughout the school.[9]

TABLE XI: Supplementary Lessons Received by *Kikokushijo* and Non-*Kikokushijo* in Fujiyama Gakuen

	Kikokushijo	non-*Kikokushijo*
Japanese language	11	1
Japanese and mathematics	12	2
Mathematics	8	8
Mathematics and one other subject	1	3
English	–	3
Science	–	1
Unspecified	1	5
TOTAL	33	23

(Sample = 166; *kikokushijo* 51%).

Fujiyama has two important differences in its academic structure from other Japanese schools: it offers supplementary lessons for slower students and streaming in English and mathematics. These facts are emphasized in the advertising to parents of *kikokushijo* who are considering attending the school. They are not, however, solely for the benefit of *kikokushijo*. Many non-*kikokushijo* students in the school also need supplementary lessons, as shown in Table XI. Apart from these factors, and the other elements discussed above, academically Fujiyama has more in common with other Japanese schools than it has differences. The lessons and methods of teaching are virtually indistinguishable from those of other schools in Japan. Moreover, perhaps the most significant element of educational philosophy in Fujiyama is still the traditional notion of the school as an institution for the passing on of a body of knowledge to the next generation. The way Fujiyama is run essentially places priority on the creation of a favourable environment for passing on this knowledge from teacher to student rather than on the creation of an atmosphere of learning which is favourable to the individual development of the students. The following two very interesting, and almost simultaneous, incidents highlight this point very clearly.

In the first of these incidents, a boy and a girl student, both in their final year, were discovered to be having sexual relations. This was the first incident of its kind uncovered at Fujiyama and it was treated with the utmost seriousness. Much discussion took place with the couple who had in the past been persistent rule-breakers and had been given numerous warnings about their conduct. Despite this, the girl was allowed to graduate from the school the following spring (although she was not allowed to attend the graduation ceremony itself) and the boy was permitted to re-enter the school to retake his final year. The main reason for this 'leniency' was the feeling on the principal's part that, despite their behaviour, the school had a responsibility to provide these students with an education.

The second incident concerned a child who joined the Jehovah's Witnesses during the summer vacation and, when school reconvened, refused to participate in *kendō* (Japanese fencing) lessons because he felt that to do so would contravene the pacifist ideals of his new religion. When he could not be persuaded to change his mind, he was asked to leave the school because, as the principal explained, 'The school philosophy is a whole, and to deny even 1 per cent of it is to deny it all.' In this case, the school was even prepared to go to court—an unusual course of action in traditionally non-litigious Japan—to defend its right to impose its own philosophy. In Fujiyama, therefore, the child has to adapt to the school, for the school has little leeway to adapt to the child. While the school feels a responsibility to provide an education for students, to the extent of allowing even the most persistent rule-breakers to remain, it is prepared to expel those who challenge its authority to pass on knowledge in the way it sees most fit.

In order to discuss how best to pass on knowledge to the students, there was an almost continuous round of teachers' meetings. Indeed, one new teacher once complained that he was spending more time in meetings than in the classroom. Every morning before school started, there was a meeting of all the teachers to announce any unusual events of the day before, or the day to come. Teachers were encouraged to announce even the most trivial events and to accompany announcements with a printed handout. This meeting was always followed by a meeting of all the full-time teachers in each grade to co-ordinate grade activities. Every Monday afternoon there was a two- or three-hour meeting of the entire full-time staff to discuss matters of school philosophy and regulation. Once a week also, heads of grades had a meeting with the principal and the three senior administrative teachers. Besides these, there were meetings of individual departments, meetings of full- and part-time teachers within each grade, and extra meetings at the beginning and end of each term. There was even a compulsory concentrated three-day *gasshuku* ('training camp') for all full-time staff in the middle of the summer vacation.[10]

The combative nature of the main teacher's union in Japan means that teachers' meetings often do not fit the images of consensus and harmony so often proposed for Japanese society (see Rohlen, 1984) There was no union representation at Fujiyama, but this did not make meetings there any smoother as the teaching staff was clearly divided into factions. The differences between them became most evident during Monday afternoon meetings, but they underlay much of school life. The two main factions were centred around the Japanese-language department (*kokugoka*) on the one hand, and the English-language department (*eigoka*) on the other. These divisions were not absolute: one member of the English department was a proponent of the philosophy held by the Japanese-language department faction. As a result, he used to sit more often at his desk in the main staffroom than in the English department, where the rest of the English teachers sat. Similarly, a new but experienced member of the Japanese-language staff dissented from the main viewpoint of that department.

The staff of the other departments tended to be rather more varied in their views and a particularly strong departmental line of thinking was not evident, although as individuals they often held strong opinions. The principal remained a generally impartial observer and arbitrator in these debates. Each side complained at times that he tended to favour the other, and one exasperated teacher once described his apparent ability to take both sides simultaneously as *zurui* (crafty).

The Japanese-language teachers were those with the best-formulated philosophy. All, except the teacher mentioned above, were members of the Seito Seikatsu Shidō Kenkyūkai (Student Life Guidance Research Association), which has some 3,000 members throughout schools in Japan, although its influence far exceeds that number. The first teacher to be appointed to the school, a former pupil of the principal, was a council member of the Seito Seikatsu

Shidō Kenkyūkai, and one of his first actions was to invite on to the staff a colleague, Azuma Chūji, a founder member and principal architect of the organization and perhaps its best-known member. Its members come from all subject departments and tend to be actively involved in school politics. In Fujiyama this was certainly the case.

The philosophy of the Seito Seikatsu Shidō Kenkyūkai is based around three main principles: leadership, grouping, and the formroom. Such a system operates in practice along these lines: a class of forty-eight children is divided into six groups (called *han*) of eight, with four boys and four girls in each; each group has two leaders, one boy and one girl, who act as intermediaries between the teacher and the rest of the group; students are encouraged to think of themselves always in relation to these groups; if somebody does something wrong then the whole group will come together to discuss why the misdeed was committed and how it can be prevented from recurring. Alternatively, success is not an individual success but that of the group.

If several children in a class, but in different groups, do something wrong, then the class as a whole will discuss the problem and how it can be solved. If several members of the same grade but in different classes commit some kind of misdemeanour, then the whole grade will be called together and the individuals may be asked to explain what they have done wrong and how they intend to do better in the future. More rarely, if several members of the school from different grades are in trouble, they may be asked to stand and recant before the whole school.

These public confessions are known as *jiko hihan* (self-criticism) or *sōgō hihan* (mutual criticism). The supporters of this approach insist that these sessions should be seen in a positive light: it is not a question of shaming the miscreants but of trying to make them see the folly of their acts and help them improve themselves. Such ideas of 'perfectibility' and the creation of the 'rounded or whole person' have a long tradition in Japan (Smith, 1985: 106–36). Nobody is perfect, there is always room for improvement, and it is the duty of one's group to help. Even when teachers make mistakes they are more likely to be offered critical advice than to be falsely reassured. However, if somebody from outside the immediate group, be it the class or the grade, were to try to criticize a member of that group, there is little doubt that the group as a whole would come to the defence of their member whether or not they thought the criticism justified.[11]

The idea of the group education system is that it reinforces ideas of equality and reduces differences among students. Everyone moves along at the same pace, and the teacher is therefore able to have tight control over a very large class. Within each grade, each class is encouraged to think of itself as a special group in relation to the other classes. As each new year starts, and students find themselves in new classes with new children, they find that they have to make new friends in that class and forget their friends of the year before.

Some of the philosophy of the Seito Seikatsu Shidō Kenkyūkai can be traced back to traditional ideas of the group in Japanese society, in particular to the *gonin gumi* of the Tokugawa period.[12] Another source of the organization's ideas appears to have been the fear, in the immediate post-war period, that everything Japanese would be thrown away in the rush to espouse western values. As Azuma complained in an article in 1985:

In the old days, the family was an important institution for education in groups, but not any more. Hence the number of children who have non-adaptation symptoms [*futekiōshō*] is increasing. Typical examples are school refusal syndrome [*tōkōkyohi*] and fear of school [*gakkōkyōfushō*]. It is to counter this that we need grouping.

It is perhaps not surprising that the group's philosophy should find its staunchest early supporters among Japanese-language teachers who saw themselves as guardians of fundamental Japanese values.[13]

Another important source for the philosophical ideas of the Seito Seikatsu Shidō Kenkyūkai lies in the communist educational philosophy of the Soviet educator, A. S. Makarenko. Ide Yūzō, head of the senior school at Fujiyama, in particular seemed to sympathize with these socialist ideas. Indeed, his style of writing and the content of his books are remarkably similar to the work of Makarenko. Like Makarenko, Ide had previously worked in a school with many delinquent students (see Makarenko, 1965). He stresses the importance of giving a class, through group education, the sense of working collectively, for with this it can develop a 'perfectly controlled, explosive power'. The group controls its individual members, yet the individual can develop within his relationship with the group.

In one particular aspect the philosophy of the Seito Seikatsu Shidō Kenkyūkai appears to be in sharp contrast to most Japanese educational thought. It seems to support the idea of original sin (*seiakusetsu*) which stands in direct contrast with the commonly accepted Japanese belief in original virtue (*seizensetsu*).[14] Ide writes that 'Children learn what to do only when they tackle a problem. When they are driven into a corner they "stand up" for the first time. That is why teachers need to drive children into a corner. It is even better, though, when children drive themselves into a corner.' Teachers are therefore encouraged by proponents of this philosophy to push children to their limits to discover their weaknesses which they can then work upon to improve. It is not felt important if the children come to dislike the teacher. Indeed, Azuma's favourite description of teachers who did not accept his way of teaching was that they were *nanjaku* (weak-kneed). Perhaps the most significant aspect of the group's philosophy, however, is Azuma's insistence that the idea of using groups in education is essentially a pedagogical technique. He is quoted in one interview as saying: 'one reason why one needs grouping is that if there are more than forty students in one class, however excellent a teacher is, it is very difficult for him or her to be able immediately to control the whole class.' This particular outcome was one which made this method of teaching especially popular with some of the younger, less experienced teachers at Fujiyama. Indeed one teacher, in a speech at Azuma's farewell party, admitted that he would have given up his job if Azuma had not taught him how to teach.

Within Fujiyama, there was, however, considerable opposition to the ideas of the Seito Seikatsu Shidō Kenkyūkai, particularly among teachers in the English department. Among their complaints were: that the system was too artificial; that it was teacher-centred simply to help control the students and did not provide opportunities for the teacher to learn anything from the students; and that it was too severe and rigorous for the good of the children. Some of its opponents also objected to its left-wing tendencies. They complained that it did not allow any room for the development of individuality. Some thought that while such a system might be successful with delinquent or difficult students, it was inappropriate for children from the kinds of background of Fujiyama students. Others felt that it might be appropriate in junior high schools but certainly not for students between the ages of 16 and 18. The most extreme opponents of the system argued that the self-criticism sessions were like something out of the Chinese cultural revolution. They tended to argue for a more liberal educational system that emphasized individualism rather than groupism.

These severe differences of opinion manifested themselves frequently in the life of the school. Even a discussion as to whether children in the dormitory should be allowed to eat instant noodles after their homework period and before they went to bed was cause for heated debate. In this particular case, the Japanese-language teachers argued that if the children were allowed noodles then they would not finish their supper, which would make them lose respect for food. Also, they felt that it was no bad thing for children to go to bed hungry since it taught the important Japanese virtue of endurance (*gaman*). The English language teachers argued that it was unreasonable for children to go to bed hungry and, moreover, the children should be able to make their own decisions about food.

Another argument arose over the running of the school festival. All students had to submit an outline of the activities they were going to carry out. From these, a list of 'dubious' activities was drawn up and their suitability was discussed by the staff for at least two hours. The Japanese-language teachers argued that some acts—such as an exhibition about pro-wrestling or a 'haunted house'—had no aesthetic or high cultural value, while their opponents insisted that any activity, if carried out diligently and carefully by the students themselves, had some educational value.

Another argument blew up over the state of English teaching in the school. The impetus for this actually came from a social-science teacher who argued that, although the students had six lessons of English a week as compared to the national average of three, there was no sign that their examination marks had greatly improved, and that it was therefore reasonable to remove one of these lessons from the senior-high-school timetable the following year. The head of the English department, however, responded that the reason Fujiyama was so special was that students were not judged purely on their examination results. Hence, they were not taught just the archaic grammar needed for the examinations, but also conversational 'living English' based on the idea of *kokusai kyōiku* (international education), and it was in this area that Fujiyama's students excelled when compared with students of other schools.

The bare outlines of these incidents, while offering something of the flavour of the philosophical differences, provide nothing of the atmosphere of the meetings themselves which sometimes degenerated into shouting on both sides, as well as tears of frustration and offers of resignation. Although there tended to be only a core of teachers who participated in the arguments, many teachers were very articulate and most of the male teachers especially were prepared to offer their opinions. It would be a mistake, however, to exaggerate the tension created. Several of the senior teachers were excellent at preventing or defusing difficult situations, and few teachers confused professional differences with personal ones. Moreover, even at the height of debate, teachers generally managed to keep their sense of humour, and most would probably recognize themselves in van Gennep's pastiche on teachers' meetings in *The Small Milk Jug* (1967: 1–6) or, perhaps more appropriately, Natsume Sōseki's account in *Botchan* (1904: esp. 91–100).

THE CREATION OF *FUJIYAMASEI* (FUJIYAMA STUDENTS)

One matter on which teachers at Fujiyama were in agreement was the pursuit of excellence, whatever their particular definitions of excellence might be. All of them saw the school as offering a different type of education from that normally available in Japan; all of them seemed to think that they were creating a special type of Japanese student.

Fujiyamasei were made aware of their special status from their first day at the school. Most Japanese schools have three terms; Fujiyama has only two. As they lined up at the entrance ceremony (*nyūgakushiki*) that begins the first term of each year, they would recognize how their Fujiyama school uniforms (smart dark-blue blazers) contrasted strongly with the brass-buttoned Prussian Navy-type jackets worn by virtually all other schoolchildren in Japan. They could see that the buildings were superior in both style and quality to the buildings of almost every other school in the country. They were also immediately told by the head of the Parent Teacher Association, a Buddhist priest, how lucky they were to be at the school. He spoke movingly as he told the children always to remember how fortunate they were that they came from good families, and that they should never forget those who were less socially blessed than themselves.

There were many other significant examples of how Fujiyama attempted to differentiate itself from other schools in Japan. Many of these centred on what might be called a 'superficial international-ness'. As we have seen, children could retain—or, if they were new to the subject, pick up a smattering of—French, Spanish, or Chinese, and one returnee from Italy also gave Italian lessons. There was also a complex school vocabulary, based on a Japanized version of English, that was comprehensible only to members of the school community. This included words like *house master, adviser, table manner, blazer coat style, common space, box, colour asphalt, pantry*—these last three referring respectively to the music practice room, the ground between the dormitory and school where *colour asphalt kutsu* (shoes) should be worn, and a room above the dining-room where students had lessons in western table manners. There was a heavy concentration on western classical music, and the school had what must be one of the few authentic harpsichords in Japan, shipped in from Europe and for which a Latin inscription (*Ars Placendi*) was specially composed. The school's two drama outings in the school year 1984–5 were to a concert given by the world's only full-time baroque dance group, visiting from Europe, and a performance of *Oedipus Rex*. Rugby football was chosen as the school's main sport, when less than 1 per cent of Japanese senior high schools and even fewer junior high schools have rugby clubs (*JEJ*, No. 31, 1987: 5), and the school became well known through television and newspaper reports for its exploits on the rugby field.[15]

Ikeda Kiyoshi's description of British public-school life in the 1940s, *Jiyū to Kiritsu* (1949), was compulsory reading for all fourth-grade students at Fujiyama. Indeed the school had preten-sions to resembling a British public school. Foreigners were sometimes invited to talk to the children and, before one such talk, the teacher in charge of international affairs told the speaker, in front of his audience: 'The purpose of inviting you here is to broaden the students' points of view because within ten or twenty years they will probably be some kind of leader in Japan.'

Elements in the creation of *Fujiyamasei*, such as the important 'Japanese' values of perseverance and effort, can also be traced back to the *samurai* tradition of the Tokugawa period: *kangeiko*, when, for two weeks in the coldest months of the year, dormitory students had to get up at 5.00 a.m. either to play rugby or to practice *kendō* in their bare feet, is a form of spartan training connected with the idea of purifying the body and soul, and is common in learning traditional Japanese arts. Other examples of traditional élite Japanese culture incorporated in the school's curriculum included Buddhist meditation training, a *karuta-kai* (a traditional New Year card game based on ancient poems) for first-grade students, and the writing of *kakizome* (the first symbolic calligraphy of the New Year) which was undertaken by all junior-high-school students in a very serious and contemplative atmosphere.

Students at Fujiyama were encouraged to create their own student culture. They learnt ideas of democracy and leadership through the running of numerous school committees. They were also nominally in charge of the festivals and ceremonies held throughout the school year. Always, though, these efforts at self-government were carefully monitored by teachers and every committee, however small, had a teacher-in-charge who would offer guidance and, if necessary, criticism on the way things were being done. The festivals and parties at Fujiyama, especially those in the dormitory, gave the students a great sense of belonging to a special group.

The idea of forming a special group of students was commonly voiced by the principal in his weekly talks either to the whole school, or to different sections of it. These talks constituted the moral education element of the curriculum, a subject which has remained politically sensitive in Japan since the War when, under the name *shūshin kyōiku* (spiritual education), it was a major force behind the dissemination of ultranationalistic ideas. I followed many of the principal's speeches throughout my year in Fujiyama. They would often last for thirty or forty minutes and would cover an enormous range of subjects. The following is an excerpt from a talk to the whole junior high school:

Compared to other schools, Fujiyama has a lot of things for students to do, and the teachers try very hard and with great purpose to allow students to be able to take advantage of these opportunities. . . . Fujiyama was built by a *dōsōkai* [group of school peers]. Now, though, half of the teachers come from other universities. The school was founded by alumni, but since they were educators they didn't have much money. However, there were many competent alumni in other areas of work, for example some in the Finance Ministry, and when the school was founded I met those people, and they promised us their utmost support. . . . This shows the importance of friendship, even friends from junior-high-school days. Fujiyama is different from other schools because it offers many chances for making friends, in the 'short-term dormitory experience', camps, clubs, etc., so it is possible to spend twenty-four hours together and make really sincere friendships. . . . The idea of friendship is very important not only for the good times but also for working together during hard times to make those hard times easier.

The following are excerpts from a talk to the whole school which followed a lecture about British public schools I had given to the fourth grade and which the principal had attended:

The fourth grade have to read a book by Ikeda Kiyoshi called *Jiyū to Kiritsu* [Freedom and Discipline]. I am now 53 years old, but it is normally those who are over 60 who stress the idea of discipline. This was very strong before the Second World War, but immediately afterwards the whole system collapsed and there was no system of discipline. It was for this reason that Ikeda decided to publish his book in 1949 because he thought that it was important to describe a value system that respects discipline and he chose the example of British public schools. The people who went to such schools learnt that they couldn't live alone in the world: that one has to learn how to co-operate and not make trouble for others, that to enjoy real freedom one must suffer discipline. . . . [*Long repetition of my talk about British public schools and their relation to British history and society before arriving at the subject of Churchill*] . . . . Churchill has often been caricatured, but he was a very unlucky leader because he was prime minister when Great Britain's colonial history was coming to an end even if she was victorious in the War. He went to Harrow and then to army school, and he was able to look at society from many angles. You must remember that at this time he was the same age as you. At army school, Churchill had the chance to look at the whole world and he thought very hard about many things, and during this period he cultivated his thoughts concerning what he would do should he be given the chance to run Britain in the future. I don't see any such qualities among you, though you are the same age as he was then. However, I do see among you a comparatively large number interested in social welfare which is something which gives me great pleasure and I want to see more like that.

Several themes ran through many of the principal's speeches: that the Japanese are naturally diligent;[16] that Japan has to develop its human resources since it has no natural ones; and that the students at Fujiyama should have pride in their school and strive to become leaders of society, and make worthy contributions to it. With a phenomenal memory for detail, the principal would interlace his talks with numerous examples, often mentioning individual students as models to be emulated or avoided.

Fujiyama was not the first school to instil a special consciousness—in this case formed by a combination of western and traditional Japanese values—into its pupils. There are important similarities between much of the system at Fujiyama and those of the Tokugawa domain schools and the pre-war Imperial high schools. Dore's account (1984: 75–7; 98–101) of the domain schools (*hankō*) for the children of the *samurai* élite in Tokugawa Japan describes the dormitories where students from all over the country lived with their teachers. Day students also had to spend some time in the sometimes very harsh dormitory regime. He also writes about the use, in these schools, of group methods in teaching (1984: 79); education in etiquette and table manners (1984: 80); the extent of student self-government (1984: 105–6); and even the importance of *kakizome* (1984: 272–3).

Donald Roden (1980: 41) stresses the similarities between Imperial high schools of the pre-war period and the Tokugawa domain schools, and also compares them to British public schools. In his description of the way the dormitories of the Imperial high schools were controlled by a combination of primitive barbarism and nationalism that centred on the sports clubs, he draws particular parallels with the British public-school system (1980: 113–22). He discusses the asceticism of these Imperial high schools' sports clubs and the early morning activities in winter (1980: 117–18); the special dormitory parties (1980: 109); the sense of the school as a 'total institution' (1980: 48); the use of symbols unique to the school to create a sense of 'separateness'—the uniforms, works of art, the school flag (1980: 59–60); the upper middle-class backgrounds of the students (1980: 69); the notion of providing a 'whole-person' education (1980: 200 ff). All of these are also features of Fujiyama Gakuen, as we have seen. Perhaps most significant, however, is Roden's suggestion (1980: 2, 44) that behind this educational philosophy of the Imperial high schools lay the aim of creating, or moulding, an élite individual, the 'cultivated man', that, according to one alumnus, 'imparted a kind of status not unlike that bestowed by birth' (1980: 250).

KIKOKUSHIJO IN FUJIYAMA GAKUEN

It is significant that in this account of Fujiyama Gakuen I have made no mention of *kikokushijo*. This reflects the conscious policy on the part of the school not to differentiate between *kikokushijo* and other students. Indeed, when I wanted to call all *kikokushijo* together to ask them some questions, I was expressly forbidden to do so on the grounds that it would heighten their awareness of being *kikokushijo* and thereby make them feel different.

In theory, up to 50 per cent of the school's places were reserved for 'children whose fathers were working overseas' (*kaigai kimusha shitei*, called *kaigaisei* for short). In practice, this quota was never reached, and the extra places were taken by non-*kikokushijo* who were known as *ippansei* (regular students). The general policy of the school was that those who fell into the *kaigaisei* category would always be considered first, but this did not mean that they would necessarily be accepted. They would be unlikely to be accepted if their deviation from the average score of that year's applicants was more than minus forty in three or more subjects. Some teachers felt, however, that this rule was too lenient and it provoked consider- able resistance in the case of students applying to enter the senior high school, since such students would only have three years to improve their scores before graduation. There were 100 places in the senior high school in 1984: of the thirty-five *kikokushijo* applicants, seventeen passed and nine actually took up places at the school. For non-*kikokushijo*, 104 out of 252 applicants were successful. In the case of the junior high school, there had been thirty *kikokushijo* applicants in 1984 and only two had been rejected. Overall, the school estimated that *kikokushijo* applicants had about a 70-per-cent chance of success, while for *ippansei* (regular students) the success rate was around 30 per cent.

But if the school particularly favoured *kikokushijo*, why were there so few applicants, and why were so many of them rejected at the senior-high-school level? The answer to the first question appears to have been concomitant on the second. When I joined a teachers' tour of Japanese junior high schools in Singapore and Jakarta, to encourage parents there to send their children to Fujiyama, the major reaction from the parents was: why did the school bother to advertise its wonderful facilities when it was clear very few of their children would be good enough to meet the entrance requirements? The problem as seen by these parents was that the school was worried about accepting too many students who might bring down its overall educational level. Argument on this subject occasionally arose at Fujiyama itself and was another aspect of the debate over what type of reputation the school should seek. Some teachers argued that it would not be fair to other students, to parents, or to the school as a whole, if too much effort had to be expended on very slow students. One teacher blamed this attitude on the formation of the Parent-Teacher Association which had led to the school's becoming increasingly oriented toward examination results. Some of the Japanese-language teachers also were not keen on taking *kikokushijo*: they were worried they would have to be responsible for providing extra language lessons for them.

On the other hand, the school made a point of advertising the number of *kikokushijo* on its register. The brochure, handed out to the parents of all prospective students, included a breakdown by main country of overseas experience of all *kikokushijo* in the school (Table XII). The principal would also use these statistics in interviews and when talking to outsiders. In the school itself, however, he would only very occasionally differentiate between *kikokushijo* and other students. Once a year he presented every *kikokushijo*—as well as every foreign teacher—with a *kaki* (persimmon) from the school tree as a symbol of how the seasons change in Japan. He would also, sometimes, be lenient in meetings towards the academic failings of *kikokushijo* on the grounds that they were returnees, though, like most teachers, he never attributed their successes to the same cause. Indeed the two best students in the school were both *kikokushijo*. One had been in America for ten years and the other in Singapore for five years; the former got directly into Tokyo University and the latter did so at the second attempt. The general attitude, though, seemed to be that this was *despite* the fact that they were returnees, not *because* of it. Perhaps understandably, teachers sometimes wished to take credit for student success and find excuses for failures.

The principal occasionally mentioned the need for *kikokushijo* to adapt to Japanese ways of doing things. In an interview with a *kikokushijo* parents' organization, he said that children who had been looked after by servants while abroad needed to learn to do things by themselves in Japan, and in response to a question about

TABLE XII: *Kikokushijo* in
Fujiyama Gakuen, by Main
Country of Overseas Experience

Asia	90
Hong Kong	15
Singapore	16
Philippines	19
Taiwan	10
Thailand	10
Indonesia	12
Nepal	1
Malaysia	3
Bangladesh	1
South Korea	1
People's Republic of China	1
India	1
Oceania	6
Australia	5
New Zealand	1
North America	86
United States	78
Canada	8
Central/South America	28
Honduras	1
Venezuela	3
Argentina	1
Peru	1
Chile	2
Brazil	16
Mexico	3
Trinidad	1
Middle East/Africa	19
Egypt	3
Saudia Arabia	4
Qatar	1
Iran	1
Kuwait	3
Kenya	1
South Africa	2
Nigeria	1
Libya	2
Sudan	1
Europe	52
United Kingdom	17
Ireland	1
France	2
West Germany	13
Italy	7
Belgium	2
Switzerland	5
Soviet Union	2

Austria	1
Czechoslovakia	1
TOTAL	281
Total School Enrolment	1209

homesickness in the dormitory, he replied: 'I can't pretend that it doesn't exist. *Kikokushijo* have a tendency to dislike groupism [*shūdanshugi*] and I think that this is often cause for a certain discordance [*futekigo*] between them and other students. They must be aware that dormitory life is a group life and they can't just do their own thing.' He also once made a negative comment about overseas experience after two students had returned to the school after a year in America. He had been horrified to discover one of the boys chewing gum while speaking to his form teacher, and he told the whole school that he hoped they would quickly help rid the boys of these *tsumaranai Americanism* (trashy/despicable Americanisms).

In general, though, the principal had a positive view of *kikokushijo* in the school and particularly of their effect on other students. As he told the *kikokushijo* parents' organization:

The *kikokushijo* give a really good stimulus [*shigeki*] to the other students [*kokunaisei*]. For example, in the whole country there are only seven or eight students selected for the ¥5,000,000 United World Colleges scholarships to study overseas, and this year three of them were from this school. One of them was an Ibaraki student living in the dormitory with no overseas experience [*futsū no kokunaisei*].

I once discussed with the principal and another teacher a television documentary about the problems faced by returnees, especially in respect to bullying. The teacher commented that this had been the main concern of the parent of a prospective student whom he had shown round the previous day, but the principal seemed to find the whole notion faintly ridiculous. If anything, he suggested, it was the other students who were teased because they had not been overseas.

In general, though, it was felt that each set of students, *kikokushijo* and *ippansei*, had something to offer the other. An article by Fujiyama's head of international affairs, Nakano Masanori, entitled *Kikokushijo ni Manabu Gakkyū Zukuri* ('Creating Classes for Teaching Returnee Children'), perhaps most clearly expresses the idea of this mutually beneficial relationship. He proposes that generally speaking the *kikokushijo* think as follows: 'I want to get accustomed to the educational environment in Japan as quickly as possible. At the same time, I don't want to lose the language, customs, and ways of doing things which I have acquired.' On the other hand, the *ippansei* think: 'I want to learn from the *kikokushijo* new things which I do not have myself. I want to acquire something from their feelings of life [*seikatsu kankaku*], from their way of doing things, from what it is that makes them different.'

Nakano, however, is less sanguine than the principal about the experiences of the *kikokushijo* in Fujiyama. In particular, he discusses the problem of non-adaptation (*futekiō*). In his experience, *kikokushijo* really want to adapt to the new school environment when they enter it, but they often become dissatisfied. He cites four main reasons for their non-adaptation: their families, especially their mothers, are often critical of Japan, creating a poor home environment for adaptation; they face language barriers because their peers and teachers talk too fast, and they end up feeling like guests (*okyakusama-teki sonzai*) and thereby lose the desire to learn; they don't like the knowledge-cramming (*chishiki tsumekomi*) style of lesson which leaves no room for their own opinions and is uninteresting; and they face teachers who do not understand their problems and may criticize them as lazy or overindulge (*amayakasu*) them as if they were foreign children who knew no Japanese at all.

According to Nakano, however, the biggest trouble with adaptation is that in actuality it means assimilation (*dōka*) and that by this process the children lose much of the 'positiveness' (*sekkyokuteki ni hatsugen suru*) they learnt overseas and end up no different from other students in the school. On this point he concludes:

The returnee children's educational problem is not necessarily a problem of *kikokushijo*, but of the education of individual human beings. . . . We should reflect on the uniformity [*kakuitsu*] of the Japanese education system. . . . Isn't there something we—as teachers, students, and guardians—should learn from these *kikokushijo*?

It was difficult to tell how representative was the view of the principal and the head of international affairs that, while *kiko-*

kushijo might face certain special problems on returning to Japanese society, these were compensated for by the positive qualities they had learnt while abroad. There was certainly no open talk in Fujiyama about the need to 'rejapanize' and 'peel off the foreignness' of *kikokushijo* which had been the common feature of the literature on *ukeirekō* I had read before beginning my fieldwork. Indeed, there was very little discussion at all about *kikokushijo* as a distinct group either in teachers' meetings or in conversations between teachers. One teacher said that it used to be a major topic of discussion in the first few years of the school, but was no longer (in the school's sixth year) a big issue. It was as a way of trying to explore opinions about *kikokushijo* and non-*kikokushijo* that at the very end of my fieldwork I circulated a short, open-ended questionnaire to all the full-time teachers at the school. Of these just less than half were returned and the answers are summarized below.

Most questions asked teachers to compare *kikokushijo* with *ippansei* at Fujiyama. It was certainly not easy visually to perceive any difference between them. All students had to wear uniforms which, together with the length and style of their hair, were constantly monitored by the teachers so as to keep to school regulations. Dormitory students were allowed to wear their own clothes during free time and while one returnee complained that teachers did not approve of the styles she wore, almost all students wore the same popular western fashions.[17] New teachers, who did not know which students were *kikokushijo* and which were not, also found it difficult to find differences between the two groups in terms of behaviour. Nevertheless, when confronted with a questionnaire, only two teachers objected to making a clear distinction between *kikokushijo* and *ippansei*. As one wrote:

I don't see that the *kikokushijo* have more problems [than *ippansei*]. . . . If there was a problem, it is not because they are *kikokushijo* but because of their own personality.

And only one teacher questioned what was meant by *kikokushijo*:

I haven't thought much about this, but there should be a difference between children who, on the one hand, went to local schools overseas [*genchikō*] and, on the other hand, those who went to full-time Japanese schools [*Nihonjingakkō*] and did not stay longer than two years overseas. The latter category should not be regarded as *kikokushijo*; they should be treated just like those who've never been abroad. Those who've been overseas longer than two years and attended the local schools should make the best use of their experience and we should help them.

Many teachers, however, were prepared to generalize about *kikokushijo*. As far as they were concerned, *kikokushijo* constituted a definable group in the school. When teachers were asked whether they found *kikokushijo* conspicuous (*medatsu*) as a group or as individuals in the school, ten out of twenty-two teachers answered positively. Significantly, this group included all the members of the Seito Seikatsu Shidō Kenkyūkai who answered the questionnnaire. This group also constituted the bulk of those who felt that *kikokushijo* had more demerits than merits. A number of specific problems faced by *kikokushijo* were mentioned:

Kikokushijo who used to live in a house with a servant or a maid tend to be lazy and make the other children angry.

Maybe they are more trouble since they cannot find their proper position in the group.

They have many problems both with learning and also getting on with other children because they lay too much stress on their own freedom.

Some of the 'problems' of *kikokushijo* as identified by the teachers, however, seemed to reflect the problems they caused for others rather than those from which they suffered directly:

Generally speaking they cause more trouble. For example, the disciplinary training at home seems to be different from that of those children who have never been abroad. *Kikokushijo* hate to be moulded [*waku ni hamerareru*].

There is such a problem with shoplifting while they are abroad, that they don't feel guilt any more [*tsumi ga nai*]. Maybe they were living in a country where civilization was of a lower level than that of Japan, and therefore they must have had a sense of élitism.

The expectations of parents of their children seem to be too great and there is a big gap between these and the children's academic achievement.

I notice that the other teachers try to force them to become ordinary Japanese.

On the other hand, six teachers felt that *kikokushijo* had more positive qualities than negative ones:

They don't hesitate to make comments which are different from the others.

They stimulate, in a positive way, students who have never been abroad.

The tendency for the teachers to fall into one of two categories—those who emphasized the lack of 'Japanese' values of *kikokushijo* and those who emphasized their 'international' qualities—was most evident in response to a request for definitions of the word *kokusaijin*. *Kokusaijin* (literally 'an international person') is currently a buzz-word in Japan and is used in a positive sense as someone who can bridge the gap between Japan and the outside world. Its exact meaning, however, is far from clear, and the staff at Fujiyama were divided over their definitions. On the one hand, there were those who felt it meant having an understanding of Japan in relation to other societies, someone who:

Does not lose Japanese identity in foreign countries and also makes the best use of experiences overseas.

Knows his own culture very well and can handle a foreign language and communicate his ideas to others.

Understands his own country and makes others understand their own country.

Is interested not only in Japan but also in other countries and is capable of understanding the different cultures and customs of other countries.

Is proud of his own customs, culture, and history and regards others as individuals.

On the other hand, others argued for a broader definition of *kokusaijin* as someone who:

Has his own self-identity, has no prejudices, biases, or preconceptions toward others, and at the same time can see others as individuals.

Regards foreigners just like one's own people: a person who can listen to different opinions and not force others to hold his opinion.

Can respect any person in any country and can co-operate with anyone for the improvement of the world.

In general, those of the first group identified closely with the philosophy of the Japanese-language teachers. The second group identified more closely with the views of the English-language department. Overall, then, it appears that the ideological viewpoints of these two groups influenced the way they perceived *kikokushijo*, although it is important to point out that these divisions were neither absolute nor even always consistent. Several teachers recognized some of the merits of the opposing position.

Nevertheless, there was clearly more than one way of thinking about *kikokushijo* education among the staff at Fujiyama.

There was one other interesting finding from the questionnaire and this was that even some of the teachers who felt positive towards *kikokushijo* held a generally negative image of *kikokushijo* experience. One new member of the school, who had never taught in high school before, suggested that there was a difference between Fujiyama's *kikokushijo* and those in other schools:

The *kikokushijo* in Fujiyama are mostly excellent in academic terms, but in other schools they have many problems such as refusal to attend school [tōkōkyohi], disciplinary problems, and they also tend to be prey to bullies.

Similarly, others emphasized the need to do more for *kikokushijo* in the belief that they generally faced serious problems on return to Japan:

At the moment recovery from the loss of academic ability rests on the shoulders of the parents. Monbushō should take more responsibility to provide more education for these children.

My brother came back from East Germany with his daughter, aged 9, who cannot speak a single word of Japanese. I am worried about whether she can make good friends with her peers. She'll be enrolled in a primary school in the countryside and she won't receive any special training in the school so her parents must be fully responsible for teaching her Japanese. As long as people in that region get rid of their sense of discrimination everything depends on her efforts to improve her situation. Maybe it's enough if there is no discrimination [sabetsushi] in that area.

It is necessary to improve the educational facilities or institutes: for example, set up classes for *kikokushijo*, since parents are always worried about the education of their children.

Japanese students are accepted with no problem when they go abroad, but, on the other hand, when they return they are not very easily accepted. Fujiyama shows that education for *kikokushijo* is regarded as of secondary importance [shūjū no jū ni] and so it is in other schools. Education for *kikokushijo* should be given more money, time, and personnel.

The results of this questionnaire raise important new questions for the understanding of the treatment of *kikokushijo*. It is clear that *kikokushijo* do suffer from certain problems on their return to Japan. But it is not clear to the teachers, when these problems are directly compared with those of other children in the school, that they are necessarily more severe, especially when one considers the offsetting positive effects of overseas experience.

The answers also suggest that some of the 'problems' of *kikokushijo* might in reality be the problems of others which have been projected on to the children themselves. Moreover, they suggest that the generally negative image of the experience of *kikokushijo* is so widely disseminated that it is accepted by some teachers even when it contradicts their own experience.

Perhaps most important, however, is the division of responses to the questionnaire into two distinct clusters of views: those who stress the need for *kikokushijo* to adapt back to Japanese culture and those who believe that *kikokushijo* should be seen, and treated, as valuable national resources. Hoshino and Niikura (1983*b*), in the only published survey of teachers' attitudes towards returnees, have found a similar division of views. They explain this division in terms of generation and gender differences. Age and gender, however, do not seem to be significant factors in the division of views of the staff at Fujiyama, where perceptions of *kikokushijo* are more closely aligned to the ideological beliefs of the two factions, discussed earlier. However, it is significant that some individuals— such as the principal—could support the idea both that the *kikokushijo* need to adapt to Japanese society and that they should retain the qualities gained overseas.

KIKOKUSHIJO AND NON-KIKOKUSHIJO IN FUJIYAMA GAKUEN

There appeared to be as little discussion among the students of differences between *kikokushijo* and non-*kikokushijo* (*ippansei*) as there was among the teachers. The discussions that did take place among *ippansei* regarding *kikokushijo* tended to reflect rather ambivalent feelings on the subject. As Nakano, Fujiyama's head of international affairs, writes:

On the one hand, the *kokunaisei* [domestic students] yearn to go overseas and envy the experience of the *kikokushijo* abroad; on the other hand there is the tendency to stigmatize [*itanshi suru*] *kikokushijo* as pitiful kids [*awarena yatsu*] who cannot speak their mother tongue and also to regard them as shameless [*hanamochinaranu*] children who unconcernedly talk to the opposite sex.

One *ippansei* complained that *kikokushijo* in Fujiyama were sometimes rather arrogant (*namaiki*). Nakano warns against this and advises teachers not to pick out *kikokushijo* in English lessons as they will become susceptible to thinking of themselves as superior and other students may become servile towards them (*hikutsu ni nattari suru*). Indeed, he goes on to suggest that because *kikokushijo* say what they think and express their opinions even when those around them do not agree with them, they are often chosen as class leaders (*shidōsha*). In particular, he writes, many members of the Fujiyama student council (*seitokai yakuin*) are *kikokushijo*.

This is just one aspect which suggests that the experience of *kikokushijo* might not be as problematic as is commonly believed. This is not to say, however, that when asked direct questions on the subject, *kikokushijo* felt that the experience was totally unproblematic. They sometimes complained about their non-*kikokushijo* peers, especially the tendency of the latter to do everything in tightly knit groups: 'They even all go to the toilet together,' one girl said. Returnees who had been in the west complained also about the habit among Japanese students of holding hands with members of the same sex.[18] Other *kikokushijo* complained about the *senpai/ kōhai* system, a traditional Japanese arrangement that extends throughout society whereby those who are new to a school or organization (*kōhai*) must be subservient to those who entered before them (*senpai*). In a school tennis club, for example, junior players, even if they are more talented, must spend much of their first year picking up balls for their seniors. This is all considered part of developing perseverance and diligence—seen by some as the 'Japanese spirit'. It involves the belief that diligent practice is often more important than natural ability and that if one is a member of a club then one should be totally dedicated to it and to its rules.[19] One returnee child who disliked the *senpai/kōhai* system wrote in an essay:

Here in Japan, you have club activities after school. You choose a club, and most people play in the same club for all their school years. If you continue, they say that you've got the spirit. If there are upper-grade class members and you see them walking towards you, you have to say hello in a term of respect. Also, you have to speak in honorifics. . . . I still can't get used to the club activities.

The *senpai/kōhai* relationship has been cause for much concern throughout Japan, with several reports of *kōhai* dying as a result of being pushed too hard by their seniors. It has been seen as a major factor behind school bullying (*ijime*) which has been the focus of a national outcry in Japan in recent years. Bullying was also seen as the biggest of Fujiyama's school problems, even though most of it was of a very minor kind such as *senpai* sending *kōhai* to do their shopping. There was never, however, any suggestion that *kikokushijo* were particularly involved in bullying, either as victims or as perpetrators.

The above worries were examples which occasionally cropped up in discussions with *kikokushijo*. There was no doubt that some *kikokushijo* did have problems in Fujiyama. But it was difficult to tell how severe these problems were, how much they were restricted to certain individuals, and how much they were connected with overseas experience. It was also difficult to tell whether the problems outweighed the felt advantages of overseas experience— or indeed whether *ippansei* found life in the school equally problematic as *kikokushijo*, or even more so.

It was in an attempt to gain a broader perspective on the issue of *kikokushijo* experience that I distributed an open-ended questionnaire to 104 students. These children were carefully divided into three almost equal groups representing students from full-time Japanese schools overseas, from local schools overseas, and from Japanese schools in Japan. Since I did not want to force answers out of children, I did not follow the questionnaires up, but, in all, seventy-two (just under 70 per cent) were returned. The questionnaire asked the students to write about the good and bad points of lessons, club activities, their friends, their teachers, dormitory life, home life, school holidays, and the school in general. There was one final question about communication problems. In examining the answers, I made a distinction between children who had had experience of an overseas educational system and those who had not. Children whose only overseas experience had been in *Nihonjingakkō* were placed in the latter category.

When I examined all the replies there were a few from *kikokushijo* that mentioned specific problems. These included complaints about the childishness of other students and the *senpai/ kōhai* relationship; the suggestion that teachers could not understand children with problems; and the complaint that teachers did not give children the chance to speak up. There were complaints about the amount of work required in the vacation, which one student described as a 'grey vacation'. Another student wrote of being unable to adapt to the group life, and two described worries about their Japanese-language ability. A couple mentioned a difference between their way of thinking and that of their peers. The most significant point, however, was that, when asked an open-ended question about their problems, only eight of the *kikokushijo* felt that problems which they could put down to being returnees were severe enough to mention. These eight were the students who had been overseas for the longest periods of time: the two who were worried about their Japanese had been in America for eleven and nine years respectively, and neither had expected ever to come back to Japan.

It was also interesting to find several answers, from non-*kikokushijo* or from *kikokushijo* who had been only to Japanese schools overseas, that were similar to those given by *kikokushijo*. Such examples were:

My ideas and those of the teachers [concerning regulations] do not go well together.

I cannot make stable friends to be with all the time in class.

Since I cannot handle Japanese so well I can't make myself fully understood and I can't make friends easily.

Human relations is the biggest problem in the dormitory: it is more difficult than washing clothes.

I have no privacy.

Students bully those teachers who have no authority.

There are too many students per class.

Teachers are not very good at teaching well. They proceed too fast.

There are many teachers who can't keep abreast of the times, especially those who are older or married. They are too sensitive about how they look.

Some teachers tend to put students into a certain mould.

To a certain extent teachers seem to be conforming too much to the image they have of being a teacher. They shout and tell off students too easily.

On the other hand, several *kikokushijo* who had been to *genchikō* expressed very positive views about the school in areas where they might have been expected to find problems:

I think the way they teach Japanese is good because they do it in groups.

I enjoy Japanese-language lessons and science because the way they are taught is different from other schools. The problem is that there are too many English lessons.

Lessons are well organized and some teachers give us short quizzes every morning and this helps me learn better.

Relations between seniors and juniors are not very formal so it is easy to make friends.

There is no discrimination between seniors and juniors.

We can do club activities every day.

There are lots of other people in the dormitory so we get very friendly with each other.

Perhaps the most interesting range of answers were given in response to the question: 'When you talk to friends or teachers, are there occasions when you cannot make yourself understood, or cannot understand what the other person is saying?' The following is a range of answers from *kikokushijo* who had been to *genchikō*:

When commuter and dormitory students talk their opinions differ sharply.

I am actually quite introvert by nature but I try to behave like an extrovert. The people around me do not seem to realize my true nature.

Nothing special. If there is any problem or misunderstanding I will talk until I make myself understood.

I have no problems with the teachers but I have with my peers because they tell me lies unlike the foreign students.

I speak too fast.

When I speak Japanese I seem to confuse the order of the words sometimes but I have noticed that some classmates also don't express clearly what they want to say.

I find it is a problem when my friends have a difference of opinion.

The above replies suggest that some *kikokushijo* see their problems as relating to their own personalities, or the personalities of those around them, rather than being the inevitable result of overseas experience. On the other hand, a number of non-*kikokushijo* expressed concerns about their ability to communicate with those around them:

Misunderstandings sometimes occur.

I tend to let my imagination run away with me about what others are thinking.

I sometimes tend to be selfish and my friends do not understand me.

I sometimes find myself feeling antagonistic towards my friends because of some differences between us.

I sometimes quarrel with peers when they differ from me in their way of thinking.

In my club, when I wore a leotard with a T-shirt I was told off and when I asked why, then [the teacher] told me that I was not yet good enough to perform in a leotard. I still don't understand why she said that.

My classmates laugh at me because I speak in a Tsuchiura dialect and I can't make myself understood very well, and I have a problem talking about TV or films even when I understand the story completely.

This last statement was also echoed by one teacher who suggested that students in Fujiyama found their peers from other parts of Japan as different as those who came from overseas. Students at Fujiyama at the time of my research came from more than half of Japan's forty-seven prefectures, as Table XIII shows.

One other interesting idea emerged from the student responses to the questionnaire and this was that Fujiyama and *Fujiyamasei* were different from other schools and other students:

I sometimes cannot follow the maths and English lessons very well because they are different from the state schools.

It's a new school, so we don't have to worry about being set in our ways by any traditions.

Sometimes when I talk to Japanese friends who go to other schools we can't enjoy our conversation at all. As Fujiyama is quite particular, we have different ways of thinking about schools so we can't understand each other very well.

The students' answers to the questionnaires were not easily quantifiable. They did, however, suggest a number of new lines of inquiry. In particular the behaviour and treatment of *kikokushijo* in Fujiyama appeared to contrast considerably with the image of *ukeirekō* the literature had led me to expect. It remained quite clear that some *kikokushijo* in Fujiyama did suffer from certain problems. What was still uncertain, however, was whether those problems were the results of their overseas experience. It was unclear whether the problems resulting from a change of country differed from the problems of Japanese children moving from one

TABLE XIII: Region of Immediately
Previous School of Fujiyama
Gakuen Students

Hokkaido	3
Iwate	1
Fukushima	2
Ibaraki	727
Tochigi	3
Saitama	11
Chiba	232
Tokyo	113
Kanagawa	15
Yamagata	2
Nagano	1
Gifu	2
Aichi	4
Shizuoka	2
Kyoto	2
Osaka	2
Hyogo	3
Nara	1
Wakayama	1
Kagawa	1
Yamaguchi	1
Fukuoka	1
Kagoshima	1
Okinawa	2
Overseas	76
TOTAL	1209

Note: although *kikokushijo*
officially constituted almost 25 per
cent of students enrolled, in fact only
6 per cent entered the school directly
from overseas. This concurs with
Table X.

part of Japan to another or from one type of school to another
within Japan. It was also not easy to determine whether the
problems from which *kikokushijo* in Fujiyama suffer—even if some
of them were specific to the experience of moving from one country
to another—were, in total, greater than the problems of *ippansei* in
the same school. There was also some doubt whether the
disadvantages of overseas experience did, in fact, outweigh the
advantages for *kikokushijo*.

Similar uncertainties about *kikokushijo* experience were
expressed in the views of the teachers at Fujiyama. They were far

from unanimous on the question whether *kikokushijo* experience should be regarded positively or negatively. Some emphasized the good points, while others concentrated on the bad points and many teachers found both good and bad features. Some felt that the children needed to be more Japanese, while others believed that their 'international' qualities should be maintained and developed. The school philosophy, as enshrined in the school brochure, attempted to incorporate both viewpoints:

In order to facilitate the readjustment of children returning to Japan, these children are, on the one hand, placed with the regular students in everyday lessons and, on the other hand, the regular students are encouraged to take advantage of the exceptional language ability, knowledge of foreign countries and positive thinking of the returnees.

What the teachers were, in almost all cases, prepared to accept was that there was a category of children called *kikokushijo* who could be credited with special qualities, negative or positive, which differed from those of other students in the school. In general, they ascribed 'western' qualities such as individualism to the *kikokushijo* and it was these attributes which were given the positive or negative evaluation. This ascription was curious because so many of the children could not be identified as different from their non-*kikokushijo* peers. This was especially the case with *kikokushijo* who had received their overseas education in *Nihonjingakkō*. This suggested that the way in which *kikokushijo* were perceived as *kikokushijo* was more important than their individual personalities and backgrounds. They appeared to be symbols in a wider debate about the nature of Japanese society. Moreover, they were symbols which could be interpreted and invoked in a number of different ways by different groups, suggesting the need for the application of a broader dynamic model in order to understand their role in Japanese society.

The treatment of *kikokushijo*, however, is only one element of the whole educational philosophy of Fujiyama and the education of *Fujiyamasei*—a special type of Fujiyama student. The students, and the teachers, are taught to see themselves and each other as different from their counterparts in other schools. Their school terms are different; the students wear different uniforms and use a different vocabulary; they are isolated from the local environment; and their education is described as radically different from that in other schools. As the school has developed, it has become clear that these differences are attractive to the general public. Particularly significant, however, is the fact that the school advertises its large number of *kikokushijo* students as a further attraction. Indeed, it is twice as difficult for non-*kikokushijo* to get a place in the school as it is for *kikokushijo*. This again seems to counter the image of *kikokushijo* as an especially problematic group of children. If they were, why would the parents of *ippansei* be so eager to send them to a school where many students are *kikokushijo*? Clearly these parents believe that there are advantages to sending their children to such an institution. Similarly, why did the school advertise so widely the number of *kikokushijo* on the register? It may have been true in part that, as the principal said, the school felt that it was a national duty to enrol such students. But in a climate where changing demographic trends make the continued existence of all private schools increasingly precarious, philanthropy cannot be the only explanation.

Even if *kikokushijo* are not given preferential treatment in Fujiyama, the way that they are perceived clearly plays an important part in the construction of what constitutes a *Fujiyamasei*. The *Fujiyamasei* is presented as a new, in Roden's words, 'cultivated man' of the current era, in whom are combined both international and Japanese values. The international (and futuristic) aspects come in part from the connection with Tsukuba Academic City and Tsukuba University, and are also provided by the foreign teachers in the school and the 'superficial internationalness' of the curriculum which was described earlier. Most importantly, however, it comes from the presence of *kikokushijo* in the school. On the other hand, Fujiyama is very clearly a Japanese school: it teaches respect for Japanese traditions; Japanese is the main language; it is part of the Japanese mainstream educational system; academically, it differs little from other Japanese schools and almost all lessons are indistinguishable from those in other institutions. Perhaps most interestingly, no teachers are specially trained in how to teach *kikokushijo*.

The fieldwork I carried out at Fujiyama Gakuen produced a picture of a *ukeirekō* which clearly differed from the general image of such schools for *kikokushijo* presented in Chapters 3 and 4. Far from being treated like inpatients of a rehabilitation centre, they appear to be being groomed for membership of a future international élite. Indeed, the special treatment of students at Fujiyama gave rise to some virulent (even if misdirected) external criticism. The treatment they receive and the problems from which they suffer do not appear to be comparable to those I had been led to expect. In order to check the validity of these observations from Fujiyama, I began to analyse *kikokushijo* in a much broader comparative perspective.

6

Kikokushijo in Comparative Perspective

Before following up some of the questions raised by the foregoing examination of Fujiyama Gakuen, it is essential to obtain some sense of how typical (or exceptional) an educational experience it offers *kikokushijo*. According to Katō (1986: 62), around 50 per cent of *kikokushijo* attend schools which are specially prepared to receive them (*ukeirekō*) while the rest attend what he calls *ippan no gakkō* (regular schools). While Fujiyama should clearly be compared with the former category, we shall also look at the experience of *kikokushijo* in the regular schools and the case of a small category of children, which Katō omits to mention, in the 'international schools'.

KIKOKUSHIJO IN REGULAR SCHOOLS

Although *kikokushijo* in regular schools tend to be widely dispersed, and it is not easy to undertake research on their experience, it was possible to find a sufficient number of such children who had returned to regular schools to obtain some idea of what happened to them.

On the one hand, there were cases of children who hid their overseas experience on returning to Japan. I heard of several cases of *kikokushijo* who were 'fluent' in English, but purposely exaggerated a Japanese accent in English lessons so as not to stand out from their peers. There were also reported cases of *kikokushijo* going to the staff room and specifically requesting the teachers not to pick them out as returnees in lessons. As one boy, who had been in the United States for two years, insisted: 'The teacher is the teacher, and I am a student.'

On the other hand, there were examples (though probably fewer) of *kikokushijo* in regular schools who became class and student leaders and organizers. According to one child: 'My friends . . . think I can do anything because I went to America.' When *kikokushijo* constitute such a small number of the students in a school, the way that they behave is clearly dependent to a large degree on their individual personalities, whether they are extroverts or introverts. It also, however, depends to some extent on the way that *kikokushijo* are perceived in such schools.

In one top-level Tokyo senior high school, the head of the English department stated that the teachers consciously avoided using *kikokushijo* (of whom there were one or two in each class) to help them in their lessons. The teachers felt that since the other students already tended to regard *kikokushijo* as 'foreigners' (*gaikokujin*) when they first entered the school, to single them out in classes would only exacerbate the problem. Moreover, individual tuition (*kobetsu shidō*) was not offered to any students, including *kikokushijo*, for fear of creating 'teachers' pets'. Teachers in the school were keen for *kikokushijo* to adapt quickly to the school environment and those who disagreed with their teachers were considered particularly problematic. It was the teachers' belief that this latter group were particularly *kikokushijo* who, when overseas, had tried to limit their contact with local people. Such students, it was felt, tended to become too family-oriented, to rely too much on their parents' opinions, and, when they returned to Japan, often did not accept what they were told by their teachers. On the other hand, those *kikokushijo* who had adapted well to life overseas were felt to possess a great 'ability to get on in new circumstances' (*junnōryoku*) and adapt to a new school.

The teachers in this particular school held an opposing view to that proffered by the Japanese branch of Unesco (1982) in their *Kokusai Rikai Kyōiku no Tebiki* ('Handbook of Education for International Understanding') in which they recommend that *kikokushijo* should be used in as many lessons as possible where their experience of life overseas can introduce a comparative angle for those who have remained in Japan. In the case of moral education lessons the handbook suggests: 'Some *kikokushijo* have had the experience of going to mission schools or churches while they were overseas. This can be useful when comparing the influence of religion on customs and family life in different countries' (Unesco, 1982: 70).

Finally, as in the case of *kaigaishijo*, the attitude of parents plays an important part in the experience of *kikokushijo* in regular schools. There is no extra provision in any of these schools for the retention of language and other skills acquired overseas. Indeed, in elementary schools there is no language tuition at all. As a result, if parents want children to retain what they learnt overseas they have to provide it, either by paying for private language schools or by forming their own groups. Those children who want to shed their 'overseas' label, however, often resist such attempts and few children remain in such classes and groups beyond the age of 12 when they enter junior high school. At this age, they can study some English at school and they find that the new responsibilities of school-club activities, homework, and often *juku* make the study of another subject, albeit one at which they excel, too great a burden.

There is clearly considerable individual variation in the attitudes and experience of *kikokushijo* who go to regular schools in Japan, though it must be said that overall their reassimilation is probably the most complete of all *kikokushijo*. This is partly due to teachers' attitudes but it may also be connected with the beliefs of their parents. In large part, however, it can be attributed to peer pressure which, as Johnson (1975) has shown in his study of adolescent peer groups, plays an important role in the Japanese educational process. The children for whom, on the other hand, reassimilation is the least complete are probably those who go to the foreign national and international schools.

KIKOKUSHIJO IN FOREIGN NATIONAL AND INTERNATIONAL SCHOOLS

There are twenty-two national and international schools in Japan, with some 7,000 students (Kitazume, *JTW*, 9 August 1986). The majority of these schools are run by North American organizations and offer an educational programme in English. There are a number of laws designed to discourage Japanese parents from sending their children to such schools. For example, they are categorized by Monbushō as *kakushu gakkō* (miscellaneous schools), along with schools for dressmaking, gymnastics, and other non-academic subjects, and this means that parents are unable to obtain loans to help meet tuition costs. It also means that qualifications from these schools are not valid for entry to a Japanese university and any student who wishes to continue to such a university must take an extremely difficult 'equivalency examination'. As a result, up to 95 per cent of those who go to international schools graduate to colleges and universities in the west (Willis, 1983: 21). International schools are also extremely expensive. School fees can be as much as twice those of Fujiyama Gakuen. But, despite these factors, around a quarter of those enrolled in international schools are Japanese (*MS*, 26 July 1985). Willis (1983: 21) offers a variety of reasons why Japanese students attend such schools, including parents' idealistic educational beliefs, a father's company having an overseas branch, or the fact that the students are offspring of mixed marriages. Ōsawa (1986), however, suggests that these schools simply constitute a last resort for children who cannot fit into (or back into) the Japanese educational system. Interestingly, the vast majority of Japanese students in international schools are girls. In part, this is a reflection of the fact that girls, as we have seen, tend to spend longer overseas than boys. In part, it may reflect the feeling among Japanese parents that it is permissible to take more risks with their daughters' than with their sons' education since the former are less likely to need to worry about future careers. In part, it may be a reflection that returning to Japan from many western countries can, in some ways, be more difficult for girls, who have been presented with images of female emancipation that differ far more from the expected role of women in Japan than do the corresponding male roles.

Teachers in the international schools generally believe that it is vital for the good of *kikokushijo* to go to these schools on their return to Japan (see Lewis, 1986; Downs, *JTW*, 12 August 1989). They often hold very negative views about Japanese education and argue that it is unreasonable to expect anyone who has received a western education to be able to adapt to the environment of a Japanese school. They cite cases of children who have had nervous breakdowns through being unable to adapt to Japanese schools, before, mercifully, being able to obtain a place in an international school. The international schools readily attribute the problems of such children to many of the basic elements of the Japanese educational system which we examined in Chapter 4: large classes; teacher-centred lessons; very strict discipline; rote-learning; little scope for imagination and individuality; excessive work loads; the belief in perseverance over ability; excessive competitiveness between classes and schools. They believe that teachers in Japanese schools punish returnees for their poor Japanese and for not using the correct terms of respect. Worst of all, they say, the children are bullied by jealous peers and even teachers, especially English-language teachers, who feel threatened by them. What the children need, the international schools argue, is to be offered the protection of an international environment where the skills and attitudes they developed in the west are allowed to flourish.

The teachers in the international schools attempt to foster a special international identity in their students. They often describe the children—and the children sometimes describe themselves—as 'Third Culture Kids' (TCKs) who belong to neither their native nor their host environment but to an international culture that is above national boundaries. Ruth Useem, who first popularized the term 'third culture', defines it as 'the way of life that is developed in the interstices between societies. . . . TCKs . . . are the minor dependants of [a], for the most part highly educated, mobile world élite' (quoted in Downs, 1976: 66).

The teachers in the international schools accept that their graduates will find it difficult fully to re-enter Japanese society. There may be a definite conflict between their home and their school life; between their grandparents and other relatives, who expect them to talk and behave in a Japanese fashion, and their non-Japanese, generally western, peers, who expect them to be like them. The teachers are doubtful whether these children will ever be considered able to act as an interface between Japan and the outside world. International schools, they accept, are not only a cocoon for such children but also a barrier. Nakatsu Ryōko (1979: 11–12), one of the best-known popular writers about *kikokushijo*, claims that international schools simply delay readjustment to Japan, and thereby deprive *kikokushijo* of a chance to become full members of Japanese society.

KIKOKUSHIJO IN *UKEIREKŌ*

Schools with special entrance systems for *kikokushijo* are generally known as *ukeirekō* and provide the most important reference group against which to judge the typicality of Fujiyama Gakuen. Fifty per cent of *kikokushijo* attend *ukeirekō* and, unlike the graduates of the international schools, almost all go on to Japanese universities. Not all *ukeirekō*, however, prepare their students to re-enter mainstream society in the same way. Nakabayashi (1981: 168) suggests there are two basic methods:

One method is to put all *kikokushijo* together in a special grade, the other is to place them with the other students who have not been overseas. . . . The former system of adaptation provides a cushion to allow them to get used to Japanese society. . . . For returnee children in this first system, there may be some psychological damage from being treated specially . . . on the other hand, for those in the second system, the environment changes radically and that can be problematic. . . . Only experience will tell which is the better method.

In actual fact, there is a third approach which combines both of the methods Nakabayashi describes, whereby *kikokushijo* are initially segregated and then integrated with the regular students at a later date. This system is practised at Ōizumi, the first state school for *kikokushijo*, which opened in Tokyo in 1964.

Ōizumi is in fact a national school, rather than a regular state school, and this distinction is a significant one. The national schools in Japan account for less than 0.5 per cent of all Japanese schools, schoolteachers, and schoolchildren. At senior-high-school level, the figure is closer to 0.2 per cent. These schools, unlike state and private schools which are under the control of local or prefectural government and certified institutions respectively, are directly administered by Monbushō. The schools are always attached to national universities and hence are generally known as *fuzoku gakkō* (attached schools). In English they are sometimes known as 'laboratory schools' and this, perhaps, gives a clearer indication of the original idea behind their conception—they were to be institutions where students could gain the necessary experience to qualify for teachers' certificates. The system of teacher training in Japan, however, has fundamentally changed and so, therefore, has the image of the *fuzoku gakkō*. The connection of these schools with national—generally the most highly rated—universities and their system for obtaining direct entry to those universities for a certain number of their students make the *fuzoku gakkō* very attractive propositions to parents anxious for their children to succeed educationally. They have therefore now become known as 'escalator schools'. If children can get on to the bottom of the 'escalator' at elementary, or even kindergarten, level they can ride it to the top. The *fuzoku gakkō* have therefore come to be considered as amongst the most élite schools in Japan. As Furuhashi Seiko (1984: 43–4), a teacher at Ōizumi, says:

Schools attached to national teachers' colleges usually have high prestige. . . . The size of the classes is kept small which means that students are blessed with a low student–teacher ratio and other aspects of a rich schooling environment. These factors attract education-oriented parents and make the entrance examination to these schools very competitive. As a result, students are mainly from upper-middle-class professional or executive families.

The decision to use an 'attached school'—Ōizumi is the attached school of Tokyo Gakugei University—for *kikokushijo* can perhaps be best explained by the fact that it was a school over which Monbushō had direct budgetary control and which, therefore, it could most easily instruct to follow a certain educational policy. Moreover, Takagi Fumio, a former president of Japan National Railways and an important figure in the creation of policy for *kikokushijo* in the early 1970s, adds that there had been rising criticism of the *fuzoku gakkō* for their increasing concentration on examination success. Hence, the decision was made to encourage *fuzoku gakkō* to be more experimental and accept *kikokushijo* (Takagi, 1977: 44).

The system of education that was first set up at Ōizumi involved a separate class for *kikokushijo*. Those who could apply had to be Japanese nationals with more than a year's residence overseas, with six years' prior schooling, and residing within an hour's commuting distance from the school. In 1965, the first fourteen students were accepted, eight of whom were returnees from the United States. In 1971 a mixed-class system, 'based on the view that mixing ordinary students with *kikokushijo* quickened the latter's adjustment', was instituted (Furuhashi, 1984: 41). The selection of *kikokushijo*, however, remained separate from that of the other students. As we have seen, the children who were selected tended to come from families with an upper-middle-class back-ground and a strong interest in education.

Ochanomizu school—which is also attached to a national university, Ochanomizu Women's University—follows a similar system to that now employed at Ōizumi. In the junior high school there is a quota of fifteen *kikokushijo* in each grade. In the first grade, these children are placed in a separate class from the regular students. These *kikokushijo* children are virtually the only entrants to the junior high school who have stepped on to the escalator half-way up, without first having competed to enter the elementary school. In the second grade, about twenty regular students join the *kikokushijo* class, but it still remains the odd class among the four in the grade. In the third grade, the *kikokushijo* are divided up so that there are about four in each class. In the second and third grades each class consists of about thirty-five children but, in the first grade, apart from the class with fifteen *kikokushijo*, the average size is about forty-five. In the first grade, therefore, as at Ōizumi, the teacher–student ratio heavily favours the *kikokushijo* who may receive up to three times as much individual attention as the other students. Some of the teachers who taught these small classes found this high teacher–student ratio an added attraction. The teacher in charge of the *kikokushijo* programme thought that it took a year to eighteen months for the students to 'adjust'. But the fact that *kikokushijo* were in a separate class in the first year relieved some of the pressure on them to speak Japanese, and although the form teacher always spoke to them in Japanese, several students, even towards the end of the year, were still talking to each other in English.

The school attached to the private Catholic Nanzan University is one of the few institutions which has an entirely separate unit for *kikokushijo*. This is known as the *kokusaibu* (international section) which takes both junior- and senior- high-school students. It had a total of some 129 *kikokushijo* in 1984, with a ratio of 2:1 in favour of girls. This again reflects the tendency among parents of *kikokushijo* to send daughters, rather than sons, to local schools abroad and generally to keep them overseas longer. The students in the *kokusaibu* spend all six years in the separate unit and they have very little contact with the other students. The curricula of the main school and the unit were, however, apart from the English language course, almost exactly the same. All *kikokushijo* had intensive Japanese-language classes when they first arrived at the school as all lessons were taught using everyday Japanese. There were minor concessions in the style of teaching in the *kokusaibu*—the English teacher was bilingual; the science teacher occasionally used *hiragana* (phonetic alphabet) when he could have used *kanji*; and the Japanese-language teacher had spent a year in Australia—but students were expected to cope with the lessons within about three months of entering the school. The result was that *kikokushijo* received very high individual attention throughout their time at the school. They also developed a stronger sense of their separate identity as *kikokushijo* than returnees in most other schools.

The final category of *ukeireko* consists of the three schools specially built for *kikokushijo* as a result of a policy committee's recommendations to Monbushō at the end of the 1970s. In many ways, these are the schools which most resemble Fujiyama Gakuen. The three schools are International Christian University (ICU) Senior High School, Gyōsei International Senior High School, and Dōshisha International Senior High School. These schools share several important characteristics. Firstly, as with Fujiyama, they are all private schools, and they are all attached to well known, long established private educational institutions from which they take their names.[1] Secondly, unlike Fujiyama, these private institutions are all Christian foundations. Thirdly, although they are private foundations with high fees, a considerable proportion of the money for their construction was provided by Monbushō in return for an agreement that the schools keep to certain guidelines. In the cases of ICU and Gyōsei, they had to be sited not more than an hour's journey from Tokyo Station, and, in all three cases, two-thirds of the students in every class had to be *kikokushijo*. Monbushō gave five hundred million yen each to ICU, Gyōsei, and Dōshisha in 1978, 1979, and 1980 respectively. For Gyōsei, this constituted about one-sixth of the total expense of building the senior high school. A fourth shared feature of the three schools is the sense of a 'total institution' which, as in Fujiyama, centres on relative isolation from the surrounding communities and the existence of dormitories. School dormitories are rare in Japan. Where they do exist, Nakabayashi (1981: 201–4) suggests that there have been two main forces behind their creation. The first is the need to provide accommodation for children of parents who have to go overseas and want to leave their children behind, or for parents who did take their children with them and believe that the boarding system provides the best environment for their readaptation to life in Japan. The second force stems from a perception that Japanese youth are being educated in a moral vacuum. Supporters of this point of view believe that boarding-schools offer an environment where a more moralistic educational system can be developed without interference from external factors. This way of thinking follows a similar vein to that of the article in *Tokyo Sports* which criticized Fujiyama Gakuen: it is, according to Nakabayashi (1981: 205, 210) related to a nostalgia for the 'spirit' (*kippu*) engendered in the pre-war Imperial high-school dormitories, and a romantic view of British institutions such as Eton College. Uji (1984) suggests that this way of thinking has become increasingly popular in Japan in recent years.

ICU, Gyōsei, and Dōshisha senior high schools all have connections with good universities which ensure direct entry for a number of students. Gyōsei has a special 'quota' from Sophia University which allows it to recommend a certain number of its students each year for direct entry. Sophia, known in Japanese as Jōchi, managed to raise its status dramatically in the 1960s and 1970s through recruiting excellent staff and students and now stands just behind the top two (Keiō and Waseda) in the hierarchy of private Japanese universities (James and Benjamin, 1988: 86). ICU, which like Sophia has a reputation for offering an 'international education', has also risen high in the hierarchy of universities and the fact that its attached senior high school can assure 15 to 20 per cent of its graduates a place in the university is a very big attraction for parents of prospective students. The most assured university entry, however, is offered by Dōshisha International School. Somewhere between 85 and 90 per cent of graduates from the school can go to either Dōshisha University (another top-ranked Japanese university) or the associated two-year college for women, Dōshisha Jogakuin, through the recommendation system (*suisen seido*).

In all three schools, it is hoped that there will be a positive pay-off between the experiences of *kikokushijo* and *ippansei*. The assumption is that the overseas experience and language ability of *kikokushijo* who have spent a long time in local schools abroad will act as a stimulant to the *ippansei*. In many cases it clearly does; sometimes, though, it can act as a source of disaffection. Entrance for *ippansei* to all three schools is extremely competitive: in the case of ICU senior high school, there are twelve applicants for each place. Those who succeed have been at the top of their classes in junior high school and it can be a shock to find themselves streamed in English far below many of their peers. Where *kikokushijo* form the majority, there is the potential for the minority group of *ippansei* to feel discriminated against. The schools, however, are keen to play down the differences between the two groups and, as at Fujiyama, try to produce students who combine the best of international and Japanese values.

Although *kikokushijo* are far from being assured entry to these special schools which provide easy access to top universities, their chances are far higher than those of the *ippansei*. At ICU in 1984, *kikokushijo* had a 50-per-cent chance of gaining entry (320 applicants for 160 places)—six times higher than their non-*kikokushijo* peers.

Despite having quota systems into good universities, all three schools offer a curriculum which differs from regular Japanese schools only in the streaming in English (and, because of traditional connections, French at Gyōsei), the provision of some supplementary lessons, and facilities for individual research projects at ICU. Since Dōshisha is under the least pressure in terms of assuring its students places in university, its insistence on keeping to the traditional Japanese system of education, when two-thirds of the students are *kikokushijo*, is particularly interesting. Teachers in the school gave a variety of reasons for sticking to the traditional path.

One teacher told me that when the school was founded they had not known that the university would offer an 85-per-cent quota, and that, given this, departing from the standard curriculum would have been too great a risk. Another teacher claimed that the school's intake was going to increase and that the university would then be able to give them only a 60-per-cent quota, hence they had to offer the standard curriculum for the benefit of the other 40 per cent of students who would have to compete for entrance to university. A similar argument was that even if the quota was 85 per cent the school still had a duty to provide a good chance for the other 15 per cent to do well in entrance examinations. A different teacher claimed that the school had no freedom in the matter because of the tight control Monbushō had over it. A further response was that the professors at the university would complain if the students coming from the school were not of the same educational background as other students. A sixth teacher said that he taught in a typical Japanese fashion simply because he did not know any other way of teaching.

This final comment is crucial in understanding the education provided by *ukeirekō*. No teachers in any of the three schools described are specially trained in how to teach *kikokushijo*. There are qualified foreign teachers and Japanese teachers with long overseas experience in all three schools, but many of these complain that they feel marginalized from the real decision-making processes in the school and unable to influence the curriculum. As with Fujiyama, these schools are closer, in terms of curriculum and structure, to the regular Japanese schools than to the international schools and are clearly part of the mainstream of the Japanese educational system. Despite this, there is a widely held belief in Japan that the *ukeirekō* are fundamentally different from other schools. One professor at Dōshisha University, for example, was apparently under the misapprehension that all lessons at the Dōshisha International Senior High School were held in English.

Where, however, there are differences between the *ukeirekō* and regular schools in Japan, these are significant. The *ukeirekō* often have smaller classes, a comparatively high teacher–student ratio, and a particularly close relationship (sometimes through a dormitory system) between staff and pupils. These special aspects appear to be utilized in *ukeirekō* to foster a strong feeling of identification with the particular school and the sense of a special status in Japanese society. As we have seen, the schools also use their special connections to offer good prospects of entry into top universities. In all the schools where a large number of *kikokushijo* are taught together with *ippansei*, the competition for places among the latter is extremely high. Although there are variations amongst these schools in terms of their different programmes, there is therefore little doubt that Fujiyama Gakuen can be considered typical among *ukeirekō*. As so many *kikokushijo* are educated in *ukeirekō*, an investigation of the issues raised by the experience of those at Fujiyama Gakuen will have ramifications for understanding the experience of a substantial proportion of all *kikokushijo*.

THE PROBLEMS OF *KIKOKUSHÌJO* IN COMPARATIVE PERSPECTIVE

Although there is no doubt that some of the *kikokushijo* at Fujiyama Gakuen faced problems, their experience did not appear to be as problematic as the literature discussed in Chapter 3 had suggested. One interesting explanation for this discrepancy suggested itself when I was able to observe a research project on *kikokushijo* being carried out at Fujiyama Gakuen by a psychiatry research student. The main aim of this project was to record the illnesses of returnees as psychosomatic evidence of their inability to readjust to Japanese society. Three medical doctors and one assistant each interviewed eight students over a two-day period. Fifteen minutes was strictly allotted to each child, and the interview consisted of the interviewer asking questions and filling in a pre-formated sheet with information derived from the child's answers. To the question, for example, 'Did you enjoy your school overseas?', the interviewer would judge the child's response on a scale from good to bad and mark the form accordingly.

The hidden question concerning physical health was almost always marked at, or near, the bad (*warui*) end of the scale. In order to justify this marking, the interviewer would sometimes go to considerable lengths, as is shown by the following exchange: the interviewee was a 12-year-old member of the junior-high-school first grade. He had spent five-and-a-half years in Canada, attending a local school during the week and a *hoshūkō* on Saturdays, and had returned to Japan just over fourteen months previously. The interviewer started by asking him about his overseas experience. Yes, he had learnt good English. He had liked the local school better than the *hoshūkō*. Most of his friends had been local children. They had lived in a town house. No, they had not had a maid. No, he had not had any special illnesses. He had been able to make friends quickly. The work at the local school, especially mathematics, seemed very easy. He enjoyed his school in Canada because he particularly liked playing ice-hockey.

The interviewer next asked the boy about his life on return to Japan. Had he had any problem with language when he returned? No, none at all because they always spoke Japanese at home in Canada, and his Japanese was always better than his English. Had he had any problems making friends when he had returned? No, he had had no problems. Had he been bullied when he came back to school in Japan? No, he hadn't had any problems. The boy stopped and thought for a moment and then added that his friends in Japan were a bit different from those he had known in Canada because they were so easily afraid of things and people, and he found this a bit strange. The interviewer asked him again: 'So you didn't have any problems with bullying then?' (*ijimeru koto wa nakatta?*). The boy again replied, no. What were the problems he had with school life? There wasn't enough time for examination preparation. What problems did he have with his studying and general educational career (*shinro*)? Well, he didn't do very well in *kokugo* (Japanese-language class) but, he added, he was, of course, very good at English.

What about his health since he had returned? Nothing special. But he had a cold now? Yes. Did he always have a cold? No, just now. Had his eyes been sore for a long time? No, it had just recently happened with the cold. Both of them? Yes. Did he mind if the interviewer took a look at his eyes? (The interviewer, a qualified physician, walked around the table and carefully inspected both the boy's eyes.) Unasked, the boy repeated that it was only a recent illness and that he also had a cough. The interviewer marked the 'bad' end of the scale for physical illness.

Did he have any family problems? No. Did he have any problems with the customs of everyday life (*seikatsu shūkan ni tsuite komatte iru ka*)? No, not really. Could he think of anything which he had found different when he had returned to Japan? No, not really (*betsu ni nai*). Was there anything else that was really bothering him? The boy thought for a bit. Well, he found that there were too many rules (*kisoku*) in Japanese schools. The interviewer asked another question: of all the problems you've talked about which is the biggest, the most distressing (*nayande iru koto wa*)? The boy gave no answer, and the next question had to be missed out since it asked how long after the return to Japan this most distressing problem had been at its worst. Well, did he think living overseas was a good thing then? Yes. Why? Because, the boy said, he liked playing ice-hockey and everything was just more relaxed in Canada (*nobinobi shimasu*). The interviewer asked one final question: if he compared his time overseas with the present, which would he say was better (*dochira ga shiawase ka*)? 'Well, when I was in Canada', the boy replied, 'I preferred Canada to Japan, but now I prefer Japan because I have made many good friends here.' After exactly fifteen minutes the interview came to an end.

Afterwards, the interviewer explained to me that all the answers were codified on the one-to-five, or good-to-bad, scale to allow them to be entered into a computer. Videos had been taken of several interviews so as to analyse the eyes and expressions of respondents to check the veracity of their answers. To assure me of the scientific nature of the research, he informed me that he had personally trained all the other interviewers.[2]

The type of research I have just described suffers from a number of serious methodological faults. These faults, moreover, are common to the majority of research projects on *kikokushijo* described in Chapter 3—large-scale quantifiable tests based on questionnaires and individual case studies alike—and perhaps go some way to explaining why *kikokushijo* experience has been described as so problematic. First of all, there is an inherent assumption that returnees have problems. Virtually all of the questions asked in the case study were related to 'problems' that the children might have had: hardly any asked directly about the benefits or positive effects that children might have gained from living abroad, though some children did mention these unasked. So, it is impossible, in these research projects to tell whether the benefits gained from overseas experience outweigh the disadvantages. The researcher simply presumes that *kikokushijo* have 'problems'; his research consists of trying to measure these 'problems'.

The techniques of measurement used in this type of research are also easy to discredit. For example, any problem which *kikokushijo* may have in the present is related to the fact that they are *kikokushijo*, regardless of where, when, and how long they were overseas. This raises an ultimately much more serious issue, namely, that this body of research lacks any control group. It is impossible to know whether the 'problems' from which the researcher 'discovers' the *kikokushijo* to be suffering might not actually be experienced by all Japanese children of their age, and be attributable to quite different reasons, such as adolescence or the strain of the Japanese educational system. As Stephen Jay Gould (1984: 242) points out in *The Mismeasure of Man*, it cannot be assumed that factors which correlate are necessarily caused by each other. Finally, the research, in its use of factor analysis, video, and scientific jargon, can only be described as pseudo-scientific. The data, from being presented in scientific terms, takes on an 'objective' nature of its own. This is particularly so in the context of Japanese society where great respect is given both to factual data *per se* and to the élite establishments which sponsor this kind of research.[3]

There is, however, a small body of research undertaken in Japan which has avoided many of the methodological faults of the case study described above. The results of this work present a very different picture of *kikokushijo* experience to the commonly accepted image described in Chapter 3. Several surveys, for example, have suggested that *kikokushijo* expect to face—and their parents expect them to face—more trouble when they return to Japan than proves to be the case. Their perceptions of the problems of being a returnee tend to surpass the actual situation. A 1982 Monbushō survey showed that the majority of parents of Japanese children overseas were very worried about returning to Japan: 40 per cent of parents with children in elementary schools overseas were worried that their offspring would not be able to keep up academically when they returned; over 50 per cent of parents with children in junior high schools were worried that their offspring would not be able to enter good senior high schools; and about 70 per cent of the total surveyed expressed uneasiness (*fuan*) about the chances of their children entering good universities.

Many children overseas had similar fears. Some 7,000 children overseas between the ages of 3 and 19 (about 14 per cent of the total) were surveyed in October 1982. Regardless of age, the biggest fears of the children were whether they would understand their lessons (34 per cent) and whether they could get into a good university or high school (23.5 per cent). The second highest response overall, about 26.2 per cent of the children, was 'No special anxiety' (*tokuni fuan wa motte inai*)—a category that does not even figure in the parents' answers (see Hasebe, 1985: 174–5). As children got older, however, their worries became more specific: around 60 per cent of children overseas in the 12 to 19 age-band were worried about how they would fare in future examinations in Japan (Monbushō, 1982: 14).

The Monbushō survey made no attempt to examine the real extent of the fears of overseas children and parents: it simply measured how their worries stood in relation to each other. Perhaps more significant is a comparison of these results with the reports of teachers of around 4,000 *kikokushijo* who had returned in the period 1979–82 (about 17 per cent of the total). Their responses seemed to suggest that the fears of overseas children and parents were rather exaggerated. The teachers polled by Monbushō rated 51 per cent of the *kikokushijo* in their classes as 'excellent or better' (*sugurete iru*), 42 per cent as 'average' (*futsū*), and only the remaining 7 per cent as 'below average' (*ototte iru*). Only 0.5 per cent of all the *kikokushijo* in the survey fell into the category of 'severely behind' (*hijō ni ototte iru*) (Monbushō, 1982: 27). As for skills in Japanese language, only about 8 per cent of *kikokushijo* were found to be handicapped to any degree, and less than 1 per cent were thought to have a major handicap(1982: 26).[4] Moreover, the areas in which *kikokushijo* did report problems—again only a measurement of relative troubles—were not those expected before returning to Japan, the biggest complaint being the lack of school holidays (28 per cent) (1982: 37).

It is important to stress how few *kikokushijo* actually have severe Japanese-language problems since they are often presented as being particularly backward in this area. In almost all families of *kaigaishijo*—as with the subject in the case study described above—Japanese is the dominant language while abroad. Inui and Sono's survey (1977: 149) of overseas-language usage showed that between 80 and 90 per cent of children used mainly Japanese at home, and up to 40 per cent used mainly Japanese while playing with friends. The fact that, as Iwasaki Mariko (1982) has pointed out, they expect to return to Japan for future education and employment means that Japanese children, even in local schools overseas, tend to be rather slower in picking up the local language than students of other nationalities. A survey by Kono Mamoru (1982) suggests that for most children the dominant language changes from Japanese only after about four years overseas, and that even after five years, children's use of English remains at about 50 per cent. Not one family of the 168 children surveyed by Kono used more English than Japanese and only 3.5 per cent used the two languages equally. It is presumably partly as a result of the concern of families to maintain Japanese-language skills while overseas, that one survey by Nakanishi, Akahori, and Matsubara (1982), which incorporated a test comparing the linguistic ability of *kikokushijo* and non-*kikokushijo*, actually suggests that in certain grades the Japanese-language ability of the former is superior. It is perhaps equally interesting that the researchers—all of them members of the community of researchers studying *kikokushijo* problems—account for this result in terms of the special help offered to returnees and concentrate their attention instead on the weak points in the responses of the *kikokushijo*.[5]

Perhaps the most interesting evidence collected to suggest that *kikokushijo* do not suffer to the extent that is commonly believed, is provided by a small number of surveys comparing the general experiences of *kikokushijo* with those of non-*kikokushijo*. In 1980, Murase published the results of a survey of 240 children, half of whom were *kikokushijo*, and among whom there were five examples from each of the four main types of school attended by returnees: regular state; regular private; *ukeirekō* (including ICU and Ōizumi high schools); and international schools. It is not surprising to find among the conclusions of this survey (1980: 81) that the older their children are the more worried their parents are about the effect going overseas may have on them, and that parents are more worried about boys than girls. However, Murase concluded (1980: 82) that the majority (94 per cent) of parents felt that their child was not very worried, or not worried at all, about having been overseas.

In 1983, Murase published an extended survey examining the assumptions underlying research on *kikokushijo*. It examined and compared *kikokushijo* and non-*kikokushijo* anxieties (*fuan*) using a modified version of the Takenshiki General Anxiety Test which is also used by Monbushō. This test looks at students' worries about school work, personal relationships, and their own bodies as well as examining feelings of solidarity, their general fears, and tendencies towards self-punishment, escapism, and violence. In this controlled survey Murase again used children from the four categories of school accepting *kikokushijo*. She states (1983: 159–72):

In comparing Japanese returnees with non-returnees, it is possible to argue that the latter may be characterized by more anxieties specific to Japanese culture and society than are the former who have lived outside of Japan and who have been somewhat removed from Japanese social and cultural influences. . . . Hence, by achieving some degree of distance and detachment from the Japanese system, the returnees are no longer as subject to all the anxieties incurred by those who remain more deeply immersed in it. . . . That returnees have specific difficulties is undeniable. That there are certain anxieties associated with their situation is substantiated by this research. However, any assumption that returnees have a disproportionate number and degree of difficulties is unjustified. There also appear to be characteristic problems for non-returnees who have been immersed in the Japanese socio-cultural-educational system.

The research by Takahagi *et al.* (1982), involving some 1,719 *kikokushijo*, offers equally interesting results. Like the work of Murase, this research has also been all but ignored by other researchers on *kikokushijo*.[6] Although the early part of the survey appears to follow the usual format for studying *kikokushijo*, including the use of video to analyse returnee behaviour both inside and outside the classroom (1982: 4), the most interesting section of the research involves the use of a control group of 216 children (1982: 20–2). Across a whole range of potential problem areas—health, home life, school and personal life, language, personality—Takahagi's research group found very little difference between returnees and non-returnees. The research did suggest that returnees' overseas experience made them less keen on organized school activities and on the amount of homework in Japanese schools and less sure that they were lucky to be born Japanese (48 per cent, as opposed to 65 per cent of non-*kikokushijo*). On the other hand, the survey suggested that the *kikokushijo* had fewer problems than non-*kikokushijo* with teachers, personal relations with peers, and language. In a section on personal relations, to the question 'Do your friends laugh at you, make fun of you, or jeer at you?', 46 per cent of the non-*kikokushijo* replied that they did, whereas only 21 per cent of the returnees answered in the affirmative. The researchers explain this by the fact that the returnees have already had such problems while overseas and that they no longer find them worrying. On the question of language, 61 per cent of non-*kikokushijo* said that they were worried that people did not really understand what they were saying, while only 24 per cent of the returnees indicated the same worry. This was put down to the returnees' self-assertiveness and confidence in expressing themselves. Similarly, 74 per cent of returnees said they had no worry about understanding what their teachers said, while only 42 per cent of the control group were equally confident. Overall, Takahagi and his researchers conclude that there appears to be very little cumulative difference in terms of daily living between children who have and who have not been overseas, although there may be differences in the types of problem faced.

Finally, Matsubara and Itō (1982), who surveyed sixty *kikokushijo* against a control group of sixty non-*kikokushijo*, came up with two interesting findings. The first of these is that, although returnees may be individualistic, this does not mean that they cannot also be group-oriented; and the second is that the fact that returnees may feel positive about (or in a sports event support) an overseas country does not mean they do not also appreciate Japan. Kumagai Fumie (1977: 46), in a study of 104 male Japanese university students, found that the longer the students were in the United States the more favourable they were towards their host country but that this was not at the expense of their appreciation of their own society and culture. Some authors (Hoshino and Niikura, 1983*a*: 190–1) have taken this idea one step further and have suggested that *kikokushijo* may have a stronger sense of Japanese identity than children who have never been overseas:

Obviously those children who have experienced a foreign culture have a better chance of understanding what Japan is and what Japanese are. . . . One child in a Turkish elementary school, before developing an internationalist mentality, made a great effort to develop a Japanese one. . . . The *kikokushijo*, in some ways, are more conscious than those who have had only a domestic education of Japan, Japanese people, and Japanese culture and history. One of their main traits could be said to be the fact that they can perceive these things objectively.

One *kikokushijo* described in an essay how the experience of having to explain Japan to those overseas, and 'keep up one's Japaneseness' while abroad, tended to reinforce Japanese identity: 'In England, whenever somebody mentioned something about me being a Japanese in a critical sort of way, I would say, "I can't help being a Japanese. I don't care, and I am proud of being one."'[7]

Azuma Hiroshi, Professor of Education at Tokyo University, undertook a survey of returnees, comparing their experiences of Japan with their time overseas, and discovered that the children had a more favourable impression of the latter than of the former. Of the children, 73 per cent said their overseas school was more fun, while 2.4 per cent chose their Japanese school; 57 per cent that they understood lessons better overseas, 7.8 per cent in Japan; 63 per cent that their overseas school friends were kinder, 2.1 per cent their friends in Japan. Azuma was initially so surprised, he claims, by his findings that he felt the children's memories must be at fault and he tried the same questionnaire on children attending a Japanese supplementary school in the United States, only to receive the same result (1979: 92–3).[8] His findings led him to become one of the first educationalists to suggest that it is not the *kikokushijo* who have problems but the Japanese educational system. As we shall see, this new perception has gained increasing popularity in recent years.

It is difficult to find evidence to support or disprove the idea that the problems from which *kikokushijo* clearly suffer are due to the fact that they are *kikokushijo*. Some of the *kikokushijo* in Fujiyama Gakuen suggested that simply moving from one educational environment to another might create problems for all children. A number of researchers on *kikokushijo* have compared the experience of *kikokushijo* with the experience of changing school inside Japan but have started out from the premiss that the experiences are qualitatively different. Kobayashi (1982*b*: 86), for example, writes that 'The adaptation of *kikokushijo* is different from that of children transferring from another school [*tenkōsei*] because the returnees are forced to adapt into a new culture while the latter adapt into a new environment in the same culture'. Nakane (1972: 13) similarly insists that moving between Japan and another country and moving within Japan are qualitatively different experiences. Unfortunately, no research has yet been undertaken to test out these contentions. Indeed, very little research appears to have been undertaken at all on the experience of so-called *tenkōsei* (transfer children) within Japan. Yokoshima has carried out a number of small projects at Utsunomiya University which suggest important similarities between the experiences of *tenkōsei* and those of *kikokushijo*. He suggests (1977: 151) that where the former have been studied there has been a strong emphasis on the negative aspects of their experience: deterioration in school work, ostracism from existing groups, refusal to go to school (*tōkōkyohi*), delinquency, and, in extreme cases, suicide. He himself, however, prefers to concentrate on the benefits of moving school as means of positive 'self-growth' (*jiko no seichō no plus*). While this research is only minimal, it does suggest that the models of Japanese society, used by those who play down the significance of moving within Japan, tend to exaggerate its social homogeneity. Indeed, as we saw at Fujiyama, the differences between peers from different regions of Japan were sometimes reported to be as great as those between *kikokushijo* and *ippansei*. Some of the 'problems' experienced by *kikokushijo* might therefore be put down to the simple fact of having changed educational environment, or region, within Japan and need not be ascribed to the fact that they have spent time overseas.

Another important question concerns the extent to which those problems from which *kikokushijo* do suffer can be ascribed to the fact that they are returning to Japanese society rather than any other. There seems to be an idea in Japan that *kikokushijo* are a uniquely Japanese phenomenon. Kobayashi (1982*a*: 38–9), in one of the few Japanese studies of returnees to other societies, concludes that their situation is not generally considered to be as problematic as it is in Japan. He examines three different groups of countries as material for his argument. In the smaller European nations, such as the Benelux countries, he concludes that, since the number of children overseas is so small and the societies are already so international and pluralistic, there is little resistance to children being educated overseas and little question of special treatment for returnees. In England, which he places in its own category, he suggests that there has been a tradition, since the days of the Empire, of parents leaving children behind in boarding-schools to complete their education. Kobayashi's third category includes the United States, West Germany, and France, from where, he admits, so many people are going abroad that they too are experiencing the full phenomenon of education for children overseas and for returnees at home. The only systematic education for *kikokushijo* of which Kobayashi has knowledge is that of West Germany where returnee children can receive a form of supplementary education in a *kolleg*. Kobayashi concludes that in these countries the issue of the children's education, apart from the immediate matter of running and administering overseas schools, is not taken so seriously as in Japan.

In fact, there is a considerable body of research, particularly in the United States, concerning returnee experience and the potential problems of such experience in countries other than Japan. This should not be particularly surprising: one estimate puts the number of children studying outside their native countries at around one million worldwide (*JTW*, 7 February 1987), and Downs (1976: 66) quotes the figure of 300,000 American children between the ages of 5 and 18 living overseas in 1976. Austin (1983) has published an annotated bibliography of 'Cross-Cultural Re-entry' with around 300 citations (the great majority published in the United States), of which only six refer to Japanese returnees. He categorizes citations in terms of the sponsorship that led to the overseas experience— corporations, federal agencies, the military, the church, and a category entitled 'international education'. Citations go back as far as 1925 (an article about returnees to China) and over 25 per cent cover the specific area of the experience of returnee children.[9]

Church (1982) has undertaken a rather more analytical review of some 300 citations on what he terms 'sojourner adjustment'. Church starts (as do many of the sources he cites) with Kalervo Oberg's (1960) famous description of 'culture shock' as an 'occupational disease' suffered by people who are suddenly immersed in a culture that is very different from their own.[10] Church then examines the vast amount of quantitative research which analyses stages of adjustment to different cultures and the background, situational, and personality variables related to these stages. Much of this work follows Lysgaard's (1955) seminal study of Norwegian Fulbright students in the United States which first introduced the concept of a U-curve of adjustment—initial euphoria, followed by a trough, followed by a period of stabilization and recovery. This pattern was extended by Gullahorn and Gullahorn (1963) into a UU (or W) curve of adjustment to take into account the effect of returning to the native culture and, as late as 1980, Bochner, Lin, and McLeod (1980: 265) were undertaking research of the kind that suggested that 'the middle of the W-curve is much flatter than either extremity'. Hardly any of this work, which still provides the methodological underpinning for much research on sojourner experience in the west, is discussed, either positively or negatively, by the researchers of *kikokushijo* in Japan.

Similarly, there is no mention in the Japanese literature of popular articles in the United States on the problems of returnees to that society (see for example Kines, 1971; Kelly, 1973; Rendahl, 1978; Eakin, 1979). Nor is there any mention of the work of the psychiatrist Sidney Werkman, probably the best-known proponent of the pathological effects of culture shock among returnees to the United States (e.g. Werkman, 1979).[11] There has, however, been one interesting research project which compared the experiences of returnees to Japan and the United States. Uehara Asako's (1985: 175) quantitative research on returnees to the United States led her to conclude that there was nothing unique about the culture shock of Japanese returnees. She believes that 'in any culture which is different from the culture of the returnee there is the possibility of the experience of returnee culture shock' and supports her contention by pointing out that many Americans in her sample (71 per cent) went to Europe but also suffered culture shock on their return to the United States. When Uehara (1986) compared the completed questionnaires of 151 Japanese and 146 American returnees, she concluded that, while in both groups females suffered a greater intensity of culture shock than males, there was no overall difference between the two groups. One must, of course, take the same precautions with all research on non-Japanese returnee problems as with work undertaken on *kikokushijo*, but nevertheless, Uehara's comparison does suggest that what is unique about the situation of *kikokushijo* is not so much that they suffer problems but that Japanese society believes these problems to be specific to Japan and to need special attention. These two factors may somehow have helped exaggerate the extent of the problems involved.

In most of the literature examined in Chapters 3 and 4 there was little discussion of the possible advantages of overseas experience outweighing the disadvantages. The case study of a research project on *kikokushijo* at Fujiyama Gakuen was perhaps quite typical in its search for the detrimental, rather than beneficial, effects of overseas experience. Even those, such as Inui and Sono (1977) and Azuma (1979), who, as we shall see, have argued for a positive view of the overseas experience of *kikokushijo*, have tended to base their case on a belief that such children more problems than their non-*kikokushijo* peers. There has, however, for some time been a body of research outside Japan which—while not perhaps directly comparable—suggests that while there may well be problems on returning to one's own society, these may be outweighed by the benefits. Furnham and Bochner (1986: 3–4) summarize this argument thus: 'Experiencing a second culture is held to be beneficial, since such exposure is said to broaden one's perspective, promote personality growth and provide insight into the culture of origin through a contrast with other world-views.' Following this positive approach, Janet Bennett (1977) redefines culture shock as a sub-category of transition shock—such as that experienced at marriage or divorce—and argues that the experience of such shocks throughout life adds to the maturation and development of individual flexibility. Deirdre Meintel (1973: 55) suggests that the experience of culture shock 'rather than being a disease to be avoided at all costs holds possibilities which are valuable for personal and intellectual growth'.[12]

It was as part of a large project on Japanese returnees by three American researchers, Bennett, Passin, and McKnight (1958), that John Bennett (1961–2) wrote an article emphasizing the innovative potential of returnees to Japan in the immediate post-war period. This project was one of the very few which studied personality variables in adjustment. It described three types of Japanese in the United States: the 'adjuster' who can adapt and assimilate to both cultures, the 'constrictor' who remains conservatively Japanese wherever he is; and the 'idealist' who is open to cultural change.[13] Since this survey, little attention has been given to the effect of individual personality differences in studies of returnees in Japan. The only recent survey (Fujiwara *et al.*, 1985) which has followed this line, however, classified 38 *kikokushijo* into three distinct personality types: those who adapt naturally and unself-consciously and are not even aware of being *kikokushijo*; those who adjust eventually to Japan, albeit unwillingly; and those who feel themselves to be strangers in Japan and cannot adapt.

The above discussions clearly bring into question many of the underlying assumptions of the research project examined earlier in this chapter as well as much of the work cited in Chapters 2 and 3. Questions are raised, for example, as to the severity of the problems faced by *kikokushijo*, and it has been shown that these are often expected to be worse than they actually are. While there is no doubt that some *kikokushijo* do face severe problems on their return to Japan, it is questionable whether the sum of these problems is greater than those of children who have not been outside Japan. It has also been shown that those problems from which *kikokushijo* suffer may not be directly connected with their overseas experience: they may be a result of the pressures of the Japanese educational system, or the effects of changing school or region within Japan. Similarly, they may be problems which are not specific to Japanese children but common to any child moving between cultures.[14] On the other hand, the experience of moving may involve more benefits than problems and indeed, one researcher (Kitsuse, quoted in Reiss, 1984: 31) on *kikokushijo* in Japan has suggested that the most interesting fact about the *kikokushijo* phenomenon is that it is considered a problem at all.

KIKOKUSHIJO AND OTHER MINORITY GROUPS IN JAPAN

Former Prime Minister Nakasone caused a furore late in 1986 when he appeared to suggest that Japan's economic success was due to racial homogeneity and that the recent decline of the United States was due to racial pluralism (see Nakasone, 1986; Weatherall, *JTW*, 13 December 1986).[15] That there are minority groups in Japan is undeniable and Nakasone's statement simply highlights the degree of discrimination which they face. The largest minority groups in Japan are the *Zainichi Kankokujin* (Japanese-Koreans), the *burakumin* ('Japanese Untouchables'), the Okinawans, and the Ainu. The way in which discrimination extends into all areas of their lives—marriage, education, employment, status, salaries— has been well covered in the literature on Japan. It is interesting, therefore, that the suggestion has been made that *kikokushijo* are simply a new form of minority group in Japan (Lebra and Lebra, 1986: xviii; Hoshino, 1983: 44; Minority Rights Group, 1983: 4). It is reasonable to describe *kikokushijo* as a minority, in the sense that they constitute a small but recognizable group in Japanese society with the common feature of overseas experience; if, however, their experience is compared with that of other minority groups in Japan—particularly in the area of education since, as we have seen, it is through education that Japanese become socially mobile—a different picture emerges. A small note of warning, however, is necessary here: the study of minority groups in Japan is a particularly sensitive subject and accurate figures are not easy to come by. This is partly because of the desire, on the part of policy- makers, to deny the existence of minority groups in Japan but is also due to a widespread belief that preferential treatment (or positive discrimination) for any one segment of the population is unacceptable in the context of the egalitarian basis of education. It is in this light that the readily available statistics on *kikokushijo*, and the special treatment afforded to them, is so interesting.

Education for the Korean minority (*Zainichi Kankokujin*) in Japan is a particularly sensitive subject. Most of the Korean residents in Japan are the families of Koreans brought over to Japan during the occupation of their country by the Japanese between 1910 and 1945. In all, Japanese-Koreans number some 600,000, almost 90 per cent of all foreign residents in Japan. It is significant that they continue to be considered as foreign residents since in the case of the descendants of the Korean 'forced labourers' (who constitute 75 per cent of the total number of Koreans in Japan) Japan and Japanese are generally the only country and the only language they know. Despite this, even this 75 per cent are treated as permanent alien residents in Japan: they have to carry alien registration cards (*gaikokujin tōroku shōmeisho*) at all times and register their fingerprints every three years at the local city hall.

The problems of the Koreans in Japan are exacerbated by a split, following the Korean war, between Koreans who support South Korea and those who support North Korea. There are altogether more than 150 schools for the children of North Korean residents in Japan (Rohlen, 1981: 186) but, like the international and foreign national schools discussed earlier, they are classified as *kakushu gakkō* (miscellaneous schools) or else they simply exist without official approval. The disadvantage of this classification, or lack of one, is that it prevents graduates from entering Japanese universities. As a result of this policy, over 75 per cent of the 125,000-plus school-age children of Korean residents in Japan attend Japanese state schools (1981: 185). The eleven schools run by the South Korean organization in Japan (*Mindan*) follow a policy of assuming the continued residence of their students in Japan and therefore follow the Monbushō curriculum, teaching Korean—about five hours a week—as a foreign language (1981: 210). As a result, these schools are accredited by Monbushō and, since the 1950s, their graduates have been permitted to enter Japanese universities. The policy of the Japanese government has clearly been to assimilate the Koreans into mainstream Japanese society.

In terms of educational achievement, the Korean children in the Japanese state system appear to do considerably worse than their Japanese counterparts. According to one survey (Rohlen, 1981: 197) in a prefecture (Hyōgo) with a large Korean population:

Korean students are (1) more likely not to go to high school at all, (2) only half as likely to enter the most desirable public academic high schools, (3) twice as likely to go to night schools (the lowest status academic schools), and (4) more likely to attend private and vocational high schools (which have lower status than state and academic schools).

Furthermore, Rohlen points out (1981: 197), while 45.8 per cent of all Hyōgo prefecture high school graduates went on to universities, only 26.3 per cent of the Korean graduates did so. Since

employment chances are so closely linked to educational background in Japan, it is not surprising that Korean graduates also fare
considerably worse in the labour market than their Japanese peers.
Adult Korean male unemployment is around 30 per cent—ten
times the official national figure—and those who are employed
tend to be in factory work, manual labour, and the service
industries. Many end up in the semi-illegal worlds of *pachinko* (pin-
ball machine) and massage parlours (De Vos and Chung, 1981:
225–7).

Despite the problems faced by Koreans in Japan, the Japanese
government has never supported special schools for these children.
Indeed, in the period 1948–54, it worked hard to close down
schools that had sprung up in the aftermath of the War when the
Koreans, seeing themselves as victors in defeated Japan, began
vigorously to express their national identity (Rohlen, 1981: 203–
4). Those schools which have continued into the present period
have relied for financial support on the local Korean community
and the North or South Korean governments, rather like *Nihonjingakkō*. The difference is, of course, that while the Japanese
children in *Nihonjingakkō* rarely intend to stay overseas, the
children at the Korean schools in Japan tend to see Japan as their
native country. While there are signs that Koreans have recently
been doing better in the Japanese educational system, this has been
a slow and gradual process of improvement brought about mainly
by changes in the Korean community rather than by government
policy. Korean children in Japan still lag behind their Japanese
peers and, for the nearly 25 per cent who go to the North Korean
schools, there is still no provision for them to enter the mainstream
Japanese educational system.

There has also been a gradual improvement in the overall
educational situation of two other minority groups in Japan: the
Ainu and the *burakumin*. Neither of these groups, however, can be
said to be faring as well as their non-minority-group peers.
Although the origins of the Ainu are not clear, it is accepted that
they were in Japan before the Japanese themselves. They have
gradually been pushed north in the face of Japanese invasions and
are now generally found in the northernmost island of Hokkaido
unless they have migrated south in the search for work. Most
unofficial surveys—there has been no post-war government survey
—give a figure of around 25,000 for the number of people in Japan

who call themselves Ainu, of whom, according to a 1986 survey (Mizuno, 1987: 147), 78.4 per cent of the relevant age-group proceed to senior high school—15.8 per cent lower than the national average. Even more significantly, only 8.1 per cent proceed to tertiary education, as opposed to the national average of over 35 per cent. Not unconnected with these figures is the fact that the percentage of the Ainu population receiving welfare benefits is around six times higher than that of the general population (1987: 147).

Mizuno Takaaki (1987: 147–8), a journalist based in Hokkaido, ascribes the problem of low educational advancement among the Ainu not to a general lack of interest in education but to a lack of finances to support that education: a vicious circle of poverty creating discrimination, and discrimination in turn giving rise to poverty. Despite repeated requests from the Ainu, the Japanese government has always refused calls for a new law that would guarantee their rights and status through affirmative action (1987: 145). This, as we have seen from Nakasone's remarks, is in line with official government policy which states that the Ainu are not a minority group. Nevertheless, since 1974 there has been a policy programme which in effect treats the Ainu as a minority group. Under the Utari Policy Programme ¥1.3 billion was administered to the Ainu in 1986 for environmental improvement projects, programmes to assist small businesses, vocational training programmes, and various scholarships. According to official sources, 'These expenditures constitute assistance . . . for the purpose of rectifying regional disparities' (1987: 146). In this way, aid could be given to the Ainu in the guise of eliminating regional differences.[16] This means, however, that Ainu not living in Hokkaido are ineligible to receive any of this aid.

The *burakumin*, of whom it is estimated there are two to three million in Japan, are best described as descendants of the outcaste class of the feudal period. They share the same racial, cultural, and national origins as the rest of their fellow Japanese and they live in some 5,000 ghettoes (known euphemistically as *dōwa chiku*— 'integration districts') throughout the whole of Japan except Hokkaido. Their outcaste status is widely believed to come from their breaking of Buddhist taboos and subsequent contamination through dealing with carcasses and dead bodies as tanners, butchers, and undertakers. In the immediate post-feudal period of the 1870s, *burakumin* were accorded commoner status as *shinheimin* (new commoners), a categorization which only served to perpetuate their outcaste status. Even today, it is common (especially in southwestern Japan), though illegal, for prospective employers, or the parents of prospective marriage partners, to investigate employees and sons- or daughters-in-law in order to exclude those with *burakumin* backgrounds.

According to Shimahara (1984: 339), the *burakumin* constitute a minority group which has, in the past fifteen years, 'dramatically improved its social mobility and educational attainment'. Even so, 10.5 per cent of *burakumin* are receiving welfare benefits. This is almost nine times the national average and very nearly twice the average for all minority groups put together (1984: 345), and, although the gap has narrowed considerably over the past fifteen years, there remain significant differences in educational attainment between *burakumin* and the majority of Japanese youth, especially at the post-secondary level. It is mainly due to a high-profile campaign waged since the end of the last century, what Shimahara (1984: 350) calls 'self-directed political mobilization', that Japanese governments have spent relatively heavily on supporting assimilation projects for *burakumin*. Cummings (1980: 9) estimates that government expenditure per *burakumin* student is three times as great as the expenditure for other children. There are no special schools for *burakumin*, however, and the extra money is spent only to ensure their smooth passage into mainstream Japanese society through improving their social status via the educational system.

The million or so Okinawans in Japan are the inhabitants of the seventy-plus islands lying between the Japanese mainland and Taiwan which constitute Japan's southernmost prefecture. The Okinawans were traditionally a distinct cultural group, though physically virtually indistinguishable from mainland Japanese, and they retain their own language (*Ryūkyūgo*), a major dialect of Japanese that is still used by the older generation. Until the thirteenth century the Okinawans also had their own empire (Dai Ryūkyū) with trade routes stretching through South-East Asia. During Japan's feudal period, the Okinawans were conquered by the southernmost domain of mainland Japan and subsumed under its control, and only really re-emerged as a separate group in the eyes of the world when they found themselves on the front line of Japan's final defence in the Second World War. At this stage, the Okinawan citizens received scarcely better treatment than the enemy from the Japanese Imperial Army and, as a result, strong anti-mainland sentiment has remained. Okinawa finally reverted to Japanese control in 1972, but there remains a strong sense among Okinawans that they face discrimination from mainland Japanese. The average salary in Okinawa remains today at around 71 per cent of that of mainland Japanese and unemployment in Okinawa, officially at 5 per cent, is double the national average (Katayama, *JT*, 21 July 1985).

One very small minority group in Japan consists of the 4,500 Vietnamese 'boat people' or, as they are known in Japan, *teijū nanmin* (resettled refugees), who by the end of 1985 were being accepted at the rate of about 500 a year. Despite heavy international pressure, Japan has refused to take more 'boat people', citing in its defence the problems these people would face in adjusting to the special nature of Japanese culture, and the potential for Japanese exclusivity to make such problems even worse. For those refugees who have been accepted, a budget of around seven million pounds per annum has been set aside (Eng, *DY*, 18 September 1984). Refugees in Japan can generally only obtain the most menial jobs whatever their personal qualifications, and the Vietnamese complain of low salaries, adjustment problems, and unfair treatment (Ohki, *JTW*, 14 December 1985). Newspaper reports suggest that the psychological stress of living in Japan under such conditions leads to mental problems, including schizophrenia (Kawabata, *JTW*, 14 December 1985). Only in 1982 was a law enacted to allow refugee children to attend schools within the compulsory-education system (*JT*, 5 September 1983). But this law does not apply to senior high schools (attended by 94 per cent of the Japanese age-band) and it is very difficult for refugee children to gain entry to such schools. When, through sheer hard work, four Vietnamese 'boat children' gained entry to a night school—the lowest level of senior high school—it raised considerable media attention. Even though programmes have been set up to help refugee children with language training, entry into the tertiary education sector remains very problematic and, as with senior high schools, there is no special system to help them gain entry.

Konketsuji (mixed-blood children) are the offspring of mixed Japanese and non-Japanese parentage. Official estimates of their numbers living in Japan range between 10,000 and 22,000, of whom about 40 per cent hold American citizenship. For the remaining 60 per cent, it has often been difficult to gain either foreign or Japanese citizenship and many, according to Strong (*KEJ*, Vol. 4, 1983: 271), 'are viewed by the Japanese government as "stateless foreigners", severely restricted in their access to equal employment opportunities and ineligible for such universal benefits as free public education, child welfare assistance, and national health insurance'. The acceptance of *konketsuji* in mainstream Japanese society is largely determined by their gender, by the stability of their family, and by their non-Japanese parentage. Children, especially girls, from stable Caucasian-Japanese backgrounds have found much greater educational and social success than boys of half-black parentage who were born out of wedlock or abandoned by their foreign fathers. Some of the former have been subsumed under the category of *kikokushijo*. In the case of the latter, there is very little in the way of assistance.

There is one other minority group in Japan which provides a particularly interesting comparison with *kikokushijo*. These are the so-called *Chūgoku zairyū koji* (war-displaced China orphans) and their children who have returned to Japan from China. In the rush to escape the Soviet advance into Manchuria at the end of the Second World War, many Japanese gave their babies and children into the care of neighbouring Chinese families. It was not until the normalization of relations between Japan and the People's Republic of China in 1972 that it was possible to consider the repatriation of these Japanese, who had been raised as Chinese and were now in their mid 30s. Those who could find relatives prepared to sponsor them were allowed to come and live in Japan. As of 1986, nearly 3,000 children of these 'orphans'—known officially as *Chūgoku kikoku koji shijo* (returnee Chinese orphan children)—were registered in over 1,000 schools throughout Japan (Monbushō, 1988: 92, 96). As with the Vietnamese, the proportion of these children in the non-compulsory part of the educational system is very low, only 5 per cent of the total enrolled in schools. Originally, these Chinese orphan children were the responsibility of the Ministry of Health and Welfare, but by 1986 programmes were being set up under the auspices of Monbushō to provide for their education. Interestingly, although they were subsumed under the work of the office for *kaigaishijo* and *kikokushijo*, they were differentiated from such children and given a separate budget. There was no suggestion that they should attend *ukeireko*. A series of Monbushō reports suggested that since they had had no contact at all with Japan before their arrival between 75 and 90 per cent of these children were facing severe language and curriculum problems in Japanese schools (*JTW*, 22 February 1986; Monbushō, 1988: 97). Moreover, accounts of these children being bullied— and even committing murder—began to appear in the Japanese media. Only 14 per cent of the schools with the Chinese orphan children, however, offer any special lessons for them, and in only 4 per cent of schools have special teachers been made available to help them. The children are more widely dispersed throughout Japan than *kikokushijo* and, in over 90 per cent of the schools they attend, there are no more than four of them on the register (Monbushō, 1988: 97). Unlike the case of *kikokushijo*, there is no suggestion in the official literature that there is anything to be learnt from such children: instead, there is a clear policy that they should be assimilated as quickly as possible into Japanese society (Lan, *JTW*, 8 July 1989).

Although, as we have seen, there are clearly specific problems associated with being a *kikokushijo*, it is doubtful whether these problems are more severe than those suffered by other minority groups in Japan. The 'boat people' and the Chinese orphans are clearly likely to suffer far worse difficulties in terms of language and curriculum. The *burakumin*, Ainu, Okinawans, Japanese-Koreans, and sections of the *konketsuji* are clearly far behind in terms of educational achievement. Yet a number of factors common to all these groups serve clearly to differentiate them from *kikokushijo*. Firstly, the amounts of money spent to further the education of these other groups is far below that spent on *kikokushijo*. The budget for a variety of projects to help Ainu in Hokkaido, only a fraction of which covered education, was, in 1986, less than 7 per cent of the sum set aside for the education of overseas and returnee children in the same year. There is no extra financial support from the Japanese government for Japanese-Koreans, whereas in the case of the pupils of overseas *Nihonjingakkō* the government was spending roughly twice the national average on each child in 1982 (Shibanuma, 1982: 154).

The one minority group in Japan which has managed to secure extra educational funding is the *burakumin*. This, however, has been achieved only after a century of mobilizing political support and has still not managed to rectify the significant discrepancies in terms of educational achievement between the *burakumin* and the majority society. The money, moreover, is clearly meant to help pacify *burakumin* and reduce complaints of discrimination. There has been no suggestion with *burakumin*, or with other minority groups, that they should be given special schools supported by the Japanese government, and encouraged to develop their own educational and cultural identities. The example of the Chinese orphans is perhaps the most telling in this context. The money provided for this group is to enable them to attend regular state schools and understand the standard curriculum with the ultimate aim of easing their assimilation into Japanese society. It is in this context that the creation of the special system of *ukeirekō* and the deliberate development and fostering of the 'special' skills of *kikokushijo* takes on particular significance.

Special schools for minority groups are suppressed by the Japanese government; they are supported in the case of *kikokushijo*. There are clearly problems in gaining entry into senior high schools and universities, even low-quality ones, for members of minority groups; in the case of *kikokushijo*, special quotas have been set up to facilitate entry into the top senior high schools and universities. Minority groups in Japan face severe problems in the labour market; *kikokushijo*, as we shall see, may have significant advantages. Clearly, therefore, it is wrong to consider *kikokushijo* as a new minority group in Japan. They may constitute a minority in terms of numbers, but they are certainly not disadvantaged in the educational and labour markets in the same way as the minority groups in Japan. It might be more accurate to distinguish between groups which are a minority in terms of numbers, and groups which are 'marginal' in terms of their access to power. By this definition, *kikokushijo* are clearly a 'minority' rather than a 'marginal' group as they are few in number but have access to considerable power within Japanese society. As a result of this, as we shall see in the next section, they are not only faring better than 'marginal' groups, but they are also doing better than average by the standards of mainstream Japanese society.

KIKOKUSHIJO IN COMPARISON WITH MAINSTREAM JAPANESE SOCIETY

Only a tiny minority of *kikokushijo* go to national schools which are the most prestigious institutions in Japan—2 per cent at elementary-school level, 7.4 per cent at junior high school, and 7 per cent at senior high school in 1983. These figures, however, were five, ten-and-a-half, and thirty-five times higher than the national average (Hasebe, 1985: 172). It is in relation to university entrance, however, that the major advantages of being categorized as *kikokushijo* become apparent. Ōkubo's survey of the universities entered by graduates of the New York supplementary school (Table XIV) shows an impressive proportion going to Sophia or Keiō

TABLE XIV: Universities Attended by Former Students of the New York *Hoshūkō*

1978–79	out of 37 children: Sophia, 8 (21.6%); Keiō, 7 (18.9%)
1979–81	out of 49 children: Sophia, 10 (20.4%); Keiō, 8 (16.3%)
1982–83	out of 63 children: Sophia, 13 (20.6%); Keiō, 14 (22.2%)

Source: Ōkubo, 1983: 22–3.

Universities—two of the top four private, and among the top ten of all, universities in Japan. The Washington *hoshūkō* appears to have been even more successful, with four or five graduates a year in recent times gaining places at Tokyo University (*Zadankai*, 1987: 289–90). In a 1984 survey of thirteen Japanese graduates from the United World College School in Singapore, three went to Sophia, five to ICU, and one to Keiō University.

Since the mid 1980s the number of universities offering a special quota to *kikokushijo* has increased dramatically—forty-three in 1984, 100 in 1986. *Kikokushijo* applicants who were entering via the special quota system (*tokubetsu waku*) were almost three times as likely to be enrolled as non-*kikokushijo* applicants—15.06-per-cent chance against 5.59-per-cent—at Waseda University, which is one of the top four institutions in the country (Waseda University Facts, 1988: 3). In 1985, just under 40 per cent of all of those who attempted to enter national universities via the *tokubetsu waku* were successful. In the case of those applying to private and public universities the figure was 50 per cent and the total success rate 48 per cent (Nakanishi, 1986: 190). In total, 90 per cent of *kikokushijo* who enrolled in Japanese universities—national, public, or private—entered those institutions through the *tokubetsu waku* (Monbushō, 1988: 87). In 1985, there were some 1,770 applicants using this system (Nakanishi, 1986: 190). Of these applicants 48 per cent gained entry to four-year university courses. This was more than 10 per cent higher than the national enrolment of 37 per cent at all higher-education institutions—including the lower-status junior colleges and fourth-year students at technical colleges—in that same year. There is little doubt, therefore, that *kikokushijo* are achieving some way above the national average in terms of university entrance.

In part because the *kikokushijo* constitute such a new social group in Japan, it is less easy to assess how they are faring in the labour market as opposed to the educational system. In the workplace, however, special quotas have also been set up to recruit *kikokushijo*. These quotas, moreover, are often to be found in the largest and most prestigious firms. As early as 1982, the eleven-company Matsushita group announced that when hiring new workers it would give priority to the children of their employees posted overseas (*MDN*, 22 April 1982). Other companies, including Ricoh, Mitsui bank, and Mitsubishi bank, as well as a series of engineering, securities, and insurance firms, have opened their doors to all *kikokushijo* (*DY*, 30 December 1986). Half of the recent intake at the prestigious Tokyo Bank were *kikokushijo* (*Zadankai*, 1987: 290). In April 1987, the Kaigai Shijo Kyōiku Shinkō Zaidan published a survey of how 163 returnees in the Tokyo area have fared in their careers: 65 per cent said that their overseas experience helped them find employment and 50 per cent said they thought that knowing a foreign language made them more attractive candidates (*JTW*, 9 May 1987).[17]

Perhaps the clearest indication of the special treatment afforded to *kikokushijo* is still, however, the setting up of the *ukeireko*. This, as we have seen, is in opposition to the ideology of equal educational experience for all Japanese children which presupposes the idea that minority groups should be assimilated into the mainstream culture. Separate provision within the mainstream of the Japanese educational system has normally been regarded as anathema. Even children who are mentally disabled are, as far as possible, integrated into the mainstream system and, where this is impossible, attend special schools (*yōgogakkō*) which endeavour to imitate the style of the mainstream schools.

Yet the *ukeireko*, which are clearly a separate provision, are supported by central and local government. They do not attempt to assimilate their students into Japanese culture; indeed, as we have seen, they are attempting to create a new type of Japanese child, sometimes called a 'Japanese-plus' (La Brack, 1983: 16), that is to say a Japanese who can be called truly Japanese and yet has something extra to offer in the line of internationalism. The non-*kikokushijo* in the *ukeireko* are there to consolidate the Japanese-ness of the *kikokushijo* and, at the same time, pick up something of their 'internationalness', a process colourfully described in one newspaper as 'chasing two hares' (*nito o ou*) (*MS*, 16 July 1985). The *ukeireko* see themselves as educating the leaders of the next generation—an international social élite. The result is that *kikokushijo* now feel proud to display their special identity as *kikokushijo* and do not have to hide it, and this is the reason why so many non-*kikokushijo* compete fiercely for places in the *ukeireko* to be educated alongside these returnee children.

The recent educational and social successes of returnees have endowed them with a new self-confidence. 'I am one of the lucky ones,' writes a returnee who spent fifteen years in the American educational system. 'True, my *kanji* is sub-par, but, in fact, I feel I have "gone ahead". . . . The children of expatriates are locked out by some doors, but hold the key to many of the bigger doors' (*JTW*, 8 March 1985). World-famous members of the Japanese artistic world—Tange Kenzō, Mori Hanae, Ashida Jun—proudly send their children to a famous boarding-school in Switzerland to become part of an international élite (*JTW*, 20 June 1987). The first All-Japan English Speech Contest for *kikokushijo* took place in 1984 (*DY*, 5 July 1984) and the contestants proudly, and with national publicity, proclaimed their differences from other Japanese: 'We *kikokushijo* can help people [of the world] understand each other' (*JT*, 7 October 1984). Special note was made of the forty *kikokushijo* who participated in the opening ceremony of the 1985 World Exposition at Tsukuba (*DY*, 17 March 1985). These images contrast defiantly with those in the literature of Chapters 3 and 4 which portray *kikokushijo* as needing to hide their overseas experience in order to reintegrate into Japanese society.

The fact that *kikokushijo* appear to be doing so well in Japan— socially, educationally, and in terms of employment—may explain the phenomenon of Japanese children going overseas with the express purpose of becoming *kikokushijo*. Abuse of the special system for *kikokushijo* is naturally not easy to uncover. One teacher in an *ukeirekō*, however, claimed that it was quite a common practice. In 1983, an article in the magazine *Shūkan Asahi*, under the title *Gaikoku no Kōkō o Dete Tokubetsu Waku de Kyōdai ni Hairō?!* ('Let's Enter Kyoto University through the Special Network by Going to an Overseas Senior High School?!'), concluded that some families were taking unfair advantage of the system: 'All of [those who go overseas to become *kikokushijo*] were persuaded by their families that they could not get into good universities if it was not for the fact that special treatment for *kikokushijo* has now expanded up to the university level' (Ichi, 1983: 169).

Kyoto University itself recognizes the argument of the above article. In an internal report on the situation of *kikokushijo* in the university who had entered via the *tokubetsu waku*, it concludes that, although the *kikokushijo* themselves fare well, the system has created two particular problems (Kinoshita *et al.*, 1985: 60–1):

Sometimes general students [*ippansei*] do not think the way *kikokushijo* entered the university is quite proper [*kokoro yoshi to sezu*] and sometimes they express what they feel towards those students. They feel jealous because they had to work hard whereas those special students worked less hard. . . . The second problem is the influence of the so-called entrance examination industry [*jukensangyō*]: in the case of the special entrance system for *kikokushijo* set up only last year, this has already been turned into a tool for entering the university more easily. Namely, while the parents stay in Japan, the children go overseas alone for two years and when they have graduated overseas they can use the special system to enter the university.

Education is big business in Japan and any way to circumvent the competitive university entrance system is seized upon eagerly. There are a number of agencies in London, for example, which specialize in placing Japanese children in British schools and act as their guardians while their parents stay in Japan. But complaints about the unfairness of the system have been very muted and where criticism has been voiced it has also been strongly contested (see *Zadankai*, 1987). Some supporters of the system insist that *kikokushijo* need special educational help; others insist that their 'international' qualities must be maintained for the good of Japan. These themes are apparent in the following exchange of letters

published in a manual for overseas education: the first is from a
mother overseas (in Hasebe, 1985: 340–1) who wonders whether the
knowledge of *kaigaishijo* that they can easily enter good schools in
Japan on their return might not actually be damaging to them:

Even after two years my son didn't really understand what was going on at
his local school overseas: his ability in English hadn't advanced beyond the
basic level. He was also going to a *hoshūkō* but not really improving much
there either. This kind of situation was the same amongst other kids who
went to the Saturday school. Yet, because of the 'adaptation system' for
returnee kids, when they go back to Japan they get the chance to enter a
prestigious school and they claim that they've made it [*isei no yoi tayori o
kureru hito mo imasu*]. . . . Recently I have heard such children talk as if
they've got a passport to those special schools for returnees, saying that if
you spend two or three years overseas you can easily enter prestigious
schools, which if you were educated in Japan would be very difficult to
enter. What an easy-going attitude! This trend is discouraging [*ashi o
hipparu*] children in Japan who have to make such enormous efforts.

Hasebe, a counsellor working for the Kaigai Shijo Kyōiku Shinkō
Zaidan, responds (1985: 345–6) by restating the normal reasons
why special systems are needed for *kikokushijo*:

There are two aspects to the special treatment for returnee children. One is
the supplementary aspect, enabling the children to catch up with the
Japanese education system: the other is our high evaluation of the skills
which the children acquire during their stay abroad, including their
language ability and . . . 'internationalness'. On top of this heterogeneous
cultural experience, we try to give them an indigenous Japanese cultural
training so that they can adapt to the future internationalization of Japan
and a future open-minded humanity. We are definitely not supporting an
easy way for returnees to enter the schools even if, as the letter says, such
an idea is a trend among parents who are overseas, which is something
which I would not like to believe. It betrays the trust of schools which
accept returnee children and also that of people who are making efforts to
promote and encourage returnee children's education. Indeed, it would
only result in the returnee children digging their own graves [*boketsu o
horu*].

Instead of complaints that *kikokushijo* have received unfair
advantages in the Japanese educational system, there continue to be
demands from important sectors of society for more to be done for
them. The annual White Paper on National Life for 1986 proposed
that *kikokushijo* should be given better educational and employment

opportunities (*JTW*, 15 November 1986). In the same year it was announced that the high-profile 'international high school' being set up by the Tokyo metropolitan government expected to enrol a large number of *kikokushijo*. In a 1989 public-opinion survey concerning measures to promote internationalization in Japan, almost a quarter of the respondents suggested further expansion of opportunities for children who had been educated overseas (*Focus Japan*, Vol. 16, No. 3, March 1989).

Perhaps most significant, however, have been the demands for better treatment for *kikokushijo* in the proposals of the National Council on Educational Reform which met, amidst a blaze of publicity, between 1984 and 1987. Under reforms for coping with Japan's internationalization, a whole section was devoted to the improvement of conditions for *kikokushijo* in Japan: there were demands for the expansion of opportunities for these children at all stages of the Japanese educational system, from elementary schools through to university, by providing larger special quotas into senior high schools and universities and more specialist staff, including foreign teachers and Japanese teachers with experience overseas. The final report of the National Council on Educational Reform (1987: 57–9) also demanded that special schools should be set up for *kikokushijo* to be educated alongside foreign children and that more money should be spent on providing educational facilities for Japanese senior-high-school students overseas.[18]

The above recommendations were outstanding in three respects. Firstly, they were among the most specific of all the recommendations to come out of the three years of deliberations. The council had been rent by disagreements from the start and the compromise reports it produced during its term of office were noticeable for their lack of concrete proposals for reform. Secondly, *kikokushijo* were the only 'minority group' to receive any discussion at all throughout the life of the council. The report contained a single, and rather vague, paragraph of recommendations for the promotion of education for the handicapped, but no other separate group received any special mention at all. Finally, *kikokushijo* were discussed under the rubric of internationalization, one of the main areas in Japanese education which the council agreed needed to be strengthened. There was agreement, therefore, that more should be done for *kikokushijo*, but this was no longer on the sole grounds of their needing help as individuals but because they constituted a valuable national asset. This, as we have seen, differs dramatically from the original perception of how *kikokushijo* should be treated. To understand why the image of *kikokushijo* appears to have changed so rapidly we need to employ a more dynamic model of the workings of Japanese society than those discussed in Chapters 3 and 4 which suggested that Japan was inherently and traditionally exclusivist. A historical review of returnees in Japan begins to provide some clues for the causes behind this changing perception of *kikokushijo* in contemporary Japan.

7

Kikokushijo in Historical Perspective

A broad historical perspective does much to counter the view that Japan is an inherently exclusivist society in which anything coming from outside (such as *kikokushijo*) is automatically resisted or attacked. Indeed, there is considerable evidence to suggest that, at certain times in the history of Japan, individuals with overseas experience have been very successful on their return home.

The first recorded Japanese missions overseas were to China in AD 57 and, from the fifth to the thirteenth century, there were numerous embassies and trading trips to China and Korea which resulted in the acquisition of much of Japan's 'culture', including a writing system, a medical system, Buddhism, and many architectural and artistic traditions. It does not appear to have been common practice for wives or children to go on these trips, even though some were of very long duration for the individuals concerned. Many young people, however, accompanied the embassies overseas and there are several examples of individuals who lived overseas in this period whose names are still well known in Japan today. Some of these individuals are named in a historical review by Bennett, Passin, and McKnight (1958: 26–7): Kibi no Makibi, who remained in China for seventeen years from AD 717 and returned to become head of the University of Nara; Takamuko no Kuromaro and the priest Bin, who returned from China in AD 640 and both became important advisers to the regent Kamatari in preparing the political and economic Taika reform of AD 645–9; Dengyō Daishi, a major figure in Tendai Buddhism, who lived in China from AD 802; Kōbō Daishi, the founder of Shingon Buddhism, who spent three years studying in China; and a variety of thirteenth-century Zen practitioners and artists such as Sesson Yūbai, Mokuan, and the painter Sesshū who spent two years in China between AD 1467 and 1469.

Bennett, Passin, and McKnight (1958: 27) point out that as early as the seventh century AD the word *ryūgakusei* had entered the Japanese language with the meaning 'overseas scholar' but with the implication of 'bearer of enlightenment from the lands beyond the sea'. There is no doubt that the Japanese were cautious in their importation of aspects of Chinese culture. This was characterized by the popular slogan for much of the period, *wakon kansai* ('Japanese spirit and Chinese technology') which supported the idea of importing knowledge gained from China without upsetting Japan's native cultural traditions. Nevertheless, there is little doubt that individuals who had had experience of living in China generally enjoyed high status on their return home.

Those who went overseas at other periods in Japanese history, however, were not given such a warm welcome on their return. In the fifteenth century, there were so-called 'Japan Towns' (*Nihonmachi*) dotted all over South-East Asia, and Tani Naoki (1985: 103–4) estimates that more than 100,000 Japanese travelled overseas during this period. These trading communities were the first real Japanese colonies overseas, although their make-up in no way reflected that of the society they had left. The picture, painted by Frederik Schdt (*sic*) (1980), of the *Nihonmachi* in Ayutthaya, capital of Siam in the seventeenth century, is of a community whose population consisted largely of peripheral members of Japanese society: many were *rōnin* (masterless *samurai* warriors), Christians escaping persecution, criminals, mercenaries, and merchants—this last being the lowest class in the Tokugawa (feudal period) social hierarchy. Fukuda (1983) writes that these Japanese did not take their families overseas with them and he compares them with the contemporary *tanshin funin*. He cites a Dutch diary from the period showing the surprise expressed by Europeans about this Japanese attitude to their families. European traders took their families with them and many of those who worked for organizations such as the East India Company, like Thomas Raffles in Singapore, settled down and played important roles in the history of the region. Many of the Japanese living in the *Nihonmachi* would not have been welcomed home; many of them probably did not want to return home. Instead, they became fully integrated into the local communities.

The ambivalence shown by Japanese society to those who returned from overseas can be explained by a number of factors: the reasons why those individuals went overseas; the reasons for their return; the general political conditions in Japan and the state of Japan's relations with the outside world at the time of their return. The history of Japan's relations with the outside world can, perhaps, be best described as one of ambivalence, and nowhere is this clearer than in its relations with the western world. Japan's foreign relations have, throughout history, been carefully controlled by those in power and rather than being continually at one extreme (total exclusion) or another (total receptiveness to foreign influence) have tended to oscillate between the two with supporters of the minority view at any given time always able, partially at least, to undermine the general orthodoxy. A knowledge of this pluralism is essential in understanding Japan's history of relations with the outside world: in general, decisions whether to be receptive or resistant to foreign influence have been based on politics and pragmatism and not on any inherent national characteristics, and have been characterized by a flexibility of response rather than a rigid adherence to a particular line.

The so-called 'Christian Century' in Japan from around 1543 to 1639 provides a clear illustration of the differing reactions of Japanese towards westerners at different periods in their history, and shows how these reactions are not necessarily the result of innate psychological tendencies towards exclusivity but of historical and political conditions. Though they must have been but little aware of it at the time, the friendly reception extended to the early European visitors, including the missionaries, in Japan was due mainly to their good fortune in arriving at a time when they had value as pawns in the internal machinations of Japanese politics. As Sansom (1950: 126) writes: 'Nobunaga's [the ruling hegemon of the time] hostility towards Buddhism gave valuable support and encouragement to the Christian community in Japan, which had suffered so much from the enmity of the monks'. The 'Christian Century' also saw the first Japanese mission to Europe: in 1584 four teenagers were sent to Portugal, Spain, and Italy under the auspices, and in the care of, the still-favoured Jesuit priests. The major significance of this mission was probably, as Lach (1968: 705) says, that 'the legates put Japan on the map for most Europeans'. The trip obviously received official blessing for Lach records (1968: 697) that 'upon their return to Japan . . . they performed on Western instruments for Hideyoshi [the Shōgun] and sang for him'.

Cooper's (1965) *Anthology of European Reports on Japan, 1543–1640* demonstrates the speed with which the European reaction towards the Japanese turned from admiration to fear as the friendship of the Japanese became hostility. Throughout the period, however, there appears to have been a pronounced ambivalence towards the Europeans: for some they were *nanbanjin* (southern barbarians) and *butterkusai* (smelling of butter)— derogatory terms coined in this period and still in use today— while, on the other hand, one shipwrecked Englishman, Will Adams, who was less dogmatic about religion than the Spanish and Portuguese, actually rose to considerable prominence in Japan because of his practical knowledge and was given both *samurai* status and his own retainers (Tames, 1983). In general, Japanese society, as in the earlier spirit of *wakon kansai*, showed greater enthusiasm for foreign skills than for foreign values. Some Japanese, however, were sufficiently impressed by the message of Christianity for the religion to be practised secretly for more than 200 years, throughout which Japan was secluded from the rest of the world and all western practices were banned on pain of death (Keene, 1952: 56).

The more than 200-year-long period of seclusion (1637–1853) is known in Japanese as *sakoku jidai*, literally meaning the 'closed-country period'. The effect of this period on the views of contemporary Japanese concerning their relations with the outside world cannot be overestimated. This period, when the only foreigners allowed in the country were Chinese and Dutch traders restricted to the artificial port of Dejima in Nagasaki, and when any Japanese who left the country could return only on pain of death, is often used to support the theory of an innate Japanese xenophobia. In fact, the policy of seclusion was a purely practical measure by the Shōgun aimed at consolidating political power in the hands of a small group. The downfall of the European missionaries at this time was as much due to the resolution of the internal struggles (in the context of which they had originally been welcomed) and the unification of the country as to the arrogance of Spanish boasts that Japan was just another colony, the Buddhist resurgence, and the Dominican-Franciscan/Jesuit squabbling. The Tokugawa rulers were so intent on stasis and peace as a means of maintaining political control that they invoked neo-Confucianism for the main ideological tenets of their view. In such a context, Christianity could only be seen as subversive and potentially disruptive, and it was therefore expedient to ban the religion and expel its proponents along with most of the cultural elements they had brought with them.[1]

Katherine Plummer (1984) has graphically described the agonies of Japanese fishermen who, swept off their normal routes to places as far away as Kamchatka, Alaska, Hawaii, and even the west coast of the United States, came to the realization that they could never return to Japan. Keene (1952) relates the story of the academies set up in Vladivostok, Irkutsk, and even elegant eighteenth-century St Petersburg, in which stranded Japanese 'fishermen-professors' were ordered to teach their dialect to generations of Russian interpreters.[2] One of these fishermen (1952: 61–7) was repatriated by the Russians in 1727 in the hope that he could help open trade links between their country and Japan, and his acceptance, along with one of his sailors, bears testimony to a relaxation by this time in the attitude of the Tokugawa leadership towards the outside world. Despite the initial attention given to this man's unusual return from abroad, scant use was made of his knowledge of the west and he himself slipped into obscurity, eventually taking employment in the Shōgun's herbary (1952: 67). A passage from Captain Wassily Golowin's *Memoirs of a Captivity in Japan During the Years 1811, 1812 and 1813* (quoted in Moloney, 1954: 86) offers a rationalization for this policy of ignoring those who had returned from abroad:

They explained to us the grounds on which their laws prohibit them from reposing any trust in Japanese subjects who have lived in foreign countries. The great mass of mankind, said they, resemble children: they soon become weary of what they possess; and willingly give up everything for the sake of novelty. When they hear of certain things being better in foreign countries than in their own, they immediately wish to possess them, without reflecting that they might perhaps prove useless, or even injurious to them.

Harumei (1985) has compared present-day *kikokushijo* with these castaways (*hyōryūmin*) who were taken overseas unwillingly and were offered such a cool reception on their return to Japan.

Even during the Tokugawa period, however, which appears to have seen the height of official xenophobia, there were important heterodox elements in Japan that challenged the mainstream view. In the outer reaches of the country (notably among the Matsumae clan in modern-day Hokkaido) and among the lower social classes there was considerable freedom and independence from the orthodox codes of behaviour. The upper classes, who had the most to lose from civil strife, tended to limit themselves to questioning the finer points of the neo-Confucian orthodoxy. There was some resistance, for example, to the fact that it was a foreign creed (Varley, 1984: 139). There was also, however, a maverick fringe who were curious about life outside the system which encased them and it is this element which Keene (1952) has described so elegantly in *The Japanese Discovery of Europe*. The curiosity of the Japanese intellectuals involved in *Rangaku* (Dutch studies) between 1720 and 1798 was a powerful undercurrent of opposition within a domineering, though not necessarily oppressive, system. This opposition, if it did not actually set into motion the Meiji Restoration of 1868—and it may well have had an influence on the event—'made possible the later spectacular changes in Japan which are all too often credited to the arrival of Commodore Perry' (Keene, 1952: 2). Moreover, evidence that the Tokugawa seclusion was not essentially xenophobic, but pragmatic, can be seen in the treatment of the few foreigners who could be found in the country during the period. This applied not only to the Dutch in Dejima, but also to the considerable number of Chinese refugees from Ming China, many of whom achieved important positions as Confucian *literati* to the *daimyō* (feudal lords), and some of whom, including the founder of the Ōbaku Zen sect in the mid seventeenth century, became important Buddhist leaders (Sansom, 1964: 82; Ching, 1979).

The official attitude, however, changed very quickly when the arrival of Commodore Perry's 'Black Ships' in Edo Bay in 1853 forced the opening of Japan to the outside world. Some of the fishermen who had unwittingly drifted overseas during the period of seclusion now returned to Japan to positions of great authority. One of these, Joseph Heco (Hamada Hikozō), played a major role in the creation of the Japanese banking system and devoted his later years to the expansion of foreign Japanese trade; Nakahama Manjirō became a teacher at the *Bansho Torishirabesho*, the forerunner of Tokyo University; Niijima Jō, who had fled to to the United States during the last years of the Tokugawa Era, having been involved in some furtive western learning, returned to form an educational group called the *Dōshisha* (Society of Likeminded) (Hunter, 1984: 57–8, 146; Plummer, 1984: 179–209). This society went on to found Dōshisha University near Kyoto, to which, as we have seen, is now attached a school with one of the largest proportions of *kikokushijo* students in Japan.

The positive reception afforded to returnees to Japan in the last quarter of the nineteenth century can again be ascribed to changes in the policy of the country's leadership. As the Meiji government eased into power following the restoration of the Emperor and the end of the Tokugawa feudal oligarchy, it promulgated a policy of increased learning from overseas. The Emperor, in a speech to noblemen in 1871, preached that 'travel in foreign lands, properly indulged in, will increase your store of useful knowlege' (Bennett, Passin, and McKnight, 1958: 30). Missions were sent to Europe and the United States to gather and bring back ideas which would be useful in Japan's now urgent drive to modernize.

The change in policy towards the outside world of the Meiji era was again, therefore, essentially pragmatic. During the first two decades of the Meiji period, a large number of Japanese were sent, at government expense, to the United States and Europe, and between three and four thousand western technicians, teachers, and experts—known as *oyatoi*—were invited to Japan (Beauchamp, 1978: 43). Some of these *oyatoi*, such as William Griffis and William Clark, are still famous in Japan today, but as Roden (1983: 50) points out the way they have been perceived has changed with time: 'Over the past century, successive generations of Japanese observers have perceived the most conspicuous *oyatoi* as symbols: symbols of "civilization and enlightenment" in the 1870s; symbols of imperialist encroachment after 1900; and symbols of renewed friendship across the Pacific in the 1960s.' Today, the *oyatoi* are sometimes described as agents of internationalization and are used to support the argument that more foreigners should be employed in Japan's universities (see Arai, 1978: 160).

During the first years of the Meiji government, almost a sixth of the annual national education budget was spent on sending officially designated *ryūgakusei* (overseas scholars) abroad and supporting them whilst they were there (Japanese National Commission for Unesco, 1966: 116). This policy had not been employed in Japan for almost 500 years. According to Kashioka (1982), a very high percentage of these *ryūgakusei* became professors in major Imperial universities on their return and were listed in the *Jinji Kōshin Roku* (Japan's *Who's Who*). To be educated overseas as a Monbushō student in this period promised almost automatic élite status on return to Japan. *Ryūgakusei* from the aristocracy were encouraged to take their wives and daughters overseas with them as there were few facilities for the education of women in Japan

(Burks, 1985: 151). These daughters can, perhaps, be considered the predecessors of today's *kikokushijo*.

The general significance of overseas experience in this period can be highlighted by the fact that for almost two years (1871–3) virtually all the leaders of the government participated in a mission, led by Prince Iwakura Tomomi, throughout America and Europe. The aim of this venture was to seek out models and ideas for the modernization of Japan (Jansen, 1980). One member of the mission who went on to study in the United States wrote that many in the group 'fervently believed that one could not become a real human being without going abroad' (Varley, 1984: 163). The greater purpose behind the mission, however, was never forgotten: Jansen (1965: 65) suggests that, rather than inspiring a sense of inter-nationalistic spirit, in many of the ambassadors the mission fostered an enhanced awareness of their 'Japaneseness'. In this period, too, there were maverick or heterodox elements in the society which did not believe in the value of overseas experience. Among such people was Saigō Takamori who, according to Morris (1980: 251), 'Of the dozen leading figures in the Meiji Government . . . was one of the only two who neither visited the west nor evinced any interest in doing so'.

Around 1890 there began something of a reaction to the previous twenty years' largely uninhibited and enthusiastic relations with the west. This marked the beginning of a period of consolidation. The national slogan, an echo of the one centuries earlier in relation to China, became *wakon yōsai* (Japanese spirit and western tech-nology). The principle, as previously with the idea of *wakon kansai*, was of adapting and applying learning and knowledge from overseas (in this case the west) without in any sense intruding upon Japan's traditional cultural values. For the next twenty-five years this meant that there was something of a withdrawal from the west and, while *ryūgakusei* continued to be sent overseas, their numbers greatly diminished, as did the number of foreign experts invited to Japan. As Conte (1977) points out, while those who went overseas in the early Meiji period tended to return to positions of public responsibility, those who went abroad later never received the same public recognition and tended to enter the private sector on their return. He suggests that, by the 1890s, a foreign education could have been a disadvantage because it was now thought inferior to that offered by Japanese schools.

Some returnees in the Meiji period chose to remain outside the government in order to take a critical stance towards it, but all of these were still from the elite sector of Japanese society. At the same time, many poorer Japanese started to go to the west coast of the United States and Hawaii to try to make their fortunes. They had very different backgrounds to those Japanese who had been to the west previously, and they tended to be an embarrassment to the upper-class Japanese living in the same area. In her historical novel *Samurai*, Matsubara Hisako concentrates on the tension between the upper-class Japanese overseas and these poor emigrants whom she calls *kimin*—garbage people'—who were 'condemned as virtual traitors, outcasts, scum' by their compatriots.

By 1910 there were 130,000 Japanese living in the United States, mostly on the west coast, and at least half were engaged in agricultural occupations, work with which they were already familiar in Japan. Their arrival provoked competition and their success provoked jealousy; in 1913, white American farmers persuaded Congress to pass the Anti-Alien Land Laws prohibiting Japanese from owning land. By 1924 a new law had been passed, fixing quotas on immigration to the United States from a number of countries: the Japanese were not given a quota at all (Wilson and Hosokawa, 1982). The élite Japanese in America found themselves caught up in the same anti-Japanese backlash. Nevertheless, those who went overseas on official sponsored trips continued to receive a much better welcome on their return to Japan than any who returned having gone overseas as economic refugees.

The anthropologist Maeyama Takashi (1984a: 185) states that the Japanese in the early decades of the twentieth century went to Europe and the United States to learn, to North and South America to emigrate, and to Asia to invade. Japan had defeated the Chinese at Port Arthur in 1895, and then, to the amazement of the whole world, become the first non-western power to defeat a western one when Admiral Tōgō destroyed the Russian fleet in the Straits of Tsushima in 1905. As a result of these victories, Japan took a foothold in Korea, finally annexing the country in 1910, and took over control of the island of Formosa (Taiwan). At the same time Japan's influence grew rapidly in Manchuria and spread throughout South-East Asia, mainly in the form of trade.

It is in this period of foreign expansion that the history of overseas Japanese schools (*Nihonjingakkō*) begins: the first such school was set up in Pusan in Korea in 1877; a school was established in Shanghai in 1897; from 1910 onwards a whole series of *Nihonjingakkō* and a university opened in Manchuria and Korea. A school opened in Manila in 1919 and another in Peru a year later (Ōkubo, 1983: 46–7).

In the 1930s, a right-wing militaristic nationalism gained a grip on Japan, condemning the models of the west that had been so significant for the past fifty years and determining to impose 'Japanese' values on its neighbours in a plan for an 'East Asia Co-Prosperity Sphere'. Eventually even the use of English words was forbidden and a whole new Japanese vocabulary had to be coined to replace the terms for essential western concepts and materials.[3]

In part, the *Nihonjingakkō* were set up to educate Japanese children overseas and maintain their close ties with the homeland. According to Quiason Serafin (1970: 215–16), writing about the Manila *Nihonjingakkō* of the mid-1930s:

The Japanese primary school [was] patterned along lines similar to the prevailing system in Japan . . . with the Japanese language as the medium of instruction. The curriculum, saddled with strong nationalistic tones, emphasized the teaching of the Code of Ethics and Morals, reverence for the Emperor, loyalty to the country, love of beauty, and obedience to parental authority. The Japanese children from about seven years of age underwent formal indoctrination in schools, and hence patriotic ideals were inculcated in the young minds. These were readily manifested in such obligatory acts as the singing of the *Kimiga-yo* [the national anthem], reading of the Imperial Rescript and bowing before the portrait of the Emperor Hirohito.

Although there were perhaps as many as two million Japanese living in colonies overseas in the 1930s, the vast majority were in their 20s and few were of school age (Hoshino, 1980: 113). The *Nihonjingakkō* therefore also played other important roles besides the inculcation of ultranationalism in Japanese children overseas. In an examination of the debate on the role of overseas schools in the history of pre-war Japan, Kojima Masaru (1981) isolates a number of recurring themes which he suggests may also be relevant to contemporary discussions on *kikokushijo*.

Kojima relates the demands of Japanese in the pre-war period to build more *Nihonjingakkō* for the re-education of anti-Japanese members of the local populations. As J. L. Fischer (1963: 516) writes, in his account of the *Nihonjingakkō* on Truk, one of the

Caroline Islands in the Pacific Ocean, these schools were established in order to 'civilize the natives and make them into loyal and
economically useful citizens of the Japanese empire'. Kojima (1981:
34) argues that the *Nihonjingakkō* were also seen as a means to
spread Japanese culture more widely as part of the process of
colonization.

Kojima (1981: 28–31) also explores the pre-war debate on the
issue of whether Japanese living in overseas colonies should remain
Japanese or assimilate (*jiminzoku chūshin ka dōka ka*). This debate
was waged primarily in Brazil and centred on the question whether
to adopt the culture of the host country was to accept a 'fall in
cultural level' (*bunka rakusa*). One side of this debate argued that
Japanese should take great care to maintain their 'Japaneseness'
overseas and not lose their culture: the other side counter-argued
that Japanese should respect the countries to which they had
emigrated. As we have seen, versions of this debate continue today.

Between 1906 and 1945 some 751 *Nihonjingakkō* were created,
545 during the last ten years of this period (Ōkubo, 1983: 47). As
the likelihood of war increased, though, the population of the
schools became more indigenous, less Japanese. In a Japanese
school in the Philippines in the late 1930s, for example, only about
16 per cent of the students enrolled were classified as pure Japanese
(1983: 39). From all over the world, Japanese children were
returning to Japan. Keimei Gakuen, the first school set up especially
for *kikokushijo*, was founded in this period in 1940 and is still
running today. The school's founder, Mitsui Takasumi, was a
member of the Mitsui dynasty who had himself spent over six years
in Oxford in the mid 1930s (Roberts, 1973: 336–7, 386–7, 411–
12). One of Mitsui's main reasons for setting up the school was his
concern for children who had been educated overseas and would
face problems on their return to Japan if they could not speak good
Japanese. He was especially concerned about boys who would have
to join the Imperial army. The school opened in Mitsui's own house
with seven returnees, all boys, one of them Mitsui's own son and
the others coming from equally élite backgrounds. By the time of
Japan's attack on Pearl Harbour in 1941, the school had some
thirty pupils. According to the current vice-principal, who was a
teacher there in the early 1940s, the school was, under Mitsui's
patronage and protection, one of the very few places in Japan at
this time where English could be freely spoken and taught.

The end of the War, and Japan's defeat, heralded another dramatic swing in Japanese official (and also unofficial) relations with the west. Disillusioned with militarism and battered by nationalism, there followed a period of receptiveness to all things western which was similar to the policy of the 1870s. Benedict (1946), attempting to explain Japan's swift turnabout from enemy to student of the west, evoked the strong Japanese sense of hierarchy in which superiors (such as victors) are regarded as teachers. During the six-and-a-half years of Allied occupation, however, there was little opportunity for the Japanese to leave their islands, and study overseas was limited. Between 1948 and 1951 there were barely 1,000 Japanese students in the United States (Bennett, Passin, and McKnight, 1958: 102). This period, though, was the heyday for all those who had already been educated overseas and spoke English as they could communicate with the occupation forces. These individuals rose quickly to important positions and acted as intermediaries between the Allied and Japanese leaderships. For some, their rise was rather too sudden and too steep and aroused considerable jealousy, particularly if they were members of minority groups such as Koreans (Kaplan and Dubro, 1987: 47–8).

As was the case, however, throughout Japan's history of contact with the outside world, there were those who upheld an opposing view and values, in this case a sense of 'Japaneseness' and the importance of Japanese traditions. As the Japanese economy began to improve rapidly in the post-war period, those who had pushed for the maintenance of Japanese values began to become more vocal and, around the mid 1960s, a new nationalism, essentially economic and not militaristic, began to emerge. As we shall see in the next chapter, it was at this time that the subject of *kikokushijo* also began to be seriously discussed and this timing had important consequences for the way the returnees came to be perceived.

A number of themes emerge from this short historical overview which are essential in our understanding of the forces behind the creation of policy on *kikokushijo* and their subsequent treatment in the post-war period. Firstly, far from having maintained a constant attitude towards the outside world, the Japanese have exhibited an extraordinary degree of flexibility, swinging between xenophobia and xenophilia. In particular, it is important to put Japan's *sakoku jidai* into perspective. As Sansom (1951: 5), with his usual lucidity, writes:

The degree of Japan's isolation may easily be overestimated if we think only in terms of the *sakoku* period; and if we exclude that period, we find that Japan shows a tendency to expand rather than to withdraw, from the earliest days of expeditions to Korean kingdoms in almost prehistoric times to the [Korean] campaigns of Hideyoshi in 1592 and 1597.

Moreover, he concludes (1951: 78): 'The fact that Japan did not enter international society until the mid-nineteenth century is . . . of no great importance to-day; since she has now for several generations shared the experience of other modern states, and much of that experience has been new to all of them.'

Secondly, it has always been possible to explain the official Japanese attitude towards the outside world at any particular period in Japan's history in terms of internal and external economic and political factors. The treatment of westerners during the so-called 'Christian Century' was a good example of this.

A third important theme apparent from a historical analysis is that even when national policy has been weighted heavily in one direction, there has always been a minor body of opinion tending in the opposite direction. This pluralism is a vital component in an understanding of Japanese history and it is important not to assume that the official line was absolute or to generalize from it to the whole population. The notion of what constituted good and bad contact with foreign countries was never static but underwent constant change and debate.

Finally, there has been a tendency to see the outside world as a source of skills and knowledge for Japanese society which could be adopted and adapted to the society without necessarily upsetting the traditional values. The importers of the outside skills, however, were sometimes regarded positively and sometimes negatively. They had to strike the appropriate balance for the period between their 'foreign' and their 'Japanese' attributes. As Bennett, Passin, and McKnight (1958: 255) write about returnees in the Meiji period:

It is apparent that persons educated abroad were in a critical position: they were expected to contribute to the official program of modernization yet they were expected to avoid the 'contamination' of western culture. At the same time, Japan's judgement of what was contamination and what was desirable was constantly changing. The opportunities for the persons educated overseas, therefore, also changed.

The treatment of returnees to Japan has not, however, been determined simply by the mainstream political view on relations with the outside world at that time but has also depended on the status of those who have gone overseas, where they have been, for how long, and why. In summary, the reception given to returnees has, throughout history, depended on a dialectic between the political and economic context at the time of their return and the individual's background. These factors have also determined the current status of *kikokushijo* in Japan.

THE CREATION OF POLICY FOR *KIKOKUSHIJO*

The first *Nihonjingakkō* to open after the war was in Taiwan in 1953, followed by another in Bangkok in 1956 and *hoshūkō* in Hamburg, Washington, and New York in 1957, 1958, and 1962 respectively. We have seen in Chapter 2 how the numbers of both *Nihonjingakkō* and *hoshūkō* have rapidly increased since then. Kida Hiroshi (1978: 78), a former vice-minister of education, comments that before the early 1960s, when the number of Japanese being sent abroad to work began to increase dramatically, going overseas and returning to Japan was considered a personal matter. From 1962, however, as well as supplying free textbooks, the government made money available for purchasing land for schools overseas and, at this time too, teachers from the schools attached to the national universities began to be sent abroad (Nakabayashi, 1981: 27). Moreover, as we have seen, the first school for *kikokushijo*, Ōizumi, was established in 1964.

Ōizumi School, though it became an important model for other schools taking *kikokushijo*, actually preceded the main debate about *kikokushijo* education by several years. Though discussion about *kikokushijo* may have started around 1960, the issue was not seriously debated until the end of the decade. There are a number of versions of the chronological development of policy for *kiko-kushijo*, among them one by Kobayashi (1978*b*), a key figure in the process, but probably the most detailed account is one pieced together by Kitsuse, Murase, and Yamamura (1984). John Kitsuse, a Japanese-American sociologist, had a particular interest in the creation of this policy in the light of an earlier theory he had propounded concerning the construction of social problems

(Spector and Kitsuse, 1977). As Spector and Kitsuse point out (1977: 12), social problems do not just emerge from a vacuum but are the result of 'the activities of specific and identifiable individuals (not "society") who are engaged in defining conditions in particular terms with specific (recorded) purposes in mind'. They propose a 'natural history of social problems' to explain how such problems are constructed. This process starts when a group or groups 'assert the existence of some condition, define it as offensive, harmful, or otherwise undesirable, publicize these assertions, stimulate controversy, and create a public or political issue over the matter' (1977: 142).

According to Kitsuse, Murase, and Yamamura's (1984) account, the issue of *kikokushijo* was first brought to public attention by the parents of these children. As we have seen, the parents living overseas tend to come from a very powerful section of Japanese society and, according to Arai (1983: 76–7), this bias was even more pronounced in the 1960s than it is today. The vast majority of parents overseas in the 1960s were diplomats, academics, businessmen, and other professionals, while those who fell into the category of *salaryman* tended to work for the biggest companies with the greatest influence in Japan. These parents complained that, while they were loyally serving their country by working abroad, their children were being handicapped through not being able to compete equally with other students on their return to Japan. They argued that, as a result of missing part of their Japanese education, their children were unable to enter the top universities from which they themselves had graduated and thus the family status was being unfairly threatened.

The first major group to define the 'problem' of the *kikokushijo* was the Zaigai Kinmusha Shijo Taisaku Kondan Kai (Overseas Employees' Childrens' Adaptation Organization) founded in 1962. This organization had an initial membership of some twenty individuals from the Foreign Ministry, international trading companies (*bōeki shōsha*), and the media world. According to Kitsuse, Yamamura, and Murase (1984: 171), 'This committee was chaired by Mr. W., a high ranking diplomat who had recently returned . . . from a post in Washington . . . [and who] transformed his personal experience of frustrating encounters with school officials into a public issue.' Other important pressure groups were created at this time by mothers of returnees: a group of wives from the Foreign Ministry, as well as mothers from many other organizations, put significant pressure on Monbushō to do something for their children.

In 1966, largely as a result of this pressure, the first statistics were collected on the number of Japanese children of compulsory school age living overseas. There were found to be some 4,159 (Kobayashi, 1978b: 15). In 1967, Monbushō initiated a system of giving subsidies to selected public and private elementary, junior, and senior high schools which accepted *kikokushijo*. Such schools were appointed *kikokushijo kenkyū kyōryokukō* (schools co-operating in research on *kikokushijo*). These schools did not provide special classes for *kikokushijo*, as Ōizumi did, but they did try to give some special attention to returnees as they proceeded through the standard educational system. By 1977, when there were some 4,000 *kikokushijo* a year returning to Japan, there was a total of twenty-two special classes and thirty-four 'co-operating schools' for them (1978b: 16).

From its inception in 1971, the Kaigai Shijo Kyōiku Shinkō Zaidan acted as an important intermediary between the various pressure groups of returnee parents and the Ministries of Education and Foreign Affairs. It was so effective that, although the Japanese House of Representatives first addressed itself to the issue of children overseas only in 1973, by 1975 52 per cent of the expenses for the forty extant *Nihonjingakkō* was being met by the government (Kobayashi, 1978b: 16). Moreover, a resolution was passed through which Monbushō took on a substantial share of the burden of running the Zaidan itself.

As a result of further deliberations between the Zaidan and Monbushō, a special committee was set up in September 1975, within Monbushō, to formulate a basic policy document on *kikokushijo*. The committee represented a balance between businessmen on the one hand and educationalists on the other. It consisted of seventeen members and included senior representatives of Japan Air Lines, Japan National Railways, Mitsui Bussan, *Nihon Keizai Shinbun* (Japan Economic Newspaper), Nihon Bōeki Kai (Japan Foreign Trade Council), and Nihon Bōeki Shinkō Kai (Japan External Trade Organization). Other members were four schoolteachers, including the principal of the Ōizumi school; three university professors, including Kobayashi Tetsuya and the head of ICU; a former diplomat; the founder of the Hatano Family School;

the head of the Kaigai Shijo Kyōiku Shinkō Zaidan; and the head of the Tokyo National Museum (Monbushō, 1985: 107–8).

The final policy document appeared in April 1976 (Monbushō, 1985: 89–106). After giving a general outline of the situation as it was in 1976, the report turned to discuss the general issue of education for Japanese children overseas. First of all, the committee recognized that there were two parallel, but conflicting, possible interpretations of overseas education. On the one hand, it was recognized that it was necessary to provide an educational system for Japanese children overseas that would not leave them educationally disadvantaged when they returned to Japan. On the other hand, the committee felt that the experience of life overseas could be seen as an advantage for children in terms of developing an 'international perspective'.

These two interpretations of overseas Japanese schooling were widely and vigorously aired during the mid 1970s, as is demonstrated by Satō Hirotake's (1978) *Kaigaishijo no Kyōiku Mondai* (*The Educational Problems of Overseas Children*). Satō (1978: 175–9) sets the debate in the context of whether *kikokushijo* should be perceived as Japanese or as 'internationalists' (*kokusaijin*). Those who supported the former viewpoint were also in favour of the creation of more *Nihonjingakkō*, believing that children overseas should study a Japanese curriculum full-time. Others argued that genuine interaction with foreign societies should be encouraged. Yoshida Teigo (quoted in Satō, 1978: 177), the eminent anthropologist, took the view that overseas experience was an excellent way for children to escape ethnocentricism, arguing that 'their internationalness should be developed so that they are Japanese of the future standing on the front line of foreign relations'. On the other hand Ogiyama, a senior member of the Kaigai Shijo Kyōiku Shinkō Zaidan (quoted in Satō, 1978: 178), was dismissive of what he considered a superficial idea of internationalness, insisting that:

It may impress intellectuals but it is only superficial theory [*tatemaeron*]. We could not admire 'little internationalists' who cannot speak Japanese and who are not really Japanese. Japanese who have lost their Japanese language are non-nationals in a bad sense. . . . Anybody who lived overseas could obtain a sense of internationalism and international understanding. To place great expectations and hopes on these children and to discard their education as Japanese is a very questionable idea.

Kitsuse, Murase, and Yamamura (1984: 178) call those of Yoshida's persuasion the *kokusaiha* (internationalist faction) while those who support Ogiyama's view they term the *kokunaiha* (parochial faction). White (1988: 50–3) shows how, even in the bastions of Monbushō which is generally considered extremely conservative, there were considerable differences of opinion at this period as to how to treat the returnees.

In its policy guidelines, the Monbushō committee suggested a compromise position. It proposed, as we have seen, that there be full-time Japanese schools in 'developing' countries and part-time schools in 'developed' ones. It decided that about 50 per cent of the general costs of running the *Nihonjingakkō* should be met by the central government, the rest to be made up by the local Japanese community. The government, however, would cover the major cost of sending teachers from Japan.

Section II–4 of the report (Monbushō, 1985: 102–4) covered measures to be taken by the government with regard to children returning to Japan. Here the committee again tried to find a compromise position between, on the one hand, complete re-adaptation to the Japanese educational and social system, and, on the other, the retention of linguistic and cultural skills learnt overseas. These latter were to be retained, it was hoped, not only for the benefit of the children themselves but also for their peers and even for their teachers who had not been overseas. The report stopped short, however, of recommending bilingual education despite support for the idea from the education minister at the time, Nagai Michio (1974–6) (Satō 1978: 210). According to Satō (1978: 210), Kobayashi's research group was particularly against this idea, arguing that:

For those who live overseas for about five years, there is some possibility of becoming bilingual. But 70 per cent of people who come back to Japan forget their language within a year. The real bilinguals are only about 10 per cent and so it is very dangerous to have some superficial idea about promoting bilingual education.

As concrete proposals, the report demanded the expansion of the existing system of special classes and mixed streams for *kikokushijo* in both state and private schools. Moreover, it was recommended that foreign qualifications be accepted when *kikokushijo* applied to the non-compulsory, and yet very competitive, senior high schools.

In particular, the report recommended the use of public money to establish a few special private high schools which could also offer boarding facilities for children whose parents were living and working overseas and who would rather remain within the mainstream Japanese educational system. These were International Christian University Senior High School, Gyōsei International High School, and Dōshisha International High School.

As a final recommendation concerning *kikokushijo*, the committee encouraged the idea of allowing September entry—the Japanese school year running from April to March—so as to facilitate the entry of the majority of *kikokushijo* from around the world.[4] It also suggested that universities should recognize the overseas certificates and credentials of returnees when considering them for entrance. Most of the institutions that accepted this idea early on were private universities. After such a scheme had been instituted by the University of Tsukuba, however, many other national universities, including the top two, followed suit—Kyoto in 1982 and Tokyo in 1984. There were a few objections that such a system might lead to making special allowances for other groups, such as handicapped applicants or housewives who wished to return to school (Kinoshita, 1985: 6–7), but they were neither loud nor effective.

There were many discussions as to the type of education which should be provided in Japanese schools overseas and for *kikokushijo* in Japan, but the fact was that very little empirical research could be produced to support many of the suggestions. Pressurized by the various groups of returnee parents to look at the situation of overseas and *kikokushijo* education, Monbushō had carried out a brief survey to uncover the extent of the 'problem' in 1974. It was this survey that Kobayashi and his research team at Kyoto University were asked to extend and complement in 1975. They were to uncover and 'measure' the extent of the *kikokushijo* 'problem' and its various facets so as to offer clearer guidelines to policy-makers. As we have seen, there was no attempt to determine whether *kikokushijo* actually had problems, or whether the problems which they did have could in reality be directly related to their overseas experience. The work that Kobayashi and his group produced between 1975 and 1978 (see 1978*a*) in effect served only to consolidate the already established view of *kikokushijo*—that they have problems on their return to Japan as a direct result of having spent time overseas.

Significantly, this paradigm reflected the belief of many of the parents of returnees that their children were suffering from various handicaps and were in need of help. The research produced helped to add substance to their case that more central government aid and direction was needed on behalf of the *kikokushijo*. It is important to point out, however, that just as many of the members of the original Monbushō committee had belonged to the pressure groups, so had some of the more important figures in the creation of this research framework. Kobayashi (1981: flyleaf), for example, admits that he first became involved in *kikokushijo* education owing to his having spent ten years overseas and his daughter having thereby received much of her education in America and West Germany. Similar personal reasons can be attributed to many others who have written about the problems of *kikokushijo*. Some are parents (Azuma, Konishi); some are teachers of returnees (Hoshino, Kubota, Sono); some are returnees themselves (Horoiwa, Muro, Nakane, Nakatsu).

Not all of the researchers, however, believed that their children needed special treatment on their return to Japan. Indeed, some argued that the Japanese educational system itself should be changed as a result of learning from the experiences of *kikokushijo*. Inui and Sono (1977: 162) end their book by calling it a single stone thrown at the Japanese educational system. They argue that *kikokushijo* should be accepted in Japan for what they are, and that if it is necessary for Japanese society to change and internationalize to accommodate them, then that would be for the good of the society. Satō (1978: 222) insists that '*kikokushijo* should not be seen as a minority education case but must be seen as a key to a new education system in Japan'. Azuma (1979: 95) proposes that 'the case of *kikokushijo* should reveal the problems of all Japanese children, and the whole of the Japanese education system, and not just be limited to the returnee children themselves'. Kobayashi (1982*b*: 100) comments that he never meant to suggest that *kikokushijo* should be forcibly adapted back to the Japanese educational system. Indeed, he says, 'the idea that it should not be a question of adapting returnee children to the Japanese education system, but adapting the education system to the returnee children has considerable merit'.

Whether they believed that the children should be given help to adapt to Japan or that the educational system should be changed to accommodate the children, those who were researching *kikokushijo* tended to emphasize their problems on returning to Japan. The evidence which they produced was used to support the idea of special help for a small group of children in a system which had regarded any discrimination, positive or negative, between individuals as anathema.

The majority view of discussing overseas and returnee children, described in Chapters 3 and 4, did not therefore occur in a vacuum but was the result of important and powerful groups creating an awareness of a social problem and bringing pressure to bear on the Japanese government to act upon that problem. This way of viewing *kikokushijo* was picked up with great energy by the Japanese media. Indeed, one of the final recommendations of the Monbushō (1985: 106) committee report was that there should be more publicity for the returnee children problem (*kikokushijo mondai*). The result, as we have seen, is the treatment of *kikokushijo* as a separate and special group of Japanese schoolchildren.

Throughout history, the treatment of returnees in Japan has depended on the political and economic conditions prevailing in the country at the time of their return and on the political and economic power of the returnees themselves. It is only through examining the interaction of these two factors that we can see, in the final chapter, how the *kikokushijo* have changed from being a downtrodden 'marginal group' to an emerging social élite.

8
The Emergence of a New Class of Japanese Schoolchildren

As discussed in Chapters 3 and 4, there is a widespread perception in Japan that *kikokushijo* suffer from serious problems and that these are the inevitable consequences of returning to Japan and Japanese society. Nakabayashi (1981: 213–14) sums up this view when he writes that:

Anthropologists say that, because Japan is a vertically oriented society of cliques, it is a place in which foreigners, as well as those who are separated from the group, such as the 'lone-wolf' [*ippiki ōkami*] and those from different cultures, find it difficult to live [*ikinikui*]. Accordingly, tolerance for alien and heretical elements has traditionally been low, and groupism has been accorded a higher value than individualism. It has been pointed out that, since Japan is essentially a homogeneous [*dōshitsuteki*] country of one language, one culture, one race . . . it is exclusive towards outsiders . . . an exclusiveness that also applies to overseas children, those who have worked overseas for a long time, and those who have returned from studying overseas.

According to this belief, it is accepted that *kikokushijo*, as a result of their problems—which have been so thoroughly researched—need special attention on their return to Japan. This special help, it is felt, is particularly necessary in relation to the educational system and hence the *ukeirekō* form part of what Ōgiya (1977: vii), among others, describes as *kyūsai kyōiku* (relief education) for these children. Yet, as we have seen in Chapters 5, 6, and 7, far from being disadvantaged children in need of help, *kikokushijo* appear to be becoming part of a new 'international' élite in Japanese society. If this is the case, then it is not only the idea that the experience of *kikokushijo* is inherently problematic that needs to be examined, but also the explanation of those 'problems'.

One answer to this apparent contradiction of *kikokushijo* on the one hand suffering from problems and on the other being seen as a new élite, can perhaps be found in another paradox which arose out of the survey of *kikokushijo* in Chapter 2 and has been touched upon in subsequent chapters. This concerns the fact that, despite wide differences in their experiences, all children who have been overseas and then returned to Japan are defined as *kikokushijo*. Over 40 per cent of *kikokushijo* attended *Nihonjingakkō* while overseas, which, if anything, are more traditional than schools back in Japan. Many of them live in communities consisting entirely of short-term Japanese overseas residents and never venture beyond these. Some of them are only out of Japan for a few months. Others went abroad only when they were very young. *Kikokushijo* in the *ukeirekō* appear to be little different from their non-*kikokushijo* peers. Certainly, their teachers are divided as to whether they stand out at all. In some cases, especially where there are few *kikokushijo* in a school, or an individual *kikokushijo* is introverted, the child very quickly disappears back into the mass and cannot be easily distinguished from his peers. Academically, the provision of limited streaming and extra language tuition is all that is required for almost all *kikokushijo* to catch up with their peers. Yet this does not explain the massive media interest in *kikokushijo* since the mid 1970s: the number of books published, articles written, conferences held, researchers employed, and money spent.

The fact is that all *kikokushijo* tend to be perceived in Japan as if they had spent fifteen years in the United States and know only a few words of Japanese on their return. *Kikokushijo* are categorized as a unified group with shared identifiable qualities often associated with western values, such as individualism and directness. Discussions about *kikokushijo* are clearly concerned with much wider issues than simply the welfare of the children themselves. What is significant about these debates is the value ascribed to the perceived qualities of *kikokushijo* by different interest groups in the context of Japan's overall political rhetoric. Indeed, the children themselves could even be described as peripheral to these debates.

As we have seen in Chapter 7, discussions on *kikokushijo* and their position in Japanese society were initiated, largely at the insistence of their parents, during the 1960s and 1970s. The complaints of these parents were widely disseminated by the media and partially supported by educators. The political rhetoric of the period as pursued by the Japanese establishment—the government, the bureaucracy, big business—was essentially one of *kindaika* (modernization) and it was this which largely determined the terms of the debate about *kikokushijo*. The values employed in support of *kindaika* were, in the main, the same as those propounded by the

Nihonjinron theorists as inherent to Japanese society. These 'Japanese' values were, in turn, used to explain the 'problems' suffered by *kikokushijo*. It is essential, therefore, to explore how this value system was created and employed.

KIKOKUSHIJO AND THE LANGUAGE OF *KINDAIKA*

The elements of *kindaika* affecting the areas which most closely concern *kikokushijo*—the family, the workplace, and the educational system—include the following: hierarchy, respect for status, social responsibility, centralization, duty, loyalty, low public status for women, equal opportunity, meritocracy, groupism, perseverance, and interdependence. These are essential elements of the Japanese 'cultural complex' and are emphasized in almost all studies of Japan, both by Japan's supporters (Reischauer, 1983; Vogel, 1983) and by its critics (Woronoff, 1983; Taylor, 1985). Such values are accepted by most Japanese to be either inherent to their culture or inherited from early contact with Chinese Confucianism, and this belief is supported by much academic and popular literature on Japan.

The values of Confucianism are not, in fact, inherent to Japanese society. Their usage has varied through their invocation by different leaders and interest groups throughout Japanese history for various political purposes: by the Tokugawa Shōgunate to aid the creation and maintenance of an essentially static society; by the Meiji oligarchy to encourage rapid development in a desire to revoke the unequal treaties Japan had been forced to sign with western nations; and, in the post-war period, to encourage rapid economic recovery. Such macro-historical perspectives are, of course, fraught with problems, not least because they tend to exaggerate the cognitive independence of the hegemony—the ability of the élite to see what the rest of the society cannot—but a brief review of the mobilization of Confucian symbols in various areas of Japanese society will help to clarify the argument.

The Confucianism of the Edo period in Japan was derived from the neo-Confucian orthodoxy of Chu Hsi. The most recognizable element of this form of Confucianism was the idea of the five levels of human relationship—ruler/subject, parent/child, husband/wife, elder/younger, and friend/friend. As Tsunoda, de Bary, and Keene

(1964: 384) point out, it is important to remember that 'Among those who upheld the orthodoxy of Chu Hsi's philosophy in Japan, there was a tendency to disregard certain aspects of this vast system of thought while emphasizing others that seemed more especially to meet Japanese needs at that time.' An essential aspect of this Confucian philosophy resulted in the division of Japanese society into four classes: the warrior-rulers (*samurai*), the peasants, the artisans, and the merchants, plus a fifth 'untouchable' class considered unworthy of inclusion within the general schema. The most important social division was that between the *samurai* and all other classes which were often classed as a single unit called *heimin* (commoners). The *samurai* were, according to Tsunoda, de Bary, and Keene (1964: 386), the acme of the society who served as 'model and leader for all the others'. They refined the neo-Confucian orthodoxy to create, within their own class, what is known as the '*bushidō* ethic'. This ethical code had its foundation 'in dedicating one's life unconditionally to one's master's service' (Furukawa, 1980: 232).

Ooms (1984), among others, has argued that *bushidō*, often regarded as the supreme refinement of Confucianism in Japanese history, was no more than the clothing in Confucian language of the indigenous behaviour of the warring élites in order to bring the potentially most volatile element of the nation, the *samurai*, into line with mainstream Tokugawa politics. The Tokugawa *bakufu* was able, through the manipulation of the *bushidō* ethic, to subdue the 6 per cent of the population who made up the *samurai* class who, in turn, could subdue the rest of the population.

While Confucianism provided the philosophical context in which many of the discussions about ethics of the Tokugawa period were carried out among the élite class, it had little effect on the social systems—occupational, educational, and kinship—of the commoners. In the Meiji period, however, a process, described by Morishima Michio (1982: 50) as the 'secularization of *bushidō*' and by Befu (1981: 50) as 'the samuraization process—the spread of the ideology of the ruling class', took place. When the early Meiji reformers set out to transform Japan speedily into a modern state with the power and prestige necessary to face any foreign nation, they quickly mobilized *samurai* values which, according to Saniel (1965: 142), hastened the modernization of the country by freezing hierarchical ties within the society and ensuring the unquestioning obedience of the people to a superior authority.

The mobilization of Confucian symbols was particularly potent in the area of industrial relations. A number of authors relate Japan's economic success to a Confucian historical legacy that has created a specifically Japanese work ethic where loyalty and hard work on the part of the employee are rewarded with benevolence from the employer (Fujihara, 1936; Abegglen, 1959; Saniel, 1965; Morishima, 1982). This theory, however, tends to ignore some basic elements of Japanese industrialization. Indeed, factories in the Meiji, Taishō, and early Shōwa periods were positively Dickensian (see Befu, 1981: 135; Hane, 1982). As Cole (1971: 8) says, there is the possibility that 'Emphasis on the "smoothing" role of tradition . . . overlook[s] the conflict, exploitation, suffering, and dislocation that occurred during Japanese industrialization.' Crawcour (1978), though, has demonstrated how the rise of labour union consciousness, and government consideration of legislation to protect industrial workers, put pressure on employers to improve their terms and conditions of employment and labour relations. This, he suggests, led to the formulation of an idea that a benevolent, paternalistic system of management is, in some way, a natural result of Japan's Confucian tradition. Union pressure on employers intensified throughout the early decades of the twentieth century, forcing them to organize in response and the result was a campaigning federation known as Zensanren. Matters reached a head during the campaign of 1931 and, according to Crawcour (1978: 236–7), 'It was in the course of this campaign against trade union legislation that the "traditional" spirit of Japanese labour relations took shape as orthodox doctrine.' The values that were taken to represent this 'traditional' system of labour relations are well documented: group consciousness; emphasis on harmony; loyalty to the firm; the company as a 'family'; and obedience to authority.

In another context in which *kikokushijo* have been discussed— the family—there is also considerable evidence to show how the samuraization process played an important role in the creation of the modern value system. The ideal attitude for the *samurai* woman in the Tokugawa period was enshrined in the *Onna Daigaku* (Great Learning for Women), which taught that 'Marriage was the only acceptable condition for women . . . [and that] the whole purpose of her education should be learning to please her future husband and especially his parents, to whom she was to become virtually a slave' (Paulson, 1976: 10–11). Nevertheless, such values were far from uniformly held throughout society, as two quotes from the early Meiji period suggest. Nitobe (1899: 150), a champion of the *samurai* ideal, admitted that 'the lower the social class . . . the more equal was the position of husband and wife', and Chamberlain (1895: 508) averred that 'the peasant women . . . have more liberty and a relatively higher position than the great ladies of the land'.

The samuraization process of the Meiji period, however, gradually led to the role of all women becoming closer to the *samurai* ideal. This was particularly powerfully inculcated through the ultranationalist rhetoric of the pre-war period, so that women, despite being granted legal rights in the Revised Civil Code of 1947, continued (and still continue) to live largely by the 'rules' that until the middle of the nineteenth century were upheld, in a rigorous form, by only a minority of the population (see Hendry, 1981: 28–30).

A third example of the samuraization process can be seen in the education system. The Tokugawa education system has been extensively analysed and researched, notably by Passin (1965) and Dore (1984). What emerges from both accounts is a picture of a bifurcated system: education for the nobility in shogunal and domain schools (*hankō*) on the one hand, and on the other, education in *terakoya* schools for the commoners. The former offered a classical Confucianist education while the latter had a much freer approach and concentrated on literacy and practical skills. The government was not completely happy with the latter type of school and tried to set up new institutions, known as *gōgaku,* to provide a Confucian education for the masses (Passin, 1965: 37–40). The fact that these *gōgaku* were considerably less widespread than the more independent *terakoya* schools, however, shows that the ruling élite were reasonably content for non-*samurai* to run their own lives, so long as they were prevented, through restrictions on their movements, from causing unrest.

As with the role of women, the Meiji samuraization process radically altered the education system in Japan. As Passin (1965: 153) says, 'The Meiji leaders set out to inculcate the *samurai* ethic as the national ethic, and the school system played the key role in this transformation.' The major purveyor of this 'message' was *The Imperial Rescript on Education* (1890) which purported to be a simple expression of Japan's natural 'tradition' (Beardsley, 1965: 333). Many of the values mobilized by the Meiji leaders in this period, in the context of education, remain in force today—the automatic promotion of students, teacher-centred lessons, education in groups, emphasis on equal potential. Moreover, as Vogel (1983: 180) says, education has played a major part in creating the sense of homogeneity and conformity which has pervaded post-war Japan.

What Moriya (1985: 136) calls the 'vocabulary of Confucianism' has therefore been manipulated for various political purposes during Japan's modernization process. During the Meiji period, it served to encourage the development of a sense of homogeneity and an acceptance of authority that was useful in both the political and the economic sphere. A number of authors argue that the *Nihonjinron* literature examined in Chapter 3 is simply a manifestation of the same political process in the post-war period (see Minami, 1973); they argue that the minimizing of differences within Japanese society and the mobilization of concepts of 'Japaneseness' and homogeneity have all played a crucial role in the rapid economic success of Japan since 1945. Kawamura (1980) describes a conspiracy between the Japanese government, élite academic institutions, and major publishing houses to spread, through the work of such as Nakane Chie, the idea that Japanese are the same as each other and different from all other people. Mouer and Sugimoto (1986) are particularly strong critics of the *Nihonjinron* literature which, they believe, in its aim of presenting Japan as a harmonious, homogeneous society, purposefully fails to take into account regional and class variations, the difference between voluntary and coerced behaviour, and the role of conflict in society. Befu (1980: 33–4) denounces *Nihonjinron* as a form of nationalism—the deliberate creation of a false social homogeneity and a sense of difference from all non-Japanese. In particular, the symbols of Confucianism mobilized in the *Nihonjinron* literature and modernization rhetoric emphasized the domination of the group—be it the work group or the whole of Japanese society—over the individual.

The way, therefore, that returnees were perceived—particularly their individualism and their heterogeneous qualities—clashed with many of the values of modernization in Japan. On a personal level, as we have seen, they posed a threat to the ideas of teachers, mothers, and employers concerning the behaviour of students, children, and employees. On a wider level, however, they posed a threat to the whole society by challenging the values on which it was based. When seen in this light the explanation given to the treatment of *kikokushijo* in the 1960s and 1970s, in terms of them needing help for their 'problems', can be more easily understood.

Merry White, who studied returnees to Japan in the mid 1970s, titled her thesis (1980) *Strangers in Their Own Land*, and subtitled her subsequent book (1988) *Can They Go Home Again?*, which reflects her general theme of the exclusive nature of Japanese society, and how this exclusivity has prevented the full reintegration of those individuals who interacted with the outside world on Japan's behalf. Such individuals were what White (1980) called 'cultural brokers', used by society to make contact with the 'impure' outside world, thereby allowing the rest of society to remain 'pure' and permitting the country to follow a policy of simultaneous 'cultural isolation and international exchange'. According to White's theory, once Japanese were contaminated by the outside world, had acquired some of its values, and had lost some of their Japanese ones, they were marked as 'different'. Various social devices were then put into play which marginalized them and removed them from the mainstream and therefore the nerve-centre of Japanese society. As a result, many returnee businessmen were transplanted into the international sections of their firms which were traditionally of inferior status to the main office; their wives were locally ostracized and excluded from social groups; and *kikokushijo* had to go to special schools before they could re-enter Japanese society. Describing this schooling for *kikokushijo* to a Japanese audience, Inui and Sono (1977: 143) used the terms *Nihonka* (Japanizing) and *somenaoshi* (redying).

Befu Harumi (1983: 247), himself a *kibei* and currently professor of anthropology at Stanford, described the phenomenon of 'rejapanization' as *gaikoku hagashi* (peeling off foreignness). Like White (1980), Befu saw the returnees as the victims of Japanese society, and, like Kawamura (1980), he perceived a conspiracy by those in power to create a strong sense of self-identity among Japanese through the promulgation of *Nihonjinron* concepts. According to Befu (1983: 243), the exclusion of *kikokushijo* from mainstream society, effected through the mobilization of *Nihonjinron* ideas, was of value to Japan's economic self-interest since 'the stubbornly maintained separation between themselves and others allow[ed] Japanese to import and incorporate foreign cultural elements at will, since the latter process [did] not threaten their racial identity'. The returnees were therefore the unfortunate victims of Japan's economic policies.

The way in which Japanese society could justify its treatment of *kikokushijo* during the period of *kindaika* (modernization) was to label them as individuals with serious problems. This labelling also happened to other groups whose presence threatened to upset, or expose, the mainstream *kindaika* values, such as children who refused to go to school. Margaret Lock (1986) has analysed the condition known in Japan as *tōkōkyohisho* (school refusal syndrome) in these terms. She has shown how the term is invoked in a wide range of circumstances by teachers, administrators, and counsellors to explain why certain children do not attend school. The term suggests that the child suffers from some kind of psychological disorder perhaps caused by stresses in the family background, such as an over-protective mother or an absent father. As a result, the fault is laid squarely with the individual child and his family, and this is reflected in the nature of the treatment provided. According to Lock, the problem of school refusal is never placed in a wider context. The question why the father is absent, or why the mother is over-protective, or whether the child is suffering as a result of the Japanese educational system, is never addressed. Instead, counsellors and therapists see their role as the recreation of a social being able to cope with the wider society. This is convenient for teachers and employers who would otherwise be forced to examine their own values, and those of their schools and companies.

Ikemi and Ikemi (1982: 233) claim that *tōkōkyohisho* is a phenomenon unique to Japan. But, as Ohnuki-Tierney (1984*a*: 192) has pointed out, 'the Japanese think of many more conditions as "illnesses" than biomedicine recognizes as "diseases" '. Drawing on Mary Douglas's (1966) concept of matter-out-of-place, she shows (1984*a*: 21–49) how those in Japan who fall outside the cultural norms are pathologized as 'cultural germs' who need special treatment before they can re-enter society. Several authors (see Hara, 1986: 53) compare *tōkōkyohisho* with *futekiōbyō*, the non-adaptation 'disease' from which *kikokushijo* are said to suffer. We have already seen why individual groups, such as teachers, who have problems with *kikokushijo* prefer to label the children themselves as having problems. Similarly, in the context of *kindaika*, it can be seen why those who have supported the education system that has been so successful in the modernization of Japan do not wish to see changes in this system and believe, therefore, that it is the children who must change. Employers in Japan might equally be said to have the same attitude. Finally, the nation's leaders, in wanting to emphasize the homogeneity of the Japanese people, might also want to emphasize that *kikokushijo*— who look Japanese, have Japanese blood, generally speak Japanese, but sometimes appear to behave differently from other Japanese— are problematic children rather than a new breed of Japanese.

As we saw earlier, the parents of *kikokushijo* played an important role in bringing the problems of their children to a wider audience and ensuring that something was done to help them. Indeed, they may even have exaggerated the problems of their children in order to ensure that special treatment was forthcoming, and that their children were not disadvantaged in Japanese society.[1] These parents were greatly aided in their efforts by the Japanese media, a large section of which sees itself (in the absence of an effective political opposition) as the defender of the people against the government. The media are often fiercely critical of the establishment in Japan, and the left-wing press, including the powerful *Asahi Shinbun*, is a virulent opponent of the post-war educational system. The problems from which *kikokushijo* are said to suffer have offered the anti-establishment section of the media an ideal platform from which to attack Japan's monolithic educational system.

Access to the media, on the one hand, and to the important establishment figures who control educational policy, on the other, was only open to the parents of *kikokushijo* because of their high status in Japanese society. It was for this reason that they were provided with financial help, in the light of which policy a system of special schools (*ukeireko*) and the special university entrance network (*tokubetsu waku*) were created. From the government's point of view, this special system of education meant not only that the qualities of *kikokushijo* were not completely lost to Japan and the demands of their parents accommodated but also that the values of homogeneity and equality—such important concepts in the political rhetoric of *kindaika*—were not damaged.

It is important to point out, however, that from the very beginning some parents of *kikokushijo* insisted that it was not their children who needed to change but Japanese society, and particularly the educational system, which needed to be more flexible and adapt to the children. Only a change in the political rhetoric, however, could allow such changes to be contemplated.

FROM *KINDAIKA* TO *KOKUSAIKA*

By the late 1970s, to modernize and catch up with the west could no longer easily be used as a political slogan in Japanese society as Japan was by then a major economic power and the world's largest creditor nation. From this period, an increasingly powerful political rhetoric for the 'internationalization' of Japan began to develop and its buzz-words were *kokusaika, kokusaijin, kokusai jidai, kokusaisei* (internationalization; the international person; the international period; internationalness). Such key words and concepts became fashionable and were common elements of contemporary Japanese debates in areas as diverse as advertising and educational or industrial reform. Everyone appeared to support the idea of 'internationalization' in Japan, but what was meant by the term was far from clear. Some of the diversity of views on the subject and definitions of the term were apparent in the surveys completed by teachers at Fujiyama Gakuen (see Chapter 5). From the teachers' replies there appeared to be a basic dichotomy apparent throughout Japanese society—those who see internationalism as based in Japaneseness and those who see it as a more global concept transcending any idea of national identity.

The authors of many of the essays in Mannari and Befu's (eds.; 1983) volume on *The Challenge of Japanese Internationalization* describe the contemporary Japanese concept of *kokusaika* as merely an extension of earlier ideas of nationalism. They see the language of internationalization being used as a means to strengthen an individual's perception of his Japaneseness and to spread the values of the Japanese 'cultural complex' throughout the world. The ultimate purpose of this vocabulary, however, they believe is to reinforce the idea of Japanese being different from all other people. As evidence in support of this argument, Befu (1983) illustrates how Japan's economic growth and success in the international market has coincided with a growth in nationalist sentiment and increasingly tighter definitions of what it means to be

Japanese. Those who view Japan's new slogan of *kokusaika* (internationalism) as simply an extension of the old slogan of *kindaika* (modernization) have identified several areas of 'boundary strengthening' in recent years. There has been a hardening of attitudes towards Japan's 'foreign' minorities—Koreans, Chinese, and Caucasians—resulting in an insistence that they submit to finger-printing and always carry alien registration cards (see Ōnuma, 1985). Tsukushi Tetsuya (1984: 70) coins the phrase *Nihon wa Saikō Syndrome* ('Japan is Best Syndrome') for a tendency he finds among Japanese to look down on the rest of the world when they travel overseas. He makes a neat pun on this change of attitude towards the west as a move from *hai* (worship) to *hai* (driving away) (1984: 59). In the field of education there have been controversial revisions of school textbooks which ignore or play down Japan's aggressive role in the Second World War. In particular, Asian neighbours of Japan have been angered by amendments to history textbooks which now describe the war in China as the result of a *shinshutsu* (advance) rather than *shinryaku* (invasion) (*DY*, 1 and 15 July 1984). There have been demands for more moral education in schools in order to emphasize 'Japanese' values (Foreign Press Center, 1985). Many other contemporary commentators also point to the fact that *kikokushijo* attend special schools on their return to Japan and face serious 'problems' as evidence of how so-called 'internationalization' in Japan has led to greater 'nationalism' (Befu, 1983: 245–50; Drifte, 1988: 79–80; Hook, 1989: 15).

This definition of 'internationalism' therefore tends to emphasize the idea of Japaneseness, but there is also a faction which defines the idea in a more idealistic global sense. In Uchiyama *et al.*'s (eds.; 1984) *Kokusaijin no Jōken* ('The Condition of Internationalists'), Tsurumi Kazuko (1984: 55) despairs of nation-to-nation dialogue in developing global understanding, concentrates on the idea of person-to-person debate, and invokes the word *minsaijin* as 'someone who knows his own problems and particular situation and, with this realization, can communicate with other people in other countries with similar problems'. Shimada Haruo (1984: 75) defines *kokusaijin* as 'those who feel the pain of others just like their own'. As Kenneth Pyle (1982) has shown, debate over the meaning of the concept of *kokusaijin* has become increasingly vocal in recent years, especially in the major intellectual journals.

Mushanokoji Kimihide (1984: 17) summarizes the two poles of the debate well when he cites Nakae Chōmin's famous distinction between two classes of *kokusaijin* (international person): those Japanese who want to introduce everything western to a Japan which they believe to be inferior (*yōgakushinshi*) and those who are too proud of their own culture to 'spoil it' by introducing anything western into it (*tōyōgōgetsu*). Wolf Mendl (1989: 25) has pointed out that this debate shows interesting parallels with debates at the end of the Tokugawa period when, as now, there were demands on Japan from outside to open up and the threat of reprisals if she failed to do so. Then, as now, Japan's leaders were divided between those who wanted to plunge into the new world and those who believed that the country's salvation lay in strengthening traditional values and repelling foreign influences. The result, as Pyle (1982: 263) states, is that 'What seems clear is that the conception of Japanese national character, Japanese nationality, is in an evolving and dynamic phase.' Put simply, the supposedly 'traditional' values are often presented as 'Japanese'; while the 'new' values are presented as 'international' or 'western'.

Kikokushijo have become an increasingly important symbol in this debate. Ebuchi (1986*b*: 321), indeed, has described the way they are treated as a 'barometer' of Japan's internationalization. This explains why they have attracted so much attention in recent years. It also explains the ferocity of some of the debates over how they should be treated. Seminars on *kikokushijo* were often very heated affairs with a number of different interest groups—parents, teachers, researchers, occasionally even *kikokushijo* themselves—presenting their ideas on how society should change to accommodate these children. The important point to emphasize, however, is how little the images of *kikokushijo* which are utilized in these debates on the nature of Japanese society actually pertain to the real individuals. They are simply Weberian 'ideal types'. Those who perceive the *kikokushijo* as in need of 'rejapanization' also support the general *status quo* in Japan and so-called 'traditional' concepts of groupism, consensus, and homogeneity. Those who support the idea of *kikokushijo* as agents of change see them as valuable assets in emphasizing concepts of individualism, creativity, and heterogeneity in Japanese society. Those who take the former conservative line would tend to see Japan as a rather closed society. Those who take a more dynamic position would see Japan as a society which is as receptive as possible to influence from the outside world. This discussion constitutes an element in what David Parkin (1978: 286–311) has termed an 'internal cultural debate' and the positive or negative connotation given to *kikokushijo* in this debate could be called their 'symbolic value'. Nakabayashi (1981: 214–15) sums up the different possible interpretations of the perceived attributes of *kikokushijo* thus:

There is a stereotype that *kikokushijo* are undisciplined, stuck up, argumentative [*rikutsuppoi*], say clearly what they like and what they don't like, a stereotype which is expressed by the teachers of these children who think that these are deficiencies for human beings. But we have to review this issue. . . . These 'deficiencies' might be perceived as returnees simply not standing on ceremony [*keishikibarazu*] or being unrestrained (*jiyū*) and individualistic.

The reasons why different groups take different positions in discussing *kikokushijo* is not easily explained. It might be seen as a defence of one's personal lifestyle: those with overseas experience might wish to emphasize the value of that experience. It might, as Hoshino and Niikura (1983*b*) suggest, relate to age and gender: their research shows that older, male teachers tended to be more traditionalist in their perception of *kikokushijo*. Among teachers also, an argument could be made to suggest that those who teach subjects at the core of Japanese culture, particularly Japanese language, tend to support what they perceive as a 'traditional' line, while those more interested in western culture, such as English-language teachers, follow a more 'international' philosophy. There are many examples, however, that do not fit these explanations. Many English teachers, as we have seen, may in fact feel more threatened by *kikokushijo* than teachers of other subjects and may therefore be more likely to play down or ignore their 'international' qualities. Takenaga (1984), on the other hand, is a good example of a Japanese-language teacher who feels he can learn a lot about his own language and culture from the essays written by *kikokushijo*.

Perhaps the simplest explanation for differences in approach to the idea of internationalism is that realists (such as businessmen) see nationalism as an important factor in Japan's economic growth, and that idealists (such as academics) look towards a genuine global community where people's similarities are more important than their differences. This distinction between realist and idealist certainly seems to reflect the debate described by Satō (1978) on how to treat *kikokushijo* in the 1970s. It also explains the policy documents drawn up by the Monbushō committee on *kikokushijo* at the same period and the National Council on Educational Reform in the 1980s, both of which were composed of a mixture of individuals from the business and education worlds. As we have seen, both the Monbushō Committee and the National Council made genuine attempts to weave together both sets of ideas on what constitutes an international Japanese. In the case of the National Council it was reported that 'The panel stressed the necessity for education which will help schoolchildren develop patriotism and a sense of internationalism' (*JT*, 3 July 1985). Similarly, the system practised in many of the *ukeireko* attempted to help the *kikokushijo* retain what they had learnt overseas whilst educating in them a sense of Japaneseness. To achieve such a synthesis is a common concern of senior administrators involved in returnee education, as the following statement by Ogiyama Shōji, head of the Kaigai Shijo Kyōiku Shinkō Zaidan, shows: 'The treasure children returning from foreign countries have brought home is . . . international-mindedness. It must be pointed out, however, that desirable international-mindedness can be obtained through living overseas only after identity as a Japanese has firmly been established' (*JT*, 9 November 1984). Former Education Minister Nishioka Takeo emphasized what he saw as the inseparable nature of the two elements when he declared that Japanese students must have a firm understanding of Japan's national identity to enable them to understand other cultures (*JTW*, 27 May 1989).

Other commentators have seen a political division between the two sides of the debate on internationalism in Japan. According to Mouer and Sugimoto (1986: 382–3), the general concept of internationalism as the extension of earlier ideas of nationalism is associated primarily with the 'establishment', while those in Japan who view the concept in more idealistic terms are 'associated primarily with anti-establishment forces'. They suggest that in most areas of contemporary Japanese life, those who support a nationalistic concept of *kokusaika* have tended to prevail. The case of *kikokushijo*, however, provides an important exception to this trend as they have become symbols of a more idealistic concept of internationalism. Unlike almost any other minority group in Japan,

the returnees have been able to manipulate their 'marked nature'—
the fact that they are viewed as different from the mainstream
society—in their own favour, which has resulted in their obtaining
important educational and social advantages.

KIKOKUSHIJO IN 'SYMBOLIC COMPETITION' WITH MAINSTREAM SOCIETY

Groups such as META, which have highlighted the issue of
kikokushijo, have played a dual function in debates on *kikokushijo*.
On the one hand, META acts as a support group for returnees and
stresses the problems faced by *kikokushijo* on their return to Japan.
As one member expressed it (personal communication, letter,
1984):

My honest feeling is that we are never able to become the Japanese we once
were, and have to suffer for the feeling that nobody will understand the
different values we attained abroad. That is why we feel the necessity of
having a *kikokushijo* friend, even though we seem to be adapted to the
pure Japanese society. Many of us feel that we are acting as if we are the
same as everybody else, but we know that we aren't.

On the other hand, the group has an active role in creating a more
positive image of returnees in Japanese society. As we saw in
Chapter 7, several writers on *kikokushijo* have argued that society
should change to accommodate the returnees rather than force the
returnees to fit into society. Such writers present *kikokushijo* as
new Japanese, often called *kokusaijin*, with a string of positive
assets, who can be leaders of Japan into the next century.
E. G. Schwimmer (1972) has described this process, whereby
minority groups present their own values as preferable to those of
the majority culture, as 'symbolic competition'.

The influence of this 'symbolic competition' is particularly potent
with regard to the educational system in Japan. As we saw in
Chapter 4, there have been strident calls for change in the Japanese
educational system: calls for greater pluralism, creativity,
flexibility, individualism, and internationalism. It was only when
big business in the late 1970s also began to demand changes
in the educational system, however, that genuine reform movements began to exert any influence. The parents, and some

educators, of *kikokushijo* were quick to stress the point that these children possessed all the qualities which were being sought in the proposed new system. When Prime Minister Nakasone's educational reform council demanded individuality, internationalism, and creativity as keys to educational reform, it was perhaps not surprising to find that *kikokushijo* were virtually the only group deemed worthy of special mention (see Hasebe, 1986). Perhaps most indicative of the public perception of *kikokushijo* was an hour-long documentary devoted to them on the national television network as part of a series discussing the possibilities for educational reform in the light of the Council's deliberations (NHK, 5 June 1985). This programme consisted entirely of interviewing *kikokushijo* on their feelings about the Japanese educational system.

Not only in the educational sphere, however, do *kikokushijo* present themselves as symbols of 'internationalism'. The picture they present is becoming increasingly fashionable, particularly to Japanese youth which has become tired of being spoon-fed images by the media of the *neaka* (bright-spirited), *sunao* (innocent), or *burikko* (bouncy) child. In recent years, there has been what White (1987: 47) calls an 'anti-*burikko* movement' and *kikokushijo*, with their wide-ranging experiences, are sometimes held up as symbols of this movement. The popularity of *kikokushijo* is portrayed, for example, in an article entitled *Kaigai.Kikokushijo no Stylebook* ('A Guide to Overseas Returnees' Style') in the popular girl's magazine *JJ* (1986). The popularity and influence of *kikokushijo* extends beyond the school career. More creative, personally meaningful jobs such as those which often attract returnees—the media, international companies, interpreting—are gaining increasingly higher status in Japan. Similarly, the demand for places with the Japan Overseas Co-operation Volunteers has been growing rapidly, and big companies are beginning actively to recruit individuals with such overseas experience (*DY*, 30 August 1984). As Takagi (1988: 433) says, being able to include experience of foreign countries on one's *curriculum vitae* is being increasingly regarded as an advantage in employee evaluations.

Companies, as was evident in their demands for education reform discussed in Chapter 4, want more creative, individualistic workers to 'invent' new products (rather than simply improve those already invented in the west) that will become the mainstay of

Japan's export market in the next decades. Exports are Japan's economic future since the country has so few natural resources. Yet, as Dore (1986: 360) remarks, there remains in Japan a perception that 'some deeply-rooted deficiency in the capacity for originality is the main problem to be overcome before Japan can make its mark as a leader in basic science'. Employers are increasingly seeing *kikokushijo* as examples of just this sort of 'inventive' worker owing to their experience overseas, and hence they are actively hiring them (see Shūshoku Jōhō, 1989: 16–19).[2]

For women who have been overseas, the new opportunities in the labour market may be particularly marked. The demographic swing which will affect high schools in the early 1990s will affect employers to the same degree—a drop of 20 per cent—only five to seven years later. In this context, talented women who until now have been largely ignored by big companies and central and local government will be perceived as a more valuable asset. It is also significant that the greater proportion of *kikokushijo* with long experience overseas are girls; and amongst *kikokushijo*, girls are more likely to have had contact with the local cultures and languages in which they lived. Such *kikokushijo*, therefore, may find themselves incorporated into the new international élite as the value of their overseas experience transcends the 'traditional' discrimination against their gender in the public sphere.

The important point, of course, about the positive image of *kikokushijo* is that many do not possess the 'international' attributes that have been ascribed to them by the rhetoric of *kokusaika*. Very few of the 10,000 *kikokushijo* who return to Japan each year are genuinely fluent in foreign languages and only a small number have any understanding of the societies beyond the 'Japan towns' in which they lived. It is the image of *kikokushijo* as individualistic, creative, and broad-minded rather than the reality which gives them their 'symbolic value'. Hara (1986: 54–8), a teacher of *kikokushijo* at ICU Senior High School who has long campaigned for better treatment for these children, includes among their individual strengths: active participation in class, frankness (*sotchoku*), individualism, creativity, ability to express themselves, willingness to help those who are weaker than themselves, leadership qualities, and a broad general vision of the world and Japan. There is no doubt that some *kikokushijo* possess some or even all of these qualities, but as we have seen it is unrealistic to ascribe them to all children who have been overseas. The children as real individuals still tend to remain peripheral to the debate about them.

The result of being perceived as having these attributes, however, has been of great social benefit to *kikokushijo* as they have become Japan's new international élite. As Kawabata (1986: 22) says, education policy for *kikokushijo* has changed in direction in recent years, from concentrating on readapting them to mainstream culture to developing their international qualities. Noda (1986: 239–40) shows how this change has been paralleled in the research on *kikokushijo* from projects in the 1970s, which emphasized a need for readaptation, to work in the 1980s which examined their broader social significance. The process by which this change of direction has been achieved illustrates how a minority group, with access to considerable power, can manipulate its own social status. It has meant the perpetuation of the class status of the *kikokushijo* family, but, contrary to the ideal of a genuine educational meritocracy, this status has been ascribed to *kikokushijo* through the fact that their fathers' work took them overseas rather than through their own educational ability. Their 'value' to society in general has been given more importance than their individual educational achievements; their personalities, their experience, and the way they are perceived are seen as more significant than their academic ability. They are being groomed as leaders.

The schools which were set up to help *kikokushijo* now realize that there are great advantages to having such children enrolled. Indeed, for many of the private schools having *kikokushijo* students may be a financial lifeline. Such schools increasingly find themselves under financial threat as the demographic swing dramatically reduces their potential intake (James and Benjamin, 1988: 56). Being able to offer an 'international' education alongside 'international' children may be the way for such institutions to survive. It is partly for this reason that the number of schools which take *kikokushijo* has mushroomed in recent years. Similarly, competition for places for non-*kikokushijo* has become increasingly fierce. Yet it is important to recognize that this 'international' education has to be founded in Japaneseness to be acceptable to mainstream Japanese society. Children who go to the international schools in Japan do not receive the same status as those who go to the *ukeirekō*.

The products of the schools for *kikokushijo* are increasingly being seen as a new social élite who will be able to take Japan into the international world of the twenty-first century. The death of the Shōwa emperor and the start of the new Imperial era, Heisei, has reinforced the idea in Japan that a new period of creativity and individuality is now beginning (Sakaiya, *JTW*, 11 March 1989). The media, which have long campaigned for better treatment for *kikokushijo*, have increasingly propagated a view of these children as cultural ambassadors (*bunka taishi*) with valuable life experience (*kichōna seikatsu taiken*) (Fujiwara, *YS*, 12 June 1984).

The debate on *kikokushijo* education is, moreover, kept alive by the commercial educational interests which have grown up in its wake. As we saw in Chapter 2, a whole industry—advice centres, research institutes, 'adaptation' schools, overseas textbook publishing houses—has sprung up in the past fifteen years which, while now downplaying the 'problems' of these children, emphasizes the fact that *kikokushijo* have 'international' qualities but that these are only of use in Japan if they are founded in 'Japaneseness'. It is this 'Japaneseness' which the 'industry' aims to provide.[3] While some parents of *kaigaishijo* and *kikokushijo* may privately question the need for this 'extra' education, few are prepared to take the risk of ignoring such provision. At the same time, other commercial interests have sprung up to capitalize on those parents who have recognized the benefits of investing in an 'international education' for their children. Such companies provide help in setting children up in overseas schools and universities and are keen to maintain the current level of interest in the whole subject of *kikokushijo*.[4]

So far the complaints against the special treatment for *kikokushijo* have been muted. The fear that it may lead to other groups being given special treatment in Japan—and thereby undermining the public perception of the equality of the educational system—is countered by the argument that other groups, such as handicapped people, do not have the skills to pass on to their peers, and Japanese society in general, which the *kikokushijo* possess (Greenlees, *TES*, 20 May 1988; Kinoshita *et al.*, 1985: 6–7). The change in the status of *kikokushijo* does not therefore necessarily herald equal changes in the status of other groups in Japan. Indeed, it might be the case that in some of the more conservative sections of the establishment, such as Monbushō, the special treatment given to *kikokushijo* is simply a sop to the demands of those idealists who want to see the complete opening up of Japan to the outside world. Monbushō can point towards its heavy investment in education for overseas and returnee children as a sign of a genuine commitment to internationalizing and relaxing the educational system, though in fact it affects only a very small number of Japanese children. This may explain why central government has invested so much in the programmes of *kikokushijo* education. At the same time, it might be argued that the leaders of big business now feel that they can draw on *kikokushijo*—and the non-*kikokushijo* peers with whom they are educated—to form an élite workforce since they are perceived to have among their western qualities the creativity which Japanese business is now seeking. Meanwhile, the rest of the nation's youth continues to be educated in the same system that produced the conformist workforce which brought about Japan's economic growth in the post-war period.

The government can, at the same time, show that it is encouraging 'internationalization' by providing better opportunities for children who have had experience overseas and also appease those on the right who insist on the importance of Japaneseness. It has found a system whereby it believes the 'international qualities' of the *kikokushijo* can be both Japanized and maintained. Once again, as we have seen throughout Japanese history, the ambivalent relationship with the outside world is resolved by the process of incorporating—adopting and adapting—foreign elements in order to strengthen the country as a whole. Japanese society has therefore attempted to create a new type of 'Japanese internationalist' who will be able to carry on a dialogue with the outside world while maintaining his 'Japaneseness'. The result of a large number of interest groups—central government, educational reformers, a group of powerful parents, the media, private schools, commercial educational interests—coming together for different reasons but with a single focus, combined with powerful demands from outside for Japan's internationalization, has been the emergence of a new class of Japanese schoolchildren.

Notes

Chapter 1

1. Throughout this book, whenever I write the words 'west' and 'western' I do so without a capital 'W'. This is because in most cases where the words are used in the Japanese literature in the context of *kikokushijo*, they imply that the west is a homogeneous whole which shares the same values and perceptions. I am keen to avoid presenting this idea of a homogeneous western culture in opposition to a homogeneous Japanese one.

Chapter 2

1. Fig. 1 shows the cumulative increase in the number of Japanese 'prolonged' expatriates over 16 years, while Fig. 2 shows the amount of overseas investment each year.
2. Minoura (1984: 15), in her study of the Japanese expatriate community in Los Angeles, has been able to show very clearly how the growth curves of Japanese imports into the United States and American exports to Japan parallel the growth in numbers of Japanese children in the Los Angeles area.
3. In their survey, Takahagi *et al.* (1982: 78) found that 81% per cent of the men were in their 40s as were 68% of the women, with 29% of the women in their 30s.
4. The survey by Takahagi *et al.* (1982: 78) showed almost exactly the same result for men, and a slightly higher percentage—75%—for women, of whom 41% had been to 2-year junior colleges.
5. The closest model to the Japanese system of education overseas is probably that of South Korea which, as of 1980, had 19 full-time schools overseas (11 in Japan) and 100 Saturday schools (53 in the USA) with no foreign children in either type. The similarity between Japan and South Korea is perhaps not surprising: a director of the Kaigai Shijo Kyōiku Shinkō Zaidan records a visit paid to his office by an official from the Korean Ministry of Education and reflects that Japan is now in a position to pass on its knowledge in such affairs to other countries (Mizuno, 1982: 169–70).

   It should be pointed out how Britain fits into this comparative account of overseas education. Britain has long had a tradition of leaving children in boarding-schools while both parents went overseas, and it is perhaps for that reason that overseas education is comparatively so undeveloped. Although there are 112 Overseas Army schools with 28,500 children, no other schools receive any government finance and this probably accounts for the fact that no official statistics are kept (Monbushō, 1988: 130). A direct comparison between Japan and Britain might lead the reader to ask why more Japanese children are not placed in boarding-schools while their parents go overseas. In this broader perspective, however, the more appropriate question might be to ask why Britain has not developed more schools overseas, as have other developed industrial powers.

6. An example of such a change is to by-pass the problem of astronomical constellations being different to those shown in Japanese textbooks (see Akahori, 1982).

7. Ōhori (1982), a teacher sent from Japan to the Japanese school in Milan, argues strongly that Japanese teachers employed locally need to be allowed to have a bigger say in the administrative and financial running of *Nihonjingakkō*. This tension between locally employed Japanese and those sent directly from Japan extends to many areas of Japanese overseas work, including overseas embassies and company branches.

8. As Martin McLean (1985: 330, 332, 337) points out, Japanese supplementary schools are not unusual in these respects, and they share many characteristics with, for example, Greek Cypriot and some Indian schools in Britain.

9. Willis (1983: 24) comments on a similar pattern for western families overseas.

10. Only about a quarter of the parents of students at Rikkyō lived in the U.K. while the majority lived in Europe and Africa; and it is not uncommon to find 3-generation families with the grandparents living in Japan, the parents in Africa, for example, and the children in England.

11. In 1987 there were 104 departments in 43 different national universities, 26 departments in 11 public universities, and an unspecified number of departments in about 70 private universities offering special entrance to *kikokushijo* (Monbushō, 1988: 83–7). Altogether, about 25% of Japan's 488 universities were part of the system.

12. Since 1985, financial support has dropped slightly (Monbushō, 1988: 26). This may partly be explained by the levelling off in the number of children going overseas and returning to Japan and the increased strength of the yen abroad.

13. Among Japanese in the United States who have written theses on the subject are Furuhashi (1984), Kunieda (1983), Minoura (1979), Muro (1987), Okamura (1981), Sakakibara (1984), and Uehara (1986). Farkas (1983) is an American brought up in Japan.

14. The three seminars were: (i) *Shōwa 59 Nendo Kikokushijo Kyōiku Kenkyū Kyōgikai*, held in Tokyo on 18 and 19 June 1984, under the sponsorship of Monbushō; (ii) *Dai Rokkai Shōwa 59 Nendo Kokusai*

Kyōiku Kenshūkai, held in Nagoya from 8 to 10 November 1985, under the private schools' sponsorship of the Shigaku Kenshū Fukushikai and the Nihon Shigaku Kyōiku Kenkyūjo; and (iii) *Ibunkakan Kyōiku Gakkai Dai Rokkai Taikai*, held in Fukuoka on 11 and 12 May 1985.

Chapter 3

1. I am grateful to Marguerite Wells for pointing out that Asai Satoru means 'shallow enlightenment' in Japanese.
2. A Nomura Research Institute report in 1978 listed nearly 700 titles as examples of this genre (Mouer and Sugimoto, 1986: 87). Certainly, in many bookshops throughout Japan there is a special section for *Nihonjinron*.
3. Nakane is herself a *kikokushijo*. She spent her teens in Peking, from the end of elementary school until the fourth year of high school (Hata and Smith, 1983: 370). She was later a research student and lecturer at London University and became the first woman professor at Tokyo University. Apart from her studies on Japan, she is well known for her anthropological fieldwork in India and Nepal.
4. This insult originates from the 16th cent. when the first westerners came to Japan. Their use of milk-based products made them appear very smelly to the Japanese who, until very recently, generally eschewed milk and butter in their diet.
5. In a sense, of course, this is simply a rephrasing of Ruth Benedict's (1946) classic thesis on the opposition between shame and guilt cultures.
6. Agnes Niyekawa (1985) disagrees with Minoura but only to propose that experiences at an earlier age can have a lasting effect on personality. In no way does she question Minoura's basic assumption concerning the relationship between culture and personality.
7. It would be a mistake to infer that this theory has not also been propounded by linguists in other societies (see Baetens Beardsmore, 1982: 90–1).
8. Lest Tsunoda's theories be considered too extreme to be taken seriously in Japan, I must say that I once heard them being taught, uncritically, to a class of returnees, as part of a demonstration lesson in Japanese language, at a conference on 'education for international understanding'.

Chapter 4

1. Much of the material for this account of the Japanese education system is drawn from 12 months' first-hand experience as a peripatetic teacher in 9 junior high schools in Yamaguchi prefecture in 1981/2.
2. The average salary of a university graduate in a firm with over 1,000

employees is 26% higher than that of a graduate in a firm with under 100 employees (James and Benjamin, 1988: 79). The overall difference, regardless of educational level, between employees in the biggest and the smallest firms is 58% (1988: 80).

3. For a detailed anthropological account of how a Japanese company operates, see Rodney Clark (1979). Ronald Dore (1973) has compared Japanese and British factories to show the differences in industrial relations in each country.

4. The expression *my homeism* is sometimes used to refer derogatorily to a man who is thought to pay too much attention to his family life (Smith, 1985: 120–2). The connotations of this word are interesting: both the use of English to express selfishness, especially the word *my* which is also found in such expressions as *my car* and *my pace* (doing things at one's own pace); and also the common suggestion that ego-centred activity has a negative connotation in Japan.

5. One informant suggested that not only did graduates of physical education make popular recruits, but so also did those who had been active in sports clubs during their university careers. As a result, one sometimes hears the expressions '*A saiyō*' and '*B saiyō*' referring respectively to those employed on the basis of 'athletic' ability or 'brains'.

6. There are a number of ways of demonstrating the different roles of men and women in Japan and how these reflect social expectations. For example, girls are not expected by their parents to go so far as boys in the educational system. According to a 1982 survey by the Prime Minister's Office, although 45% of parents wanted their sons to receive a university education, only 19% had the same aspirations for their daughters. In the employment system, only 1% of managerial positions are filled by women, who also in 1984 constituted only 11% of doctors and dentists, 3% of judges and lawyers, and less than 2% of Members of Parliament. The pressure in Japan for women to marry means that while women tend to marry slightly later than their peers in other industrially advanced countries, the proportion of women unmarried by the age of 30 tends to be significantly lower. Explanations for the position of women in Japan range from the Confucian belief in their inherent inferiority, to a strong sense that male and female roles should be separated—expressed in the pre-war maxim *ryōsai kenbo* ('a good wife and wise mother') as the ideal woman, and the incompatibility of raising a family and giving complete loyalty to the company (Foreign Press Center, 1986: 12, 20–2, 28–9).

7. Johan Galtung, in the 1971 OECD survey of Japan, used the term 'educational degreeocracy' (OECD, 1971: 138–42) to emphasize that status is not determined by an individual's total educational achieve-

ment, but by success at one particular point (age 18) in the educational system.

8. Fig. 10 does not show this proportion of children in kindergarten because it only includes pre-school institutions of the category *yōchien* which are administered and licensed by Monbushō, while the remainder go to *hoikuen* which come under the control of the Ministry of Health and Welfare. According to Hendry (1986: 61), however, 'the purpose of early childhood education is considered to be the same in both types of institution'. For a good overview of the Japanese preschool system, see Boocock (1989).

9. It is not easy to give an accurate figure here, as senior high schools prefer not to take account of the *juku* and *yobikō* systems, and when students move from a *yobikō* to a university, the high school from which they graduated a year, or even more, earlier will tend to take the credit for their success. According to James and Benjamin (1988: 37), about 40% of new entrants to good universities each year have spent 1 to 3 years as *rōnin*. In particularly competitive fields, such as dentistry, the figure may be as high as 60%.

10. Moeran (1985: 98) points out that 'baddies' in television dramas set in the feudal period (*jidaigeki*) are often *rōnin*.

11. In some areas, however, this authority is vigorously contested by Nikkyōso, the largest Japanese teachers' union, perhaps the most powerful union in Japan (see Duke, 1973; Thurston, 1973).

12. Although technically illegal, physical punishment is still relatively common in Japanese schools as a means of control. A newspaper report in 1984 read *Gakkō Taibatsu Hadomenashi: Shō, Chū, Kō de 97% Taiken* ('No Brake on Physical Punishment in Schools: 97% of Schools Have Instances') (*AS*, 30 May 1984), the most common methods being hitting with a flat hand (40.3%); with knuckles/fist (20.1%); with a bamboo stave (18.1%); and forcing students to kneel on the floor in the upright posture (*seiza*) for a long period (12.5%). The most common areas of the body to receive punishment were apparently the face, including ears (44.2%); head (40.1%); and legs (7.5%). Between 1985 and 1988, 5 students died from assaults by teachers, and in 1986, 189 teachers were sacked for excessive violence and a further 900 received official warnings (Greenlees, *TES*, 28 October 1988).

13. It is important to point out that the idea of perfecting a form is central to all Japanese traditional arts from judo to flower arranging. It has a positive connotation, not the negative one often reflected in western phrases such as 'copycat'.

14. The book sold 5 million copies through more than 50 print-runs in 16 months. It has been translated into English as *Totto-chan: The little girl at the window*.

Chapter 5

1. Fujiyama Gakuen is a pseudonym, which I use interchangeably with its shortened form, Fujiyama. The use of a pseudonym is partly because it is anthropological convention with studies of literate societies, but also because I want to emphasize that I am more interested in the general significance of this type of school than in the particular details of a single institution. For the same reasons, the teachers have also all been given pseudonyms.

2. The governors' fears did not totally register with the teaching staff, some of whom pointed out that local and central government, in recognition of the problem of keeping up with public demand for education, has been very supportive of private education. According to James and Benjamin (1988: 65–7), there has been a policy to provide the private-school sector with access to very favourable loans. Similarly, there has been considerable local and central government subsidization of private education. At Fujiyama the subsidy in 1985 from the Ibaraki prefectural government ran to ¥100,000 a year for each junior-high-school student and ¥180,000 a year for each senior-high-school student: in other words, local government paid about 25% and 50% respectively of the fees of commuting junior- and senior-high-school students, and 15% and 25% respectively of the fees of boarding junior- and senior-high-school students.

3. In recent years, Monbushō has instructed schools in Japan to raise the *hinomaru* flag at school entrance and graduation ceremonies. Some, however, particularly on the left wing, argue that the use of the *hinomaru* (a red circle on a white background) is only convention and that it is not designated as Japan's national flag in the post-war constitution.

4. Overall, however, there have been dramatic salary increases in the private sector, and whereas in the 1970s private-school teachers earned less than their counterparts in state schools, by 1980 the situation was reversed (James and Benjamin, 1988: 172).

5. Annual fees at Fujiyama in 1984/5 were ¥390,000 (plus a ¥600,000 entrance fee) for commuting students and ¥690,000 (plus a ¥820,000 entrance fee) for boarding students.

6. Chamberlain (1895: 302), writing at the end of the 19th cent., commented amusingly on the notion that there was no reduction in price for large orders since 'If . . . Messrs. Smith and Co., instead of ordering only one bale of silk, order a hundred, that shows they are badly in want of it, and must be able to pay a good price.'

7. Scholarships are rare in Japan. Indeed, the Japanese word for scholarship—*shōgakukin*—can have a pejorative meaning, implying that the recipient is from a poor background and unable to afford the normal fees. It perhaps has something of the sense of 'bursary'. The

English word 'scholarship' is sometimes used in Japanese in a rather more positive sense. Fujiyama had a fund raised by the Parent–Teacher Association (*fubokai shusai*) which was used to support children who had already entered the school but subsequently had financial problems—for example on the death of a parent.

8. In 1986, junior-high-school entrants in Japan (12-year-olds) numbered 2,050,000. The equivalent figure in 1994 will be 1,510,000.

9. According to Sakakibara (1988: 7), 50% per cent of the 3,700 Tōdai entrants each year come from just 37 schools and the rest from only 470 of Japan's 5,400 senior high schools. A school which can place a student in Tōdai is, therefore, by this criterion automatically in the top 10% of Japanese senior high schools.

10. In most Japanese schools teachers are required to give a list of where they expect to be on each day of the school vacation. In most schools also, they need to obtain permission (from the local board of education in the case of state schools) if they wish to go abroad, even for a holiday. Many teachers come to school almost every day during the vacation to supervise club activities and few of them take more than a few days away from home as a holiday. Students also are required to do a great deal of homework during the summer vacation and have little opportunity for an extended holiday away.

11. This is a distinction which is sometimes generalized to one between Japanese 'particularistic' ethics (which change depending on the situation) and western 'universalistic' ethics (which remain absolute in all contexts).

12. Under this system villages were divided into groups of 5 households and a misdemeanour by any one member of any one household could lead to the punishment of all the members of all the households in the group.

13. In order to protect the anonymity of individuals in the school, I have decided not to include references to their work. For a full exposition of the philosophy of the Seito Seikatsu Shidō Kenkyūkai, see Zenseiken Jōniniinkai (1975).

14. Yamamura (1986: 35) points out that while there has traditionally been a view of children as essentially good, some writers, such as Kaibara Ekken, the author of *Onna Daigaku* ('The Greater Learning for Women') in the Tokugawa period, viewed human nature as essentially evil.

15. Such superficial westernization has a tradition among the élite in Japan at least as far back as the Meiji period when those in important positions took to wearing western clothes and learning ballroom dances in the famous *Rokumeikan* (Deer Hall Pavilion) built by Meiji leaders to impress western visitors (Barr, 1965).

16. The principal sometimes explained this diligence as due in part to the

fact that the Japanese are kept busy preparing for the changes brought about by the country's four distinct climatic seasons, while for those who live in tropical climes there is no need to prepare for seasonal changes and, as a result, they end up being naturally lazy. This is a not uncommon theory in Japan.

17. The only clear physical distinction I could find was that a number of *kikokushijo* who had been in the west wore orthodontic braces on their teeth, compared to very few among their non-*kikokushijo* peers. It has been stated that while 60% of children in the United States start orthodontic treatment in their early teens, only 10% of Japanese children do so (Campbell, *JTW*, 21 June 1986). In Japan, slightly protruding, overlapping teeth, known as *yaeba*, are thought to be rather attractive, especially in girls, and are a common feature of pop idols.

18. Barnlund (1975) has shown exactly how American and Japanese touching patterns differ. Holding hands among members of the same sex in Japan has few of the homosexual connotations it has in some western countries.

19. Whiting (1984) offers a particularly graphic description of the differences between playing baseball in Japan and in America, differences which pertain to other sports as well.

Chapter 6

1. Takagi (1977: 44), who gave the explanation cited earlier as to why national schools were chosen for *kikokushijo*, adds that private schools were also considered appropriate because they were much freer than most state schools in deciding their own system of management and were more independent of local demands.

2. I should make clear that my purpose here is not to denigrate the work of a fellow researcher. Indeed, the method used did generate a large amount of information in a very short time, and it is perhaps not surprising that a psychiatrist should search for the pathological rather than the normal. Moreover, the questionnaire was largely based on that of the research student's supervisor's general theory about *kikokushijo*, and the hierarchical nature of Japanese university departments makes it extremely difficult for students to take a line that differs much from that of their teachers. It is the underlying assumptions of the research, however, which make it such an interesting case study.

3. It must be stressed that such pseudo-objectivity is far from uncommon outside Japan too. Gould (1984) gives numerous examples from western research that contain the same problems. In particular, he points out the basic flaw inherent in factor analysis, an approach that is especially popular in profiling *kikokushijo*: although it is possible to

cross-reference any two variables the results do not necessarily pertain to reality but are merely a reflection of the researchers' original preconceptions.

4. Inui and Sono's survey (1977: 138), which appears to be looking for *kikokushijo* language problems in support of their argument that more needs to be done for returnees, seems to show that only around 3% had severe problems in any area of Japanese language (i.e. reading, writing, speaking, or listening) and under 20% had mild disabilities.

5. There is also considerable evidence from other societies to contradict the idea proposed by Nomoto and Hatano (see Chapter 3) that bilingualism is necessarily debilitating. This argument seems to confuse education with intellect. Alison Elliot's (1981: 56) summary of comparative work on monolinguals and bilinguals tends towards the view that the latter do better 'on measures of cognitive flexibility, creativity or divergent thought'. In the case of bilinguals, therefore, the value ascribed to such measures—flexibility, creativity, and divergent thought—in the educational system may be as important as the individual child's intellectual and linguistic ability.

6. The only citations of the work of Takahagi *et al.* that I have come across are quoted approvingly in Murase (1984: 3), and disapprovingly in Saitō (1986: 255) who considers the work rendered useless by the fact that it contains no practical advice for *kikokushijo*.

7. The idea that only by stepping outside one's culture can one really understand it is quite common in anthropological literature. As Anthony Cohen (1985: 69) says: 'People become aware of their culture when they stand at its boundaries: when they encounter other cultures, or when they become aware of other ways of doing things, or merely contradictions to their own culture.'

8. A similar survey in 1986 produced the same findings (see *JTW*, 21 March 1987).

9. The children of missionaries, in particular, have been, and continue to be, extensively studied: in January 1987 there was a Second International Conference on Missionary Kids (MKs) held at Quito in Ecuador. This was an enormous event with around 100 seminars, papers, and panel discussions ranging from 'Terrorism and MK Schools' to 'College Entrance and Career Development for MKs'.

10. Even earlier sources for Oberg's medical paradigm, however, might be Durkheim's (1897) classic study of suicide which related excessive social mobility to an increase in mental illness, or Park's (1928) work on the 'marginal man' caught between two cultures. The concept of the expatriate suffering from 'jungle fever' has doubtless been around even longer.

11. A comprehensive overview by Kawabata *et al.* (1986: 364–74) of

research on *kikokushijo* does not include a single reference to returnees in other societies than Japan among its 191 citations.

12. It is significant also that none of the researchers in Japan consider *kikokushijo* in the category of third culture kids—Useem's 'mobile world élite'—which is such a popular concept in other societies. The only teachers who discuss *kikokushijo* in such terms are those in international schools in Japan (see Enloe and Lewin, 1984). Researchers in Japan seem keen to maintain the idea of classlessness when discussing *kikokushijo*.

   There is also in the literature on overseas sojourners in the west the idea that complete immersion in the overseas culture leads to more successful adaptation on return home (e.g. Adler, 1981). In contrast, all the work in Japan suggests that the less contact individuals have with overseas cultures, the smoother their adaptation will be on their return home (e.g. Kobayashi, 1982*b*: 99; Tsukamoto, 1987). This provides a good rationale for Japanese parents overseas to keep themselves in tight-knit Japanese communities.

13. Nash and Shaw's (1963) analysis of Japanese immigrants in Cuba, with another invocation of three personality types—the 'autonomous', the 'traditional', and the 'transitional'—shows remarkable similarities to the work of Bennet, Passin, and McKnight. It is interesting that, apart from a reference in Hoshino's (1982) overview of the concept of 'culture shock' in his essay for *Gendai no Esprit*, there appears to be no reference anywhere in the Japanese literature to the work of Bennett, Passin, and McKnight.

14. It would, for example, be a mistake to think that the attitude of Japanese teachers to *kikokushijo* is unique, as I discovered through interviewing returnees to the British educational system and their parents. Most of the British children said that at least part of their overseas experience was denied by British teachers. One boy who had just returned from an international school in the Philippines was asked sarcastically by his teacher, when he was unable to do a mathematical problem, whether he had just returned from 'Bongo-Bongo Land'. Similarly, peers would tease children who had been overseas, giving them a nickname that associated them with the experience, such as 'Froggy' for a boy who had lived three years in France. At a potentially more serious level, Woods (1986: 16–17) describes how in England children whom teachers classify as trouble-makers are sometimes put in a separate class for 'preferential treatment'.

15. In the ensuing uproar, Nakasone defended his assertion that there were no minority groups in Japan by claiming that his own bushy eyebrows (the Ainu are thought by the Japanese to be particularly hirsute) showed that even he had Ainu blood in him (*JTW*, 13 December 1986). Not surprisingly, Ainu rights leaders were doubly indignant!

16. Despite central government redistribution through the tax system, there remain significant regional educational differences in Japan at the post-compulsory level (see James and Benjamin, 1988: 149–65). In rural farming and fishing communities there is considerably less pressure to succeed in the educational system than in the urban centres.

17. Moreover, contrary to the general image of overseas experience projected by White (1980, 1988) and Sussman (*JTW*, 12 October 1985), Ishida's (1983: 74) survey of fifty overseas employees in 1982 found that 84% felt that the experience of working overseas was beneficial to their future careers. Similarly, the adjective most commonly used in essays written by 150 fathers on their overseas experience—collected by the Kaigai Shijo Kyōiku Shinkō Zaidan (1983)—were 'precious' (*kichō-na*), 'blessed' (*megumareta*), and 'worthwhile' (*yūigi-na*). These findings provide an interesting comparison with a mere 10% of young employees of large Japanese firms who were keen to accept overseas postings—this low figure being due to problems they anticipated on their return to Japan (Hulme, *DY*, 30 September 1984).

There is evidence to suggest that overseas experience may be a boon, particularly in the case of career women. Six out of the ten successful career women in Lebra's (1981) survey were returnees. Also, in certain areas of employment such as the media, returnees may be considered especially attractive. According to one former executive, NHK (Japan's foremost broadcasting station) actively recruits *kikokushijo*, believing not only that there are benefits from their overseas experience but also that the problems they have faced and overcome on their return to Japan make them more complete individuals than those who have passed through the normal educational system (Yamashita, 1988).

A manual for employees prepared for the Bank of Tokyo personnel department by the head of its educational advice section—written in the form of hypothetical questions and answers—confirms the view that it can be advantageous (*yūri*) to be a *kikokushijo* when looking for employment. The reasons given relate, in part, to the changing economic situation—the internationalization of Japanese companies—but also to the individual qualities of the *kikokushijo*—their positiveness (*sekkyokusei*), independence (*jishusei*), rational way of thinking (*gōrisei*), and cheerfulness (*meirōsei*). Indeed, according to the manual, not only do *kikokushijo* have a high success rate when applying for jobs, but certain medium and small-sized companies have begun positively to search them out as recruits (Sōgabe, 1989: 208–9).

18. In 1988 Monbushō established a new year-long council of 14 educationalists and other intellectuals specifically to study the problems of *kaigaishijo* and *kikokushijo*. The council was detailed to

examine a number of specific issues: whether overseas Japanese senior-high-school children should be encouraged to attend local schools or whether special Japanese schools should be provided for them; whether, if special schools are provided, the government should subsidize them since, constitutionally, they are outside the compulsory-education sector; how the existing overseas Japanese schools should be made more international; and what could be done to help *kikokushijo* on their return to Japan (*JTW*, 21 May 1988).

Chapter 7

1. According to Storry (1983: 66), 'Apart from a number of new words that were incorporated in the Japanese language, the only important permanent legacies of the Portuguese were the musket—and tobacco.' To which list should be added what Morris (1980: 202) describes as 'Crucifixion, that precious import from the west', a common death for leaders of uprisings throughout the Tokugawa (1603–1868) period.

2. The Japanese learnt in these academies proved, when in later years the interpreters met Japanese diplomatic parties, to be as useless as the Dutch manfully learnt by the Japanese scholars who found their way, or were ordered, to Dejima, proved when the first Americans arrived in Japan.

3. Taid O'Conroy (1936: 35–6), in Japan during this period, even suggested that western ideas were being reinvented, recounting the case of a Japanese given an award by the War Ministry for inventing the aeroplane, and citing the case of another who sued the Ford Motor Company for stealing his invention of the motor car. Even in this climate, though, there remained pro-western groups in Japan, such as the Institute of Pacific Relations, a group of intellectuals whose distinguishing features were their élite status and their ability to speak English and communicate with western leaders (see Wilson, 1987).

4. In a 1978 Unesco survey, only 9 out of 213 countries (4.2%) were like Japan in having a school year which began in April, whereas 98 countries (46%) had a school year starting in September (Nihon Zaigai Kigyō Kyōkai, 1981: 24).

Chapter 8

1. It should be pointed out, however, that while parents trying to help their children often exaggerated their problems this sometimes only created more problems. Similarly, researchers could to some extent be blamed for having exacerbated rather than explored the problems of *kikokushijo*, thus creating what Murase (1980: 53) described as a self-fulfilling prophecy (*yogen ga tekichū suru yō ni*). Some *kiko-kushijo* became lazy and defeatist and blamed their problems on the fact that they had lived overseas. One girl at Fujiyama Gakuen who

had failed her university entrance examinations the first time round insisted that this was because she was a returnee and had not been able to readjust to Japanese society. Her whole experience overseas, however, had been at the Japanese school in Jakarta and she had had no local Indonesian friends nor had she learnt anything of the language. Yet she felt that she had picked up the local culture while she was travelling on the buses and that this had greatly affected her. One of her teachers told me that he had found her a rather lazy student and he ascribed her failure to this rather than to her overseas experience.

2. See also the 1984 report by the Keizai Dōyūkai (Japan Committee for Economic Development) entitled *Sōzōsei, Tayōsei, Kokusaisei o Motomeru* ('In Pursuit of Creativity, Diversity and Internationality') in Foreign Press Center (ed.), 1985: 35–42, esp. 36–7.

3. A cram school (*juku*) for *kaigaishijo* was set up in 1986 in New York to follow a school already established in Hong Kong. The latest idea is a home-linked fax service to help *kaigaishijo* keep up with their Japanese homework.

4. The number of children going overseas on educational exchange programmes for more than 3 months while at senior high school—normally considered the riskiest time, in educational terms, to be outside Japan—has risen dramatically in recent years to around 4,000 children in 1988, and annual increases of between 30 and 40% are expected for the next few years. A council was set up in 1989 to suggest measures to introduce greater flexibility into the Japanese school system for the benefit of these returning students (*JTW*, 1 September 1989).

There are also a number of agencies which specialize in helping students enrol in overseas (particularly European and North American) institutions of higher education. Recruit International, moreover, provides counselling and financial services for overseas students and will lend them up to £20,000 to pay for overseas education and living expenses (Greenless, *TES*, 15 July 1988). Similarly, in recent years, there has been the sudden appearance in Japan of new campuses of American universities, such as Temple University in Tokyo. Although only a few have so far been established, their success has led to a further 134 foreign universities demonstrating interest in the idea (*JTW*, 31 December 1988), despite the fact that Monbushō does not recognize the degrees awarded by such establishments. The problem of lack of accreditation also applies to those Japanese colleges (such as Gyōsei in Reading, England) established overseas. Nevertheless, in all cases as far as the individual student is concerned an 'international' education is perceived to be a sound investment.

Glossary

Sources for the glossary include: *Kenkyusha's New Japanese–English Dictionary* (1982); *Kodansha Encyclopaedia of Japan* (1983); and Hunter, *Concise Dictionary of Modern Japanese History* (1984).

The pronunciation of Japanese vowels is similar to Italian vowels. Vowels are given double length when modified by a macron (e.g. Ō, ō, ū). Consonants are pronounced similarly to English. Each element of a double consonant (e.g. pp, kk) should be treated separately—by a slight pause after the first consonant and the release of a small explosion of breath with the final consonant. Words are pronounced in an even fashion with little variance in pitch. G is hard (For more detail, see Seward, 1983: 30–5.)

Ainu: early inhabitants of the Japanese islands, gradually pushed back to the northernmost island of Hokkaidō where their current numbers are estimated at around 25,000. Very few are of pure Ainu blood.

bakufu: 'military government', the administration headed by the shōgun.

burakumin: 'hamlet people', euphemistic term used in most western-language literature to describe members of Japan's outcaste class who were officially distinguished by their low-status occupations until 1870.

bushidō: the feudal-military Japanese code of behaviour, the ethical system of the *samurai*.

Chūgoku kikoku koji shijo: children of the *Chūgoku zairyū koji*.

Chūgoku zairyū koji: Japanese left as children in China by their parents fleeing from the advancing Russian army at the end of the Second World War.

daimyō: feudal lord in direct vassalage to the shōgun.

Edo period: period between 1603 and 1868 when the centre of national power was based in Edo (present-day Tokyo) under the Tokugawa *bakufu*. Also known as the Tokugawa period.

Fujiyamasei: students of Fujiyama school.

futekiō byō: literally, 'non-adaptation sickness'. Often used in the context of *kikokushijo*.

futsū no jidō: 'normal children'. Sometimes used in opposition to *kikokushijo*.

fuzoku gakkō: schools attached to the national universities in Japan.

gaikokujin (or *gaijin*): generic word for foreigners, but normally referring to westerners.

gakkō: public or private school(s).

gakuen: literally 'academic campus', frequently denoting a private school.

genchikō: term for all non-Japanese schools outside Japan.

gōgaku: 'village schools', educational institutions set up during the Edo period which later became incorporated into the state education system in the Meiji period. Divided into two types, *hankō* and *terakoya*.

gonin gumi: a five-family mutual responsibility unit of local political organization during the Edo period.

haiku: a verse form consisting of three metrical units of five, seven, and five syllables respectively.

han: a 'group' or 'corps' used in both a military and an educational context.

hankō: domain schools set up in the Edo period under the control of domainal authorities for the education of domainal retainers and their children.

heimin: 'commoners', term given to all those below nobility and warriors following the abolition of the feudal class system in 1869 during the Meiji restoration. Those who had previously been considered outcastes were known as *shinheimin* (new commoners).

Heisei period: name given to the new Imperial era beginning with the accession to the throne of Emperor Akihito in 1989.

hinin: 'non person', term previously used to designate sections of Japan's outcastes.

hoshūkō: overseas Japanese supplementary schools.

hyōryūmin: castaways in the Tokugawa period who were unable to return to Japan because of the policy of seclusion.

ICU: International Christian University, a private Protestant university established in Tokyo in 1953.

ippansei: 'regular students', term frequently used in opposition to *kikokushijo*.

Jōchi: also known as Sophia University, a private Catholic university established in Tokyo in 1913.

juku: tutoring or cram school(s).

Kaigai Shijo Kyōiku Shinkō Zaidan: known in English as Japan Overseas Educational Services, set up in 1971 to act as an intermediary between groups of returnee parents and the Ministries of Education and Foreign Affairs. Now acts largely as a counselling service for overseas and returnee parents.

kaigaishijo: generic term for all overseas Japanese schoolchildren.

kakizome: symbolic first calligraphy of the New Year.

kakushu gakkō: 'miscellaneous' schools, including institutions for dress-making and gymnastics. All schools which are not accredited by Monbushō, including the foreign national and international schools, fall into this category.

kangeiko: mid-winter, generally early-morning, training exercises.

kanji: Chinese ideographs used in writing Japanese.

Kansai: 'West of the Barrier', the Kyoto-Osaka area.

Kantō: 'East of the Barrier', the Tokyo area.

keimōsho: popular accounts of serious research written for the enlightenment of the general public.

kendō: Japanese fencing.

kibei: Japanese-Americans who receive their education in Japan.

kikokushijo: Japanese returnee schoolchildren.

kikokushijo mondai: 'the returnee children problem', general term for the whole returnee children debate.

kindaika: modernization process.

kōhai: one's juniors in a school, club, or company.

kokunaiha: 'parochial faction', those who take a conservative line on the subject of internationalization in Japan.

kokunaisei: 'domestic students', sometimes used in opposition to *kikokushijo*.

Kokusai Jidō Bunko Kyōkai: organization founded in 1979 by a group of returnee mothers to help *kikokushijo* maintain their overseas language skills.

kokusaibu: international section of a school or company.

kokusaiha: 'international faction', those who take a liberal line on the subject of internationalization in Japan.

kokusaijin: an 'international person'.

kokusaika: internationalization process.

konketsuji: children with one Japanese and one non-Japanese parent.

kyōiku: education.

Meiji period: period between 1868 and 1912 when Japan was formally ruled by the Emperor Meiji.

META: organization set up in 1983 as a mutual support group for returnees.

Monbushō: Japanese Ministry of Education.

Nihon: Japan; also pronounced Nippon, especially in the pre-war period.

Nihongo: the Japanese language as taught to foreigners; it is normally distinguished from *kokugo* (the national language) which is taught to Japanese children.

Nihonjingakkō: full-time overseas Japanese schools.

Nihonjinron: 'theories of Japaneseness', genre of literature which examines what it means to be Japanese.

Nihonmachi: 'Japan towns', areas of towns outside Japan with a high concentration of Japanese inhabitants.

Nikkyōso: Japan's main teachers' union.

nisei: second-generation Japanese-Americans.

nyūgakushiki: school entrance ceremony held in April.

Okinawans: inhabitants of the chain of Ryūkyū islands to the south-west of the Japanese mainland, the largest of which is Okinawa, originally an independent kingdom.

oyatoi or *oyatoi gaikokujin*: foreign employees of the Meiji period.

Rangaku: 'Dutch studies', western learning in the Edo period through the study of Dutch books and limited contact with the few Dutch merchants who were trading at the island of Dejima in Nagasaki.

rōnin: 'masterless samurai', term used in the contemporary period to refer to high-school graduates who failed to enter a college and are preparing to retake the entrance examinations.

ryōsai kenbo: 'good wife, clever mother', traditional ideal role for women in pre-war Japan.

ryūgakusei: Japanese student studying abroad.

Ryūkyūgo: indigenous language of the people of Okinawa.

sakoku jidai: 'closed country period', the policy of seclusion of the Tokugawa *bakufu* from the mid-seventeenth century until the arrival of Commodore Perry's ships in 1854.

salaryman: term for Japanese white-collar workers in contrast to self-employed or manual blue-collar workers.

samurai: feudal retainer, warrior class of pre-modern Japan, particularly identified with the Tokugawa period.

senpai: one's seniors in a school, club, or company.

sensei: 'one who goes before', general term of respect towards seniors used to schoolteachers.

setsumeikai: 'explanation meetings', term used, for example, for meetings to explain to parents of prospective students the attractions of a particular school.

shingakkō: schools which concentrate almost entirely on helping their students to succeed in the university entrance examinations.

shōgun: abbreviation of *seii taishōgun* (barbarian-subduing great general), title awarded to the emperor's military deputy. From 1192, the holders of the title were often in effect the rulers of Japan. The title was held by members of the Tokugawa family from 1603 to 1868 when political power was officially restored to the emperor.

Shōwa period: period between 1926 and 1989 when Japan was formally ruled by the son of the Taishō emperor.

sōdan shitsu: name given to the counselling centres for *kikokushijo* and their parents.

suisen seido: 'recommendation system', system whereby certain universities award a quota to certain schools to recommend some of their students for direct entry to the university. The same system is also sometimes used by senior or junior high schools when recruiting students from junior or elementary schools.

Taishō period: period between 1912 and 1926 when Japan was formally ruled by the third son of the Meiji emperor.

tanka: Japanese verse of thirty-one syllables, consisting of five lines in the pattern 5–7–5–7–7.

tanshin funin: phenomenon of husbands who live away from home during the week because of their work. Also applies to those who go overseas for long periods and leave their families in Japan.

teijū nanmin: Japanese term for the Vietnamese 'boat people'.

tekiō: adaptation to a new environment.

tenkōsei: students who change school within Japan.

terakoya: temple schools, generic term for schools established for the education of the general populace in the Edo period.

Tōdai: Tokyo University.

tōkōkyohi(sho): 'school refusal syndrome', psychological problem ascribed to children who refuse to attend school.

tokubetsu waku: special quota for *kikokushijo* provided by Japanese universities. Also applies to the quotas offered in some senior high schools.

Tokugawa period: period between 1603 (when Tokugawa Ieyasu was awarded the title of shōgun) and 1868. Also known as the Edo period because the military government headed by the shōgun, known as the Tokugawa *bakufu*, was based in Edo (present-day Tokyo) while the Imperial family in Kyoto was virtually powerless.

ukeirekō: 'reception schools', generic term for schools which are part of the special educational provision for *kikokushijo*.

wakon kansai: Japanese spirit and Chinese technology, the ideal of using knowledge gained from China in accordance with Japan's native cultural traditions.

wakon yōsai: Japanese spirit and western knowledge, the ideal of adopting and applying western learning and knowledge to native Japanese cultural traditions.

yobikō: cram schools for *rōnin* preparing for university entrance examinations.

zainichi Kankokujin: Koreans resident in Japan, generally with Korean nationality.

References

ABEGGLEN, JAMES C., 1959. *The Japanese Factory: Aspects of its Social Organization* (Asia Publishing House, India).

ADLER, NANCY J., 1981. 'Re-Entry: Managing Cross-Cultural Transitions', *Group and Organization Studies*, 6/3, 341–56.

AKAHORI, KANJI, 1982. 'Kaigai Nihonjingakkō Muke no Tentai Kyōzai no Kaihatsu (The Improvement of Teaching Materials in Astronomy for the Science Curriculum in Japanese Schools Overseas)' *Tōkyō Gakugei Daigaku, Kaigaishijo Kyōiku Centre Kenkyū Kiyō*, No. I, pp. 95–110.

ARAI, IKUO, 1978. 'Kyōshi no Kokusaika (The Internationalization of Teachers)' in Mori, Iwashita, and Kita (eds.), *Kyōiku no Kokusaika to Kyōiku Gyōsei (The Internationalization of Education and Educational Administration)* (Kyōdō Shuppan, Tokyo).

—— 1983. 'Ibunka ni Sodatsu Kodomotachi no Kyōiku Mondai (Educational Problems of Children Brought Up in a Different Culture)' in Kobayashi (ed.), *Ibunka ni Sodatsu Kodomotachi (Children Brought Up in a Different Culture)* (Yūhikaku, Tokyo).

Asahi Evening News and the Japan Trade Board (Nihon Bōeki Kai), 1978. *Chiisana Kokusaijin: Kaigaikko no Yorokobi to Kanashimi (Little Internationalists: The Joys and Miseries of Overseas Children)* (Asahi Evening News, Tokyo).

AUSTIN, CLYDE N., 1983. *Cross-Cultural Re-entry: An Annotated Bibliography* (Abilene Christian University Press, Abilene, Tex.).

AZUMA, HIROSHI, 1979. 'Kikokushijo Kyōiku no Kadai (The Subject of Returnee Children's Education)' in *Kaigaishijo Kyōiku o Kangaeru: Symposium Dai II kai (Thoughts on the Education of Overseas Children: 2nd Symposium)* (Tokyo Gakugei Daigaku Kaigai Shijo Kyōiku Centre).

BAETENS BEARDSMORE, HUGO, 1982. *Bilingualism: Basic Principles* (Tieto Ltd., Brussels).

BARNLUND, DEAN C., 1975. *Public and Private Self in Japan and the United States: Communicative Styles of Two Cultures* (The Simul Press, Inc., Tokyo).

BARR, PAT, 1965. *The Deer Cry Pavilion: A Story of Westerners in Japan, 1868–1905* (Macmillan, London).

BEARDSLEY, R. K., 1965. 'Religion and Philosophy' in J. W. Hall and R. K. Beardsley (eds.), *Twelve Doors to Japan* (McGraw-Hill, New York).

BEAUCHAMP, EDWARD R., 1978. 'Griffis in Japan: The Fukui Interlude, 1871' in E. R. Beauchamp (ed.), *Learning to be Japanese: Selected Readings on Japanese Society and Education* (Linnet Books, Hamden, Conn.).

BEFU, HARUMI, 1980. 'A Critique of the Group Model of Japan', *Social Analysis*, No. 5/6 [Special Issue: *Japanese Society: Reappraisals and New Directions*], pp. 29–43.

—— 1981. *Japan: an Anthropological Introduction* (Tuttle, Tokyo).

—— 1983. 'Internationalization of Japan and Nihon Bunkaron', in Mannari and Befu (eds.), 1983 (see below).

—— 1986. 'The Social and Cultural Background of Child Development in Japan and the United States' in Stevenson, Azuma, and Hakuta (eds.), *Child Development and Education in Japan* (W. H. Freeman and Company, New York).

BENEDICT, RUTH, 1946. *The Chrysanthemum and the Sword: Patterns of Japanese Culture* (Routledge and Kegan Paul, London, repr. 1977).

BENNETT, JANET, 1977. 'Transition Shock: Putting Culture Shock in Perspective', *International and Intercultural Communication Annual*, Vol. 4, pp. 45–52.

BENNETT, JOHN W., 1961–2. 'The Innovative Potential of American-Educated Japanese', *Human Organization*, vol. 20–1, pp. 246–51.

—— PASSIN, H. and MCKNIGHT, R. K., 1958. *In Search of Identity: The Japanese Overseas Scholar in America and Japan* (University of Minnesota Press, Minneapolis).

BESTOR, THEODORE C., 1989. *Tokyo Neighborhood* (Stanford University Press, Stanford, Calif.).

BOCHNER, S., LIN, S., and MCLEOD, B. M., 1980. 'Anticipated Role Conflict of Returning Overseas Students', *Journal of Social Psychology*, vol. 110, pp. 265–72.

BOOCOCK, SARANE SPENCE, 1989. 'Controlled Diversity: An Overview of the Japanese Preschool System', *Journal of Japanese Studies*, 15/1, 41–65.

BOOTH, ALAN, 1985. *The Roads to Sata* (Weatherhill, New York and Tokyo).

BRANDT, VINCENT S. R., 1971. *A Korean Village: Between Farm and Sea* (Harvard University Press, Cambridge, Mass.).

BURKS, ARDATH, 1985. 'Japan's Outreach: The Ryūgakusei' in A. Burks (ed.), *The Modernizers: Overseas Students, Foreign Employers and Meiji Japan* (Westview Press, Boulder and London).

CALDAROLA, CARLO, 1979. *Christianity: The Japanese Way* (E. J. Brill, Leiden).

CHAMBERLAIN, BASIL HALL, 1895. *Things Japanese: Being Notes on Various Subjects Connected with Japan* (Tuttle, Tokyo, repr. 1980).

CHEUNG, LINDA MEE-YAN, 1976. 'A Study of the Ignored Variables in the Traditional Paradigm of Assimilation', (MA thesis, University of Maryland).

CHING, JULIA, 1979. 'The Practical Learning of Chu Shun-shui', in W. T. de Bary and I. Bloom, (eds.), *Principle and Practicality: Essays in Neo-Confucianism and Practical Learning* (Columbia University Press, New York).

CHRISTOPHER, ROBERT C., 1983. *The Japanese Mind: The Goliath Explained* (Pan Books Ltd., London).

CHURCH, AUSTIN T., 1982. 'Sojourner Adjustment', *Psychological Bulletin*, 91/3, 540–72.

CLARK, RODNEY, 1979. *The Japanese Company* (Yale University Press, New Haven and London).

COHEN, ANTHONY P., 1985. *The Symbolic Construction of Community* (Ellis Horwood Ltd., Chichester, and Tavistock Publications, London and New York).

COLE, ROBERT E., 1971. *Japanese Blue Collar: The Changing Tradition* (University of California Press, Berkeley).

CONNOR, JOHN W., 1977. *Tradition and Change in Three Generations of Japanese Americans* (Nelson Hall, Chicago).

CONTE, JAMES THOMAS, 1977. *Overseas Study in the Meiji Period: Japanese Students in America, 1867–1902* (Ph.D. thesis, Princeton University [Dissertation Abstracts International, 38/9, 1978]).

COOPER, MICHAEL, (ed.), 1965. *They Came to Japan: An Anthology of European Reports on Japan, 1543–1640* (University of California Press, Berkeley).

CRAWCOUR, E. S., 1978. 'The Japanese Employment System', *Journal of Japanese Studies*, 4/2, 225–45.

CUMMINGS, WILLIAM K., 1978. 'The Conservatives Reform Higher Education' in E. R. Beauchamp, (ed.), *Learning to be Japanese: Selected Readings on Japanese Society and Education* (Linnet Books, Hamden, Conn.).

—— 1980. *Education and Equality in Japan* (Princeton University Press, NJ).

DALE, PETER N., 1986. *The Myth of Japanese Uniqueness* (Croom Helm and the Nissan Institute, London, Sydney, and Oxford).

DE VOS, GEORGE, and CHUNG, DAE KYUN, 1981. 'Community Life in a Korean Ghetto' in De Vos and Lee, *Koreans in Japan: Ethnic Conflict and Accommodation* (University of California Press, Berkeley).

DŌMOTO, AKIKO, 1987. 'Student Returnees, Student Misfits', *Japan Quarterly*, 34/1, 34–8.

DORE, R. P., 1973. *British Factory–Japanese Factory: The Origins of National Diversity in Industrial Relations* (George Allen and Unwin, London).

—— 1982. *The Diploma Disease: Education, Qualification and Development* (George Allen and Unwin, London).

—— 1984. *Education in Tokugawa Japan* (Athlone Press, London).

—— 1986. 'Where will the Japanese Nobel Prizes come from?', *Science and Public Policy*, 13/6, 347–61.

DOUGLAS, MARY, 1966. *Purity and Danger: An Analysis of Concepts of Pollution and Taboo* (Penguin, Harmondsworth, repr. 1970).

DOWNS, RAY F., 1976. 'A Look at the Third Culture Child', *Japan Christian Quarterly*, 43/2, 66–71.

DRIFTE, REINHARD, 1988. 'Nihon no Kokusaika (The Internationalization of Japan)', *Fukuoka Unesco Kyōkai*, No. 23, pp. 70–88.

DUKE, BENJAMIN C., 1973. *Japan's Militant Teachers* (University Press of Hawaii, Honolulu).

DURKHEIM, EMILE, 1897. *Suicide: A Study in Sociology* (trans. by John A. Spaulding and George Simpson; Routledge and Kegan Paul, London and Henley, 1979).

EAKIN, KAY BRANAMAN, 1979. 'The Real Culture Shock: Adolescent Re-Entry to the U.S.', *Foreign Service Journal*, August 1979, pp. 20–2.

EBUCHI, KAZUKIMI, 1980. 'Tōnan Asia no Nihonjin: Genchi Bunka e no Tekiō Pattern no Mondai o Chūshin toshite (Japanese in South-East Asia: The Problem of Adaptation Patterns to the Local Culture)' in Sofue (ed.), *Gendai no Esprit: Nihonjin no Kōzō (L'Esprit d'aujourd'hui: The Structure of the Japanese)*.

—— 1983. 'Kodomotachi no Ibunka Sesshoku (Children's Contact with Different Cultures)' in Kobayashi (ed.), *Ibunka ni Sodatsu Kodomotachi (Children Brought Up in a Different Culture)* (Yūhikaku, Tokyo).

—— 1985. *Kikokushijo no 'Tekiō' o Dō Toraeru ka? Bunkajinruigaku no tachiba kara (How should the 'Adaptation' of Returnee Children be Approached? From the Viewpoint of Cultural Anthropology)* (paper delivered to the Sixth Ibunkakan Kyōiku Gakkai, Fukuoka, 11 May 1985).

—— 1986a. 'Kikokushijo Kyōiku Kiso Kenkyū no Kadai (Themes in the Basic Research on Returnee Schoolchildren)' in Kawabata *et al.*, 1986a (see below).

—— 1986b. 'Kikokushijo o torimaku Nihon Shakai no Kankyōteki Tokushitsu ni kansuru Kenkyū: Nihon Shakai no Sakokusei to Kikoku-shijo (Research Concerning the Environmental Special Circumstances of Japanese Society Surrounding Returnee Schoolchildren: The Isolation-ism of Japanese Society and Returnee Schoolchildren)' in Kawabata *et al.* 1986b (see below).

Economist Rinji Zōkan (Economist Special Edition), 1984. *59 Nenji Keizai Hōkoku Yori: Waga Kuni Kaigai Chokusetsu Tōshi no Sui-i (1984 Annual Economic Report: The Change in the Country's Direct Overseas Investment)*, 8/27.

ELLIOT, ALISON J., 1981. *Child Language* (Cambridge University Press, Cambridge).

ENLOE, WALTER, and LEWIN, PHILIP, 1984. 'Educating the Bi-Cultural Child: Problems of Re-Adaptation for Children Returning to Japan' in Dai San Bunka no Kodomo o Sodateru Kai (ed.), *Third Culture Children: Hiroshima no Kaigai.Kikoku Jidō.Seitotachi*, vol. 1.

FARKAS, JENNIFER BURKHARD, 1983. *Japanese Overseas Children's American Schooling Experience: A Study of Cross-Cultural Transition* (Ph.D. thesis, Ohio State University. [Dissertation Abstracts International, 44/11, 1984]).

FISCHER, J. L., 1963. 'The Japanese Schools for the Natives of Truk, Caroline Islands' in G. D. Spindler (ed)., *Education and Culture: Anthropological Approaches* (Holt, Rinehart and Winston, New York, etc.).

Foreign Press Center (ed.), 1978. *Education in Japan* (Foreign Press Center/Japan, Tokyo).

—— (ed.), 1982. *Japan's Mass Media* (Foreign Press Center/Japan, Tokyo).

—— (ed.), 1985. *Discussions on Educational Reform in Japan* (Foreign Press Center/Japan, Tokyo).

—— (ed.), 1986. *Japanese Women Yesterday and Today* (Foreign Press Center/Japan, Tokyo).

FUJIHARA, GINJIRO, 1936. *The Spirit of Japanese Industry*, trans. by Fukukita Yasunosuke (Hokuseido Press, Tokyo).

FUJIWARA, KIETSU et al., 1985. 'Kikokushijo no Tekiō Katei ni kansuru Shinrigakuteki Kenkyū (Psychological Analysis of the Adjustment Processes of High School Returnees from Overseas)', *Tōkyō Gakugei Daigaku Kiyō*, Section 1, vol. 36, pp. 71–81.

FUKUDA, YUSUKE, 1983. 'Jo (Foreword)', in Kaigai Shijo Kyōiku Shinkō Zaidan, 1983 (see below).

FURNHAM, ADRIAN and BOCHNER, STEPHEN, 1986. *Culture Shock: Psychological Reactions to Unfamiliar Environments* (Methuen, London and New York).

FURUHASHI, SEIKO, 1984. 'Foreign in Their Own Land: Returnee Children's Patterns of Adjustments into Japanese Schools', (M.Ed. thesis, University of Hawaii).

FURUKAWA, TESSHI, 1980. 'The Individual in Japanese Ethics' in C. A. Moore (ed.), *The Japanese Mind: Essentials of Japanese Philosophy and Culture* (Tuttle, Tokyo).

FYFIELD, J. A., 1982. *Re-Educating Chinese Anti-Communists* (Croom Helm, London).

GLAZER, NATHAN, 1976. ' "There are no Dropouts in Japan": The Japanese Educational System', in H. Patrick, and H. Rosovsky (eds.), *Asia's New Giant: How the Japanese Economy Works* (Brookings Institution, Washington, DC).

GOLDSTEIN, BERNICE Z., and TAMURA, KYOKO, 1975. *Japan and America: A Comparative Study in Language and Culture* (Tuttle, Tokyo).

GOULD, STEPHEN JAY, 1984. *The Mismeasure of Man* (Penguin Books, Harmondsworth).

GULLAHORN, J. T. and J. E., 1963. 'An Extension of the U-curve Hypothesis', *Journal of Social Issues*, 19/3, 33–47.

HAMILTON, ALEXANDER, *A New Account of the East Indies: 1688–1723* (ed. by W. Foster, vol. II, Argonaut Press, London, 1930).

HANE, MIKISO, 1982. *Peasants, Rebels and Outcastes: The Underside of Modern Japan* (Pantheon Books, New York).

HARA, KIMI, 1983. 'Sociological Observations of the Problems Encountered by the Japanese in Understanding the Southeast Asia "Multi-Ethnic Society" ' (paper presented at the Sub-Regional Workshop on Education for International Understanding on *The Study for 'Multi-Ethnic Society' and its Implications for Intercultural Education*, Kyoto University, Japan, 14–15 July 1983).

HARA MAKOTO, 1986. 'Kikokushijo Kyōiku no Jissen Mokuhyō toshite no Tokusei no Hoji.Shinchō (The Development and Maintenance of Special Qualities as the Objective of the Practice of Education for Returnee Schoolchildren)', in Kawabata *et al.*, 1986 (see below).

HARUMEI, OSAMU, 1985. 'Sekai o Mite Shimatta Kodomotachi (Children who have Seen the World)', *Zenkoku Kaigai Shijo Kyōiku Kenkyū Kyōgikai: Kaihō*, No. 20, p. 1.

HASEBE, SHŌJI (ed.), 1985. *Kaigaishijo Kyōiku Manual (Parents' Manual for Educating Children Overseas)* (Kaigai Shijo Kyōiku Shinkō Zaidan, Tokyo).

—— 1986. 'Kyōiku Kaikaku to Kaigai Shijo Kyōiku (Educational Reform and Overseas Children's Education)', *Kaigai Shijo Kyōiku*, No. 155, pp. 98–100.

HATA, HIROMI, and SMITH, WENDY A., 1983. 'Nakane's "Japanese Society" as Utopian Thought', *Journal of Contemporary Asia*, 13/3, 361–88.

HATANO, KANJI, 1973. *Sekai no Gakkō, Nihon no Gakkō: Taikenteki Hikaku Kyōikugaku (Schools around the World, Schools in Japan: Comparative Pedagogy from Personal Experience)* (Shōgakukan, Tokyo).

HENDRY, JOY, 1981. *Marriage in Changing Japan: Community and Society* (Croom Helm, London).

—— 1986. *Becoming Japanese: The World of the Pre-School Child* (Manchester University Press, Manchester).

HIDAKA, ROKURŌ, 1984. *The Price of Affluence: Dilemmas of Contemporary Japan* (Kodansha International Ltd, Tokyo).

HIRANO, KICHIZŌ, 1984. *Kokusai Jinji Kanri Jidai: Kaigai Chūzaiin no Shitei no Kyōiku Mondai no Mirai (The Era of International Personnel Affairs: The Future of the Education of the Children of Overseas Employees)* (Eiko Shuppansha, Tokyo).

HOOK, GLENN D., 1989. 'Internationalization of Contemporary Japan', *The Japan Foundation Newsletter*, 17/1, 13–16.

HOROIWA, NAOMI, 1983a. 'Kaigai Seichō Nihonjin no Tekiō to Sentaku: Life History ni yoru Kenkyū (Adaptation and Choices of Japanese Growing

Up Overseas: A Study of Life Histories)' (MA thesis, University of Tsukuba).

—— 1983*b*. Kaigai Seichō Nihonjin no Identity Hensen to Tekiō: Life History Kenkyū kara (Adaptive Strategies and Changing Identities of Japanese Growing Up Overseas)', *META Report I* (META Culture no Kai, Tokyo).

—— 1985. 'Metacultural Perspective: An Alternative for Multiculturals', *Flux*, vol. 2, ed. 2, pp. 10–14.

HOSHINO, AKIRA, 1980. 'Kikoku Nihonjin no Seikatsu Tekiō to Identity (Life Adaptation and Identity of Returnee Japanese)' in Sofue (ed.), *Gendai no Esprit: Nihonjin no Kōzō* (*L'Esprit d'aujourd'hui: The Structure of the Japanese*).

—— 1982. 'Gaisetsu: Culture Shock (A General Outline: Culture Shock)' in Hoshino, (ed.), *Gendai no Esprit: Culture Shock* (*L'Esprit d'aujourd'hui: Culture Shock*), No. 161.

—— 1983. 'Kodomotachi no Ibunka Taiken to Identity (Children's Experience of Different Cultures and Identity)' in Kobayashi (ed.), *Ibunka ni Sodatsu Kodomotachi* (*Children Brought Up in a Different Culture*) (Yūhikaku, Tokyo).

—— and NIIKURA, RYŌKO, 1983*a*. 'Atarashii Kata no Nihonjin no Tanjō: Ibunka no naka de Sodatsu Kodomotachi (The Birth of a New-style Japanese: Children Brought Up in a Different Culture)' in Ogino and Hoshino (eds.), *Culture Shock to Nihonjin: Ibunka Taiō no Jidai o Ikiru* (*The Japanese and Culture Shock: Living in an Era of Cross-Cultural Communication*) (Yūhikaku Sensho, Tokyo).

—— 1983*b*. 'Kaigai Kikoku Jidō.Seito Ukeire ni kansuru Shōgakkō. Chūgakkō Kyōshi no Ishiki Chōsa (The Views of Teachers on Specialised Education for Overseas Children)' in *Tōkyō Gakugei Daigaku Kaigaishijo Kyōiku Centre Kenkyū Kiyō, Dai II Shū*, pp. 21–53.

HOUSER, MICHAEL, 1982. 'The Japanese School in Camden Town', *Japan: Review of the Anglo-Japanese Economic Institute*, No. 76, pp. 15–20.

—— 1984. 'Tsukuba: Birth and Early Years of a Technopolis', *Japan: Review of the Anglo-Japanese Economic Institute*, No. 79, pp. 11–16.

HUNTER, JANET, 1984. *Concise Dictionary of Modern Japanese History* (Kodansha International Ltd., Tokyo).

HURST, G. CAMERON III, 1984. *Japanese Education: Trouble in Paradise?* (University Field Staff International Reports, No. 40 (Asia).

ICHI, YŪKI, 1983. 'Gaikoku no Kōkō o Dete Tokubetsu Waku de Kyōdai ni Hairō?! (Let's Enter Kyoto University through the Special Network by Going to an Overseas Senior High School?!)', *Shūkan Asahi*, 11 April 1983, pp. 167–9.

IKEDA, KIYOSHI, 1949. *Jiyū to Kiritsu: Igirisu no Gakkō* (*Freedom and Discipline: School in England*) (Iwanami Shoten, Tokyo, repr. 1983).

258   *References*

IKEMI, YŪJIRŌ and IKEMI, AKIRA, 1982. 'Some Psychosomatic Disorders in Japan in Cultural Perspective', *Psychotherapy and Psychosomatics*, vol. 38, pp. 231–8.

INAMURA, HIROSHI, 1982. *Nihonjin no Kaigai Futekiō (The Non-Adaptation of Japanese Overseas)* (NHK Books, Tokyo).

—— and ARAKI, HITOSHI, 1983. 'The Adaptation States of Temporary Japanese Residents in Latin America', *Latin American Studies*, No. 7, pp. 143–59.

—— and TAMURA, TAKESHI, 1987. 'Kaigaishijo.Kikokushijo no Tekiō ni kansuru Rinshōteki Kenkyū (A Clinical Study on the Adaptation Problems of Overseas and Returnee Children)', *Ibunkakan Kyōiku*, No. 1, pp. 55–66.

INUI, SUSUMU and SONO, KAZUHIKO, 1977. *Kaigai Chūzaiin no Shijo Kyōiku: Kage o Otosu Shingakkō Kyōsō (Education for the Children of Overseas Employees: Under The Shadow of the Education Rat-Race)* (Nihon Keizai Shinbunsha, Tokyo).

ISHIDA, HIDEO, 1983. 'Takokusekika to Kaigai Haken Yōin no Motivation (The Multi-nationalization and the Motivation of Employees Sent Overseas)', *Shūkan Tōyō Keizai*, Special Edition, Series 65, pp. 72–9.

—— (n.d.). 'Kaigai Keieisha no Yōken to Career (The Requisites and Careers of Overseas Managers)', *Keiō Gijuku Keiei Kanri Gakkai Kikanshi*, 1/2, 21–42.

ISHIDA, TAKESHI, 1971. *Japanese Society* (Random House, New York).

IWASAKI, MARIKO, 1982. 'New York Kyojū Nihonjin Shijo ni Miru Bilingualism: Sono Dokkairyoku ni kansuru Kenkyū (A Study of First Language Maintenance and Second Language Acquisition of Kaigaishijo in New York)', *Tōkyō Gakugei Daigaku Kaigaishijo Kyōiku Centre Kenkyū Kiyō, Dai I Shū*, No. 1, pp. 47–66.

JAMES, ESTELLE and BENJAMIN, GAIL, 1988. *Public Policy and Private Education in Japan* (Macmillan Press, Basingstoke).

JANSEN, MARIUS B., (ed.), 1965. *Changing Japanese Attitudes toward Modernization* (Princeton University Press, Princeton, NJ).

—— 1980. *Japan and its World: Two Centuries of Change* (Princeton University Press, Princeton, NJ).

Japanese National Commission for Unesco (ed.), 1966. *The Role of Education in the Social and Economic Development of Japan* (Tokyo).

JJ, 1986. 'Kaigai Kikokushijo no Stylebook (A Guide to Overseas Returnees' "Style")', November 1986, pp. 223–7.

JOHNSON, THOMAS WAYNE, 1975. *Shōnendan: Adolescent Peer Group Socialization in Rural Japan*, Asian Folklore and Social Life Monographs, vol. 68 (Oriental Cultural Service, Taipei).

KAIGAI SHIJO KYŌIKU SHINKŌ ZAIDAN (ed.), 1980. *Kaigai Shijo Kyōiku Shinkō Zaidan Jūnenshi (Ten Year History of the Japan Overseas Educational Services)* (Kaigai Shijo Kyōiku Shinkō Zaidan, Tokyo).

—— (ed.), 1983. *Watashi no Kaigai Kinmu Jidai: 150 Nin no Chichioya ga Kataru Ko Zure Funin Taikenki* (*My Period of Overseas Service: A Diary of their Experiences as Told by a Hundred and Fifty Fathers Taking Up a New Appointment with their Children in Tow* (Kaigai Shijo Kyōiku Shinkō Zaidan, Tokyo).

—— (ed.), 1984. *Chikyū ni Manabu: Dai Gokai Kaigai Shijo Bungei Sakuhin Concours* (*Learning around the Globe: The Fifth Overseas Children's Literary Works Competition*) (Kaigai Shijo Kyōiku Shinkō Zaidan, Tokyo).

KAMATA, SATOSHI, 1984. *Japan in the Passing Lane: An Insider's Account of Life in a Japanese Auto Factory* (Unwin Paperbacks, Counterpoint, London).

KAMIJŌ, MASAKO, 1983. 'Nihon ni Okeru Bilingual Kyōiku Keikaku ni Kansuru Hikakuteki Kenkyū: Kaigai.Kikokushijo Kyōiku Mondai to Kaiketsusaku (Planning Bilingual Education in Japan—A Comparative Study: The Education Problems of Overseas and Returnee Children and a Practical Solution)', *Tōkyō Gakugei Daigaku Kaigaishijo Kyōiku Centre Kenkyū Kiyō*, No. 2, pp. 3–20.

—— and MCLEAN, MARTIN, 1983. 'The Japanese Community and Japanese Supplementary Schools' (paper presented to the Comparative Education Society of Europe XIth Conference, Würzburg, July 1983).

KANAZAWA, MASAO, 1984. 'Kachikan ga Sōtaika shita Jidai no "Kokusaika" Ron (The "Internationalisation" Theory in an Era of Relativised Senses of Values)' in Uchiyama *et al.*, 1984 (see below).

KAPLAN, DAVID E., and DUBRO, ALEC, 1987. *Yakuza: The Explosive Account of Japan's Criminal Underworld* (Macdonald/Queen Anne Press, London).

KARABEL, JEROME, and HALSEY, A. H., 1977. 'Educational Research: A Review and an Interpretation' in Karabel and Halsey (eds.), *Power and Ideology in Education* (Oxford University Press, New York).

KASHIOKA, TOMIHIDE, 1982. *Meiji Japan's Study Abroad Program: Modernizing Elites and Reference Societies* (Ph.D. thesis, Duke University [Dissertation Abstracts International, 43/5, 1982]).

KATŌ KŌJI, 1986. 'Kikokushijo Kyōiku no Jissen (The Practice of Returnee Children's Education)' in Kawabata *et al.*, 1986 (see below).

KAWABATA, MATSUNDO *et al.*, 1986. (Tokyo Gakugei Daigaku Kaigaishijo Kyōiku Centre: Kikokushijo Kyōiku Mondai Kenkyū Project) *Kokusaika Jidai no Kyōiku: Kikokushijo Kyōiku no Kadai to Tenbō* (*Education in the Era of Internationalization: Themes and Views on Returnee Children's Education*) (Sōyūsha, Tokyo).

—— and SUZUKI, MASAYUKI, 1981/2. 'Kaigai Nihonjin no Jidō, Seito no tame no Kyōiku ni kansuru Kisoteki Kenkyū (Towards a General Theory of Education for Children Overseas)', *Kōbe Daigaku Kyōiku Gakubu Kenkyū Shūroku*, No. 68 (1981), pp. 29–39 (Part I), No. 69 (1982), pp. 21–31 (Part II).

KAWABATA, MATSUNDO, SUZUKI, MASAYAKI, AND NAGAOKA, KEIZŌ, 1982. 'Kaigai Nihonjin Jidō. Seito no Ibunka Rikai to Oya no Ishiki: Sūryōteki Bunseki ni yoru Kōsatsu (Cross-Cultural Understanding of Japanese Children and Students Overseas and Parental Consciousness: An Inquiry via Quantitative Analysis)', *Nihon Hikaku Kyōiku Gakkai Kiyō*, No. 8, pp. 43–50.

KAWAMURA, NOZOMU, 1980. 'The Historical Background of Arguments Emphasizing the Uniqueness of Japanese Society', *Social Analysis*, No. 5/6 [Special Issue: *Japanese Society: Reappraisals and New Directions*], pp. 44–62.

KEENE, DONALD, 1952. *The Japanese Discovery of Europe: Honda Toshiaki and other Discoveries, 1720–1798* (Routledge and Kegan Paul Ltd., London).

KEIZAI KŌHŌ CENTER, 1985. *Japan 1984: An International Comparison* (Japan Institute for Social and Economic Affairs, Tokyo).

KELLY, THOMAS F., 1973. 'Who's the Kid's Advocate?', *Foreign Service Journal*, September 1973, pp. 16–19 and 32.

KIDA, HIROSHI, 1978. 'Kyōiku no Kokusaika to Gyōsei Shisaku (The Internationalization of Education and Administrative Policy)' in Mori, Iwashita, and Kida (eds.), *Kyōiku no Kokusaika to Kyōiku Gyōsei (The Internationalization of Education and Educational Administration)* (Kyōdō Shuppan, Tokyo).

KINES, LINDA B., 1971. 'The Shock of Coming Home', *The Commission*, August 1971, pp. 12–13.

KINOSHITA, TOMIO *et al.*, 1985. *Kyōto Daigaku ni okeru Tokubetsu Senbatsu Seido no Keika to Hyōron (The Progress and Criticism of the Special Selection System at Kyoto University)* (Kyōto Daigaku Kyōiku Yōbu).

KITSUSE, JOHN I., MURASE, ANNE E., and YAMAMURA, YOSHIAKI, 1984. 'Kikokushijo: The emergence and institutionalization of an education problem in Japan' in Schneider and Kitsuse (eds.), *Studies in the Sociology of Social Problems* (Ablex Publishing Corporation, Norwood, NJ).

KOBAYASHI, TETSUYA, 1976. *Schools, Society and Progress in Japan* (Pergamon Press, Oxford).

—— (ed.), 1978a. *Zaigai.Kikokushijo no Tekiō ni Kansuru Chōsa Hōkoku (A Report of Research on the Adaptation of Overseas and Returnee Children)* (Department of Comparative Education, Kyoto University, Kyoto).

—— 1978b. 'Japan's Policy on Returning Students', *International Education and Cultural Exchange*, 13/4, 15–16 and 47.

—— (ed.), 1979. *Zaigai Nihonjin Jidō no Tekiō to Gakushū: Manila. Singapore ni Okeru Zaigai Nihonjin Community to Sono Shitei no Kyōiku ni Kansuru Chōsa Hōkoku (The Learning and Adaptation of Overseas Japanese Children: A Report on the Education of the Children of the Overseas Japanese Community in Singapore and Manila*) (Department of Comparative Education, Kyoto University, Kyoto).

—— 1980. 'Into the 1980s: The Japanese Case', *Comparative Education*, 16/3, 237–44.

—— 1981. *Kaigaishijo Kyōiku, Kikokushijo Kyōiku: Kokusaika Jidai no Kyōiku Mondai* (*Overseas Children's Education, Returnee·Children's Education: An Education Problem in an Internationalizing Age*) (Yūhikaku, Tokyo).

—— 1982*a*. 'Kaigai.Kikokushijo no Kyōiku no Kaikaku ni tsuite (On the Reform of Education for Overseas and Returnee Children)', *Nihon Hikaku Kyōiku Gakkai Kiyō* No. 8, pp. 37–41.

—— 1982*b*. 'Kaigai Kikokushijo no Tekiō (Overseas and Returnee Children's Adaptation)' in Hoshino (ed.), *Gendai no Esprit: Culture Shock* (*L'Esprit d'aujourd'hui: Culture Shock*), No. 161.

—— 1983. 'Hajime (Preface)' in Kobayashi (ed.), *Ibunka ni Sodatsu Kodomotachi* (*Children Brought Up in a Different Culture*) (Yūhikaku, Tokyo).

KOJIMA, MASARU, 1981. 'Senzen no Zaigai Shitei Kyōikuron no Ronchō (The General Tone of the Debate over the Education of Overseas Children before the War)' in Kobayashi (ed.), *Kyōiku ni Okeru Bunkateki Dōka to Tayōka: Multi-Cultural Education no Kenkyū. Kenkyū Kirokushū II* (*Diversification and Cultural Assimilation in Education: Research on Multi-Cultural Education. Research Report II*) (Department of Comparative Education, Kyoto University, Kyoto).

KONDŌ, HIROSHI, 1984. *Culture Shock no Shinri: Ibunka to tsukiau tame ni* (*The Psychology of Culture Shock: How to Get On in Different Cultures*) (Sōgensha, Osaka).

KONISHI, SAYAKA, 1983. *Futatsu no Kuni ni Sumu Kodomotachi* (*Children who Live in Two Countries*) (Bunka Shuppan Kyoku, Tokyo).

KONO, MAMORU, 1982. 'Zaibei Nihonjin Shijo no Nigengo Shiyō to Kyōka Gakushū (Bilingualism and Academic Language Proficiency of Japanese Children in the United States)', *Tōkyō Gakugei Daigaku Kaigaishijo Kyōiku Centre Kenkyū Kiyō*, No. 1, pp. 25–45.

KUBOTA, ETSURŌ, 1985. 'Tōdaisei no Nise "Kaigai Kyōiku Taikenki" no Hakushindo (The Verisimilitude of the Fake "Diary of Overseas Educational Experience" of a Tokyo University Student)', *Asahi Shūkan*, 1 February 1985, pp. 24–7.

KUBOTA, MORIHIRO, 1983. 'Kikokushijo no Seishin Kōzō (The Psychological Structure of Returnees)', *Nihon Hikaku Kyōikukai Kiyō*, No. 8, pp. 59–64.

KUMAGAI, FUMIE, 1977. 'The Effects of Cross-Cultural Education on Attitudes and Personality of Japanese Students', *Sociology of Education*, vol. 50, pp. 40–7.

KUNIEDA, MARI, 1983. *Japanese School Children in New York: Their Assimilation Patterns* (Ph.D. thesis, Columbia University Teachers' College [Dissertation Abstracts International, 44/11, 1984]).

KUROYANAGI, TETSUKO, 1982. *Totto-chan: The Little Girl at the Window*, trans. by Dorothy Britton (Kodansha International Ltd., Tokyo).

KUSAHARA, AKIRA, 1984. 'Daisan Sekai to Nihon no Kyōiku (The Third World and Japanese Education)', *Kyōikugaku Kenkyū*, 51/3, 18–27.

KUSANAGI, HIROSHI, 1980. '*Kikokushijo no Nihongo Go-i Unyō Nōryoku* (The Ability of Japanese Language Use of Returnee Children)', in Higa (ed.), *Nihon ni okeru Bilingualism* (*Bilingualism in Japan*) (Tsukuba Daigaku Bilingualism Kenkyūkai).

LA BRACK, BRUCE, 1983. 'Is an International Identity Possible for the Japanese?' (paper presented at the International Education Center, Tokyo, 21 May 1983).

LACH, DONALD F., 1968. *Japan in the Eyes of Europe: The Sixteenth Century* (reproduced from Lach, D. F., 'Asia in the Making of Europe': Part III, ch. VIII, vol. I, pp. 651–729) (Phoenix Books/University of Chicago Press, Chicago).

LEACH, E. R., 1954. *Political Systems of Highland Burma: A Study of Kachin Social Structure* (G. Bell and Sons Ltd., London, repr. 1964).

LEBRA, TAKIE SUGIYAMA, 1981. 'Japanese Women in Male Dominant Careers: Cultural Barriers and Accommodations for Sex-Role Transcendence', *Ethnology*, 20/4, 291–306.

—— 1982. *Japanese Patterns of Behavior* (University of Hawaii Press, Honolulu).

——, and LEBRA, WILLIAM P., (eds.), 1986. *Japanese Culture and Behavior: Selected Readings* (University of Hawaii Press, Honolulu).

LEWIS, CORRINE, 1986. 'Expensive International Schools', *Tokyo Journal*, September 1986, pp. 16–17 and 20.

LOCK, MARGARET, 1986. 'Plea for Acceptance: School Refusal Syndrome in Japan', *Social Science and Medicine*, 23/2, 99–112.

LYSGAARD, S., 1955. 'Adjustment in a foreign society: Norwegian Fulbright grantees visiting the United States', *International Social Science Bulletin*, No. 7, pp. 45–51.

MAEYAMA, TAKASHI, 1984a. 'Ishitsu no Mono e no Katarikake no Shiza— Zainichinikkei Nihonjin no Ron (A Viewpoint for Talking to Heterogeneous Elements: A Theory of Overseas Japanese in Japan) in Uchiyama *et al.*, 1984 (see below).

—— 1984b. 'Brazil Nikkeijin ni okeru Ethnicity to Identity: Ninshikiteki. Seijiteki Genshō toshite (Ethnicity and Identity of the Japanese in Brazil: Politico-Cognitive Phenomena)', *Minzokugaku Kenkyū*, 48/4, 444–58.

MAKARENKO, ANTON S., 1965. *Problems of Soviet School Education* (Progress Publishers, Moscow).

MANNARI, HIROSHI and BEFU, HARUMI (eds.), 1983. *The Challenge of Japan's Internationalization: Organization and Culture* (Kwansei Gakuin University and Kodansha International Ltd., Tokyo).

MATSUBARA, HISAKO, 1978. *The Samurai* (trans. from German by Ruth Hein; Robin Clark, London, 1982).

MATSUBARA, TATSUYA, 1980. 'Kikokushijo no Gakushū Tekiō ni kansuru Kenkyū (A Study of Returnee Children's Adaptation to School Education)' in Higa (ed.), *Nihon ni okeru Bilingualism (Bilingualism in Japan)* (Tsukuba Daigaku Bilingualism Kenkyūkai, Tsukuba University).

—— 1984. 'Kikokushijo ga Kakaeru Mondai (The Problems which the Returnee Children Have)', *Eigo Kyōiku: Tokushū—Kikokushijo to Eigo Kyōiku (English Language Education: Special Edition on English Language Education for Returnee Children)*, 33/4, 19–21.

—— and ITŌ, SAKIKO, 1982. 'Kaigai Kikokushijo no Minzokuteki Kizoku Ishiki.Shūdan Dōchōsei.Kojin Shikōsei no Kenkyū (A Study of Overseas Returnees' Ethnic Identity, Group Conformity and Individual Directivity)', *Tōkyō Gakugei Daigaku Kaigaishijo Kyōiku Centre Kenkyū Kiyō*, No. 1, pp. 5–24.

MCLEAN, MARTIN, 1985. 'Private Supplementary Schools and the Ethnic Challenge to State Education in Britain' in C. Brock and W. Tulasiewicz (eds.), *Cultural Identity and Educational Policy* (Croom Helm, London and Sydney).

MEINTEL, DEIRDRE A., 1973. 'Strangers, Homecomers and Ordinary Men', *Anthropological Quarterly*, 46/1, 47–58.

MENDL, WOLF, 1989. 'Independence and Interdependence: Japan in a Changing International Environment', *Annals of the Institute of Social Science, University of Tokyo* (Special Issue), pp. 25–39.

MILLER, ROY ANDREW, 1982. *Japan's Modern Myth: The Language and Beyond* (Weatherhill, New York and Tokyo).

MINAMI, HIROSHI, 1973. 'The Introspection Boom: Whither the National Character?', *Japan Interpreter*, 8/2, 159–84.

Ministry of Education, Science and Culture (Monbushō), Research and Statistics Division, Government of Japan, 1982. *Education in Japan: A Graphic Presentation* (Gyōsei Publishers, Tokyo).

Minority Rights Group, 1983. *Japan's Minorities (Burakumin, Koreans, Ainu, Okinawans)* (Report No. 3).

MINOURA, YASUKO, 1979. 'Life In-Between: The Acquisition of Cultural Identity among Japanese Children Living in the United States' (Ph.D. thesis, University of California).

—— 1984. *Kodomo no Ibunka Taiken: Jinkaku Keisei Katei no Shinri Jinruigakuteki Kenkyū (Children's Experience of Different Cultures: A Psycho-Anthropological Study of the Process of Personality Formation)* (Shisakusha, Tokyo).

MIYAKAWA, YASUO, 1985. 'The Metamorphosis of Japan's Industrial System and the Development of the International Division of Labour' in *United Nations Industrial Development Organization Symposium Papers* (Vienna).

MIZUNO, FUJIO, 1982. 'Fu no Kokusaisei no Sonzai (The Existence of Negative Internationalism)' in Yamazaki (ed.), *Kokusaiha Shuryū Sengen: Stop.Out kara no Hassō (Declaration of the Mainstream Internationalist Faction: Conceptions from the Stop Out)* (Nihon Recruit Centre Shuppanbu, Tokyo).

MIZUNO, TAKAAKI, 1987. 'Ainu: The Invisible Minority', *Japan Quarterly*, 34/2, 143–8.

MOERAN, BRIAN, 1983. 'The Language of Japanese Tourism', *Annals of Tourism Research*, 10/1, 93–106.

—— 1984. 'Individual, Group and *Seishin*: Japan's Internal Cultural Debate', *Man*, 19/2, 252–66.

—— 1985. 'Confucian Confusion: The Good, the Bad and the Noodle Western' in D. Parkin (ed.), *The Anthropology of Evil* (Basil Blackwell, Oxford).

MOLONEY, JAMES CLARK, 1954. *Understanding the Japanese Mind* (Greenwood Press, New York, repr. 1968).

MONBUSHŌ, 1982. *Kaigai Kinmusha Shijo Kyōiku ni kansuru Sōgōteki Jittai Chōsa Hōkokusho (Final Research Report Concerning the Education of the Children of Japanese Working Overseas)* (Tokyo).

—— 1985. *Kaigai Shijo Kyōiku no Genjō (The Current Situation of Education for Overseas Children)* (Monbushō Kyōiku Joseikyoku Zaimuka Kaigai Shijo Kyōikushitsu, Tokyo).

—— 1988. *Kaigai Shijo Kyōiku no Genjō (The Current Situation of Education for Overseas Children)* (Monbushō Kyōiku Joseikyoku Zaimuka Kaigai Shijo Kyōikushitsu, Tokyo).

MORISHIMA, MICHIO, 1982. *Why has Japan 'Succeeded'?: Western Technology and Japanese Ethos* (Cambridge University Press, Cambridge).

MORITA, AKIO, REINGOLD, EDWIN M., and SHIMOMURA, MITSUKO, 1987. *Made in Japan: Akio Morita and Sony* (Collins, London).

MORIYA, TAKESHI, 1985. 'The Ideology of the Samurai' in Umesao (ed.), *Seventy-Seven Keys to the Civilization of Japan* (Sōgensha Inc., Osaka).

MORRIS, IVAN, 1980. *The Nobility of Failure: Tragic Heroes in the History of Japan* (Penguin Books, Harmondsworth).

MOTOBAYASHI, YOSHIMASA, 1977. *Sabaku no Nihonjingakkō: Ikyō ni Sodatsu Kodomotachi (A Japanese School in the Desert: Japanese Children Brought Up in a Different Environment)* (Nihon Keizai Shinbunsha, Tokyo).

MOUER, ELIZABETH KNIPE, 1976. 'Women in Teaching' in J. Lebra,

J. Paulson, and E. Powers (eds.), *Women in Changing Japan* (Westview Press Inc., Colorado).

MOUER, ROSS and SUGIMOTO, YOSHIO, 1986. *Images of Japanese Society: A Study in the Structure of Social Reality* (KPI, London).

MURASE, ANNE E., 1978. 'The Problems of Japanese Returning Students', *International Education and Cultural Exchange*, 13/4, 10–14.

—— 1980. 'Kikoku Seito ni kansuru Chōsa Hōkoku: Yottsu no Kotonaru Type no Gakkō ni tsuite no Yobiteki Kōsatsu (Survey Report: Japanese Children Returning from Overseas: A Preliminary Study of Four Different Types of Schools)' in Kobayashi (ed.), *Kyōiku ni Okeru Bunkateki Dōka to Tayōka: Multi-Cultural Education no Kenkyū. Kenkyū Kirokushū I (Diversification and Cultural Assimilation in Education: Research on Multi-Cultural Education. Research Report I)* (Department of Comparative Education, Kyoto University, Kyoto).

—— 1983. 'Kikokushita Kodomotachi no Fuan (Anxiety Levels among Japanese Returnees)' in Kobayashi (ed.), *Ibunka ni Sodatsu Kodomotachi (Children Brought Up in a Different Culture)* (Yūhikaku, Tokyo).

—— 1984. 'Higher Education and Life Style Aspirations of Japanese Returnee and Nonreturnee Students', *Jōchi Daigaku Gaikokugo Gakubu Kiyō*, No. 19, pp. 1–34.

MURO, MARIKO, 1987. 'Acquiring the American Way of Learning: The Adjustment of Japanese Students at an American School' (Ph.D. thesis, Stanford University).

MUSHANOKOJI, KIMIHIDE, 1984. 'Sekai System no naka no Kokusaijin (The International Person in a Global System)', in Uchiyama *et al.*, 1984 (see below).

MUSIKASINTHORN, RENUKA, and RESSLER, PHYLLIS, 1980. 'The Japanese Community in Bangkok', *Sawaddi*, July–August 1980, pp. 16–19.

NAGAI, MICHIO, 1985. 'Educational Reform: Developments in the Postwar Years', *Japan Quarterly*, 32/1, 14–17.

NAGASHIMA, NOBUHIRO, 1973. 'A Reversed World: Or Is It? The Japanese Way of Communication and their Attitudes towards Alien Cultures' in R. Horton and R. Finnegan (eds.), *Modes of Thought: Essays on Thinking in Western and Non-Western Societies* (Faber and Faber, London).

NAKABAYASHI, KATSUO, 1981. *Sekai no Nihonjingakkō (Japanese Schools around the World)* (Sanshūsha, Tokyo).

NAKANE, CHIE, 1970. *Japanese Society* (Penguin Books, Harmondsworth, repr. 1973).

—— 1972. *Tekiō no Jōken: Nihonteki Renzoku no Shikō (The Conditions of Adaptation: The Contemplation of Japanese Continuity)* (Kodansha Gendai Shinsho, Tokyo).

NAKANISHI, AKIRA, 1985. 'Kikokuseito oyobi Boston Zaijū Nihonjin Jidō Seito no Hogosha kara Mita Nihon to Ō-Bei no Bunkateki Kankyō no Chigai (Cultural Differences between Japan and Western Countries as Perceived by the Returnee Students and Japanese Parents Living in Boston)', *Tōkyō Gakugei Daigaku Kaigaishijo Kyōiku Centre Kenkyū Kiyō*, No. 3, pp. 1–24.

—— 1986. 'Kikoku Jidō.Seito no Ukeire no Jittai (The Actual Conditions for Receiving Returnee Students and Children)' in Kawabata *et al.*, 1986 (see above).

—— AKAHORI, KANJI and MATSUBARA, TOMOKO, 1982. 'Kikokujidō no Nihongoryoku no Kōsatsu: Cloze-hō o Mochiite (A Study of the Japanese Language Proficiency of Returnee Children through a [Japanese] Cloze Test)', *Tōkyō Gakugei Daigaku Kaigaishijo Kyōiku Centre Kenkyū Kiyō*, No. 1, pp. 67–93.

NAKASONE, YASUHIRO, 1986. ' "Chiteki Suijun" Kōen (Lecture on "Levels of Intellect")', *Chūō Kōrōn*, No. 11, pp. 146–62.

NAKATSU, RYŌKO, 1979. *Kodomo.Gaikokugo.Gaikoku: Aru hi Totsuzen Eigo ni natte shimatta Ko (Children, Foreign Countries, Foreign Languages: A Child who one day could suddenly speak English)* (Bungei Shunjū, Tokyo).

NASH, D. and SHAW, L. C., 1963. 'Personality and Adaptation in an Overseas Enclave', *Human Organization*, vol. 21, pp. 252–63.

National Council on Educational Reform (Government of Japan), 1987. *Fourth and Final Report on Educational Reform.*

NATSUME, SŌSEKI, 1904. *Botchan* (trans. by Sasaki Umeji; Tuttle, Tokyo, 1980).

NIHON ZAIGAI KIGYŌ KYŌKAI, 1981. *Kaigai Hakenmono no Shijo Kyōiku Mondai ni kansuru Teigen (A Proposal concerning the Educational Problems of Children of Individuals Sent Overseas)* (Tokyo).

NISHIMURA, HIDETOSHI, 1987. 'Universities—Under Pressure to Change', *Japan Quarterly*, 34/2, 179–83.

NITOBE, INAZŌ, 1899. *Bushidō: The Soul of Japan. An Exposition of Japanese Thought* (Knickerbocker Press, New York, repr. 1905).

NIYEKAWA, AGNES M., 1985. 'Seijin shita katsute no Kikokushijo no Kako Saikentō (Re-Evaluation of Past Experiences by Former Returnees as Adults)' in Tōkyō Gakugei Daigaku Kaigai Shijo Kyōiku Centre (ed.), *Bilingual.Bicultural Kyōiku no Genjō to Kadai: Zaigai.kikokushijo kyōiku o chūshin toshite (The Topic and Condition of Bilingual and Bicultural Education: As the basis for the education of overseas/returnee children)* (Tokyo).

NODA ICHIRŌ, 1986. 'Kikokushijo Kyōiku no Kisoteki Kenkyū no Ayumi (Stages in Basic Research on Returnee Children's Education)' in Kawabata *et al.*, 1986 (see above).

NOMOTO, KIKUO, 1985. *Kikokushijo no 'Tekiō' o dō Toraeru ka? Gengo-*

gaku no Tachiba kara (*How should the 'Adaptation' of Returnee Children be Approached? From the Viewpoint of Linguistics*) (paper presented to the Sixth Ibunkakan Kyōiku Gakkai, Fukuoka, 11 May 1985).

OBERG, K., 1960. 'Cultural Shock: Adjustment to New Cultural Environments', *Practical Anthropology*, vol. 7, pp. 177–82.

O'CONROY, TAID, 1936. *The Menace of Japan* (Paternoster Library, No. 6, London).

O.E.C.D. (Organization for Economic Co-Operation and Development), 1971. *Reviews of National Policies for Education: Japan* (O.E.C.D., Paris).

ŌGIYA, SHŌZŌ (ed.), 1977. *Zaigai Shitei no Kyōiku: Genjō to sono taisaku* (*The Education of Overseas Children: A Counterplan of the Present Situation*) (Aoba Shuppan, Tokyo).

OHNUKI-TIERNEY, EMIKO, 1984*a*. *Illness and Culture in Contemporary Japan: An Anthropological View* (Cambridge University Press, Cambridge).

—— 1984*b*. 'Monkey Performance: A Multiple Structure of Meaning and Reflexivity in Japanese Culture' in E. Bruner (ed.), *Text, Play and Story: The Construction and Reconstruction of Self and Society* (American Ethnological Society, Seattle).

ŌHORI, SATOSHI, 1982. 'Nihonjingakkō Un'ei no Arikata ni Kansuru Kōsatsu: Milan Nihonjingakkō ni okeru Kyōiku Jissen o Moto ni (A Study of the Administration of Japanese Schools Overseas: The Example of the Japanese School in Milan)', *Tōkyō Gakugei Daigaku Kaigaishijo Kyōiku Centre Kenkyū Kiyō*, No. 1, pp. 111–30.

OKAMURA, FUMIKO, 1981. *Mother Tongue Maintenance and Development among the Japanese Children Living in the United States* (Ph.D. thesis, University of California, Los Angeles [Dissertation Abstracts International, 42/10, 1982]).

ŌKUBO, SHIZUTO, 1983. *Hoshū Jugyō Kō* (*Supplementary Lesson Schools*) (Fukazawa Kyōkai Insatsubu, Tokyo).

Ō-NICHI KYŌKAI, 1984. *Europe, Chūkintō ni Sumu Kodomotachi no Seikatsu to Iken: Dai Yonkai Shō.Chūgakusei Sakuhin Concours Nyūsen Sakuhinshū* (*The Opinions and Lives of Children who Live in Europe, the Middle and the Near East: A Selection of Works from the Fourth Elementary and Junior High School Students' Competition*) (Ō-Nichi Kyōkai, Tokyo).

ONO, YASUKATSU, 1983. 'Genchikō ni okeru Americajin Kyōshi no Zaibei Nihonjingakkō Shijo e no Kyōikuteki Taiō Shisei (Teachers' Verdicts on Japanese Children in American Schools)', *Tōkyō Gakugei Daigaku Kaigaishijo Kyōiku Centre Kenkyū Kiyō*, No. 2, pp. 79–97.

ONODA ERIKO and TANAKA KAZUKO, 1988. 'Ibunkataiken no Chōkiteki Ishiki (A Long-Term Perspective on the Experience of Other Cultures)', in Kobayashi (ed.), *Kikokushijo no Tekiō ni kansuru Tsuiseki Kenkyū* (*Follow-Up Research on the Adaptation of Returnee Children*) (Kyōto Daigaku Kyōiku Gakubu).

ŌNUMA, YASUAKI, 1985. 'Tanitsu Minzoku Shakai no Shinwa o Koete (Going Beyond the Myth of a Single-Race Society)', *Chūō Kōron*, No. 9, pp. 104–28.

OOMS, HERMAN, 1984. 'Neo-Confucianism and the Formation of Early Tokugawa Ideology: Contours of a Problem' in Nosco (ed.), *Confucianism and Tokugawa Culture* (Princeton University Press, Princeton, NJ).

ŌSAWA, CHIKAKO, 1986. *Tatta Hitotsu no Aoi Sora: Kaigai.Kikokushijo wa Gendai no Sutego ka? (Under The One Blue Sky: Are Kaigai.kikokushijo Abandoned Children of the Modern Era?)* (Bungei Shunjū, Tokyo).

ŌTA, HARUO, 1983. 'Kodomotachi no Tekiō (Children's Adaptation)' in Kobayashi (ed.), *Ibunka ni Sodatsu Kodomotachi (Children Brought Up in a Different Culture)* (Yūhikaku, Tokyo).

OZAKI, ROBERT S., 1980. *The Japanese: A Cultural Portrait* (Charles E. Tuttle Company, Tokyo).

PARK, ROBERT E., 1928. 'Human Migration and the Marginal Man', *The American Journal of Sociology*, 33/6, 881–93.

PARKIN, DAVID, 1978. *The Cultural Definition of Political Response: Lineal Destiny among the Luo* (Academic Press, London)

PASSIN, HERBERT, 1965. *Society and Education in Japan* (Teachers' College, Columbia University).

PAULSON, JOY, 1976. 'Evolution of the Feminine Ideal' in J. Lebra. J. Paulson, and E. Powers (eds.), *Women in Changing Japan* (Westview Press Inc., Colo.).

PLUMMER, KATHERINE, 1984. *The Shōgun's Reluctant Ambassadors: Sea Drifters* (Lotus Press, Tokyo).

PYLE, KENNETH B., 1982. 'The Future of Japanese Nationality: An Essay in Contemporary History', *Journal of Japanese Studies*, 8/2, 223–63.

REISCHAUER, EDWIN O., 1983. *The Japanese* (Tuttle, Tokyo).

REISS, SPENCER, 1984. 'Japan's Lonely Outsiders: A Generation of Expatriate Children come Home as Strangers to their own Land', *Newsweek*, 27 February 1984.

RENDAHL, PAT, 1978. 'Where Do I Hang My Head? Cultural Discontinuity during the Teenage Years', *Foreign Service Journal*, June 1978, pp. 14–16 and 43–4.

ROBERTS, JOHN G., 1973. *Mitsui: Three Generations of Japanese Business* (Weatherhill, New York and Tokyo).

RODEN, DONALD, 1980. *Schooldays in Imperial Japan: A Study in the Culture of a Student Elite* (University of California Press, Berkeley).

—— 1983. 'Commentary: on the Oyatoi' in C. L. Beck and A. W. Burks (eds.), *Aspects of Meiji Modernization: The Japan Helpers and the Helped* (Rutgers University, NJ).

ROHLEN, THOMAS P., 1981. 'Education: Policies and Prospects' in C. Lee and

G. De Vos (eds.), *Koreans in Japan: Ethnic Conflict and Accommodation* (University of California Press, Berkeley).

—— 1983. *Japan's High Schools* (University of California Press, Berkeley).

—— 1984. 'Conflict in Institutional Environments: Politics in Education' in E. S. Krauss, T. P. Rohlen, and P. G. Steinhoff (eds.), *Conflict in Japan* (University of Hawaii Press, Honolulu).

SAITŌ KŌJI, 1986. 'Tekiō no Shosokumen (The various sides of adaptation)', in Kawabata *et al.*, 1986 (see above).

SAKAKIBARA, JUNKO, 1988. 'The Paper Elite', *Tokyo Journal*, 8/7, 5–7 and 26–7.

SAKAKIBARA, YOSHITAKA, 1984. *A Study of Japanese Students at the University of Southern California, 1946–80: Vocational Impact of American Academic Experience on Japanese Students after returning to Japan* (Ph.D. thesis, University of Southern California [Dissertation Abstracts International, 45/1, 1984]).

SANIEL, JOSEFA M., 1965. 'The Mobilization of Traditional Values in the Modernization of Japan' in R. N. Bellah (ed.), *Religion and Progress in Modern Asia* (Free Press, New York).

SANSOM, GEORGE B., 1950. *The Western World and Japan* (Tuttle, Tokyo, repr. 1984).

—— 1951. *Japan in World History* (Tuttle, Tokyo, repr. 1981).

—— 1964. *A History of Japan: 1615–1867* (Cresset Press, London).

SANUKI, KAZUIE, 1984. 'Kokusaika Shakai ni okeru Kyōiku Kadai no Shiten to Tenbō (Views on the Subject of Education in an Internationalizing Society)', *Kyōikugaku Kenkyū*, 51/3, 1–9.

SATŌ, HIROTAKE, 1978. *Kaigaishijo no Kyōiku Mondai (The Educational Problems of Overseas Children)* (Gakkensha, Tokyo).

SATŌ, YŌKO, 1985. 'Kaigai Ijū, Tenkō, Chichi no Tanshin Funin . . . . Haha o Koroshita Ichi Rōsei no "Fukugō Gen'in" (Migration Overseas, Change of School, Father Living Away for Work . . . . The "Composite Causes" for a First-Year Exam Retake Student who Killed his Mother)', *Sunday Mainichi*, 31 March 1985, p. 201.

SCHDT (*sic*), FREDERIK L., 1980. 'Nipponmachi', *Sawaddi*, July–August 1980, pp. 36–40.

SCHOPPA, LEONARD, 1988. The Limits of Change in the Japanese Political System: The Case of Education Reform, 1967–87 (D.Phil. thesis, University of Oxford).

SCHWIMMER, E. G., 1972. 'Symbolic Competition', *Anthropologica*, 14/2, 117–55.

SERAFIN, QUIASON D., 1970. 'The Japanese Community in Manila: 1898–1941', *Philippine Historical Review*, 5/3, 184–222.

SEWARD, JACK, 1983. *Japanese in Action* (rev. ed., Weatherhill, New York and Tokyo).

—— 1984. *America and Japan: The Twain Meet* (Lotus Press, Tokyo).

SHIBANUMA, SUSUMU, 1982. 'Tenki ni Tatsu Kaigaishijo Kyōiku (Overseas Children's Education at the Turning Point)' in Yamazaki (ed.), *Kokusaiha Shuryū Sengen: Stop.Out kara no Hassō (Declaration of the Mainstream Internationalist Faction: Conceptions from the Stop Out)* (Nihon Recruit Centre Shuppanbu, Tokyo).

SHIMADA, HARUO, 1984. 'Motomerareru Sekai to sono Taiwa (Dialogue with a Desired World)' in Uchiyama *et al.*, 1984 (see below).

SHIMAHARA, NOBUO, 1984. 'Toward the Equality of a Japanese Minority: the case of Burakumin', *Comparative Education*, 20/3, 339–53.

SHŪSHOKU JŌHŌ (Europe), 1989. *Japanese Students in Europe*, vol. 3.

SMITH, ROBERT J., 1985. *Japanese Society: Tradition, Self and the Social Order* (Lewis Henry Morgan Lecture Series, Cambridge University Press, Cambridge).

SOFUE, TAKAO, 1980. 'Nihonjin no Kōzō: Shinri Jinruigakuteki Kyōdō Kenkyū (The Structure of the Japanese: Psycho-Anthropological Joint Research)' in Sofue (ed.), *Gendai no Esprit: Nihonjin no Kōzō (L'Esprit d'aujourd'hui: The Structure of the Japanese)*.

SŌGABE YASUSABURŌ (ed.), 1989. *Kaigaishijo Kyōiku Q and A (Overseas Children's Education: Question and Answer)* (Nikkeiren Kōhōbu, Tokyo).

SOUTH, 1987. 'The Rising Sun: Cutting Out Asia', *South*, No. 76, pp. 57–9.

SPECTOR, MALCOLM and KITSUSE, JOHN I., 1977. *Constructing Social Problems* (Cummings Publishing Company, Calif.).

STOETZEL, JEAN, 1955. *Without the Chrysanthemum and the Sword: A Study of the Attitudes of Youth in Post-War Japan* (Heinemann, London).

STORRY, RICHARD, 1983. *A History of Modern Japan* (Penguin Books, Harmondsworth).

SUGIMOTO, YOSHIO and MOUER, ROSSE., 1989, *Constructs for Understanding Japan* (Kegan, Paul International, London and New York).

SUKITA, ALEN, 1984. 'Kikokushijo no Sanninshō Tansū no Ninshō Daimeishi no Shiyō: Eigo no Eikyō ni yotte Shōjiru "Kare/Kanojo" no Shiyō (The Use of the Third Person Singular Personal Pronoun by Returnee Children: The Use of "He/She" due to the Influence of English)', (MA thesis, Tsukuba University).

SUZUKI, MASAYUKI, 1984. 'Kaigai.Kikokushijo no Kyōiku (The Education of Overseas and Returnee Children)', *Kyōikugaku Kenkyū*, 51/3, 38–47.

SUZUKI, NORIHISA, 1974. 'Christianity' in Arai *et al.*, *Japanese Religion: A Survey by the Agency for Cultural Affairs* (Kodansha International Ltd., Tokyo and Palo Alto).

TAKAGI, FUMIO, 1977. 'Kikokushijo Kyōiku ni tsuite Kangaeru Koto (Some Thoughts about the Education of Returnee Children)', *Monbu Jihō*, No. 1205, pp. 39–46.

TAKAGI, NOBUO, 1988. 'Japanese Abroad: Armed with Slippers and Soy Sauce', *Japan Quarterly*, 35/4. 432–6.

TAKAHAGI, YASUJI *et al.*, 1982. *Kaigai.Kikokushijo ni okeru Culture Shock no*

Yōin Bunseki to Tekiō Programme no Kaihatsu.Shikō (*The Trial and Development of a Programme for Adaptation and Fundamental Analysis of Culture Shock among Overseas and Returnee Children*) (Tōkyō Gakugei Daigaku Kaigaishijo Kyōiku Centre, Tokyo).

TAKENAGA, YOSHIMASA, 1984. *Kikokushijo no Kotoba to Kyōiku* (*Returnee Children's Language and Education*) (Sanseidō, Tokyo).

TAMES, RICHARD, 1983. *Servant of the Shōgun* (Paul Norbury Publications Ltd., Tenterden, Kent).

TANI, NAOKI, 1985. 'Trade with the Continent' in Umesao (ed.), *Seventy-Seven Keys to the Civilization of Japan* (Sōgensha Inc., Osaka).

TAYLOR, JARED, 1985. *Shadows of the Rising Sun: A Critical View of the 'Japanese Miracle'* (Tuttle, Tokyo).

TEMPLEMAN, MAX, 1979. *Kibei: A Novel* (Daimax Publishing House, Honolulu).

THURSTON, DONALD R., 1973. *Teachers and Politics in Japan* (Princeton University Press, Princeton, NJ).

TRAINOR, JOSEPH C., 1983. *Educational Reform in Occupied Japan: Trainor's Memoirs* (Meisei University Press, Tokyo).

TSUKAMOTO MIEKO, 1987. 'Haha Oya no Ibunkataiken (Mothers' Different Cultural Experience)', *Tōkyō Gakugei Daigaku Kaigaishijo Kyōiku Centre Kenkyū Kiyō*, No. 4, pp. 33–59.

TSUKUSHI, TETSUYA, 1984. 'Datsu.Kokusuijin no Jōken (The Conditions for becoming a Former Ultra-Nationalist)' in Uchiyama *et al.* 1984 (see below).

TSUNODA, RYŪSAKU, DE BARY, W. THEODORE, and KEENE, DONALD, 1964. *Sources of Japanese Tradition*, vol. 1 (Columbia University Press, New York and London).

TSUNODA, TADANOBU, 1985. *The Japanese Brain: Uniqueness and Universality*, transl. by Yoshinori Oiwa (Taishūkan Publishing Company, Tokyo).

TSURUMI, KAZUKO, 1984. 'Minsaijin no Jōken (The Condition of Humanists)' in Uchiyama *et al.*, 1984 (see below).

UCHIYAMA HIDEO *et al.*, 1984. *Kokusaijin no Jōken* (*The Condition of Internationalists*) (Mitsumine Shobō, Tokyo).

UEHARA, ASAKO, 1985. 'Americajin no Gyaku Culture Shock: Kaigai Kikoku Gakusei ni kansuru Yobichōsa yori (American's Return Culture Shock: A Preparatory Survey of Overseas-Returnee Students)', *Kyōtō Daigaku Jinruigaku Kenkyūkai Kikan.Jinruigaku*, 16/3, 158–80.

—— 1986. *Comparison of Re-Entry Adjustment between Japanese and American Students: An Interactionist Perspective* (Ph.D. thesis, University of Minnesota [Dissertation Abstracts International, 47/4, 1986]).

UJI, YOSHIO, 1984. ' "Ninki Kyūjōshō" Zenryōseidō Kōtō no Genzai ("Boosting Popularity": The Current Complete Dormitory System in High Schools)' *Chūō Kōron*, No. 12, pp. 244–54.

Unesco Nihon Kokunai Iinkai, 1982. *Kokusai Rikai Kyōiku no Tebiki* (*A Handbook of Education for International Understanding*) (Tokyo Hōmei Shuppan, Tokyo).

272 *References*

VAN GENNEP, ARNOLD, 1967. 'The Small Milk-Jug: or Comparative Esthetics' in *The Semi Scholars*, trans. and ed. by Rodney Needham (Routledge and Kegan Paul, London).

VARLEY, H. PAUL, 1984. *Japanese Culture: A Short History* (Tuttle, Tokyo).

VOGEL, EZRA F., 1963. *Japan's New Middle Class: The Salary Man and his Family in a Tokyo Suburb* (University of California Press, Berkeley and Los Angeles).

—— 1983. *Japan as Number One: Lessons for America* (Tuttle, Tokyo).

WAKABAYASHI, SHINSUKE *et al.* n.d. *The New Century English Series II* (Sanseidō, Tokyo, Teachers' Version).

Waseda University, 1988. *Waseda University Facts*, 1988.

WERKMAN, SIDNEY L., 1979. 'Coming Home: Adjustment Problems of Adolescents who have Lived Overseas' in Feinstein and Giovacchini (eds.), *Adolescent Psychiatry* (Developmental and Clinical Studies, vol. 7, University of Chicago Press, Chicago).

WHITE, MERRY, 1980. 'Stranger in his Native Land: Group Boundaries and the Japanese International Returnee' (Ph.D. thesis, Harvard University).

—— 1987. *The Japanese Educational Challenge: A Commitment to Children* (Free Press, New York).

—— 1988. *The Japanese Overseas: Can They Go Home Again?* (Free Press, New York).

WHITING, ROBERT, 1984. *The Chrysanthemum and the Bat: The Games Japanese Play* (Permanent Press, Tokyo).

WILLIS, DAVID, 1983. 'International Schools in Japan', *International Schools Journal*, No. 5, pp. 21–5.

—— 1984. 'Strangers in their own Country—the Misfit Returns', *Far Eastern Economic Review*, 19 January 1984, pp. 67–8.

WILSON, ROBERT A. and HOSOKAWA, BILL, 1982. *East to America: A History of the Japanese in the United States* (Quill, New York).

WILSON, SANDRA, 1987. *Pro-Western Intellectuals and the Manchurian Crisis of 1931–1933* (Nissan Occasional Paper Series, No. 3, Nissan Institute, Oxford).

WILTSHIRE, RICHARD, 1989. 'Going Around in Circles: Migration and Internal Labour Markets in Japan', *Japan Education Journal*, No. 40, pp. 9–10.

WOODS, PETER, 1986. *Inside Schools: Ethnography in Educational Research* (Routledge and Kegan Paul, London and New York).

WORONOFF, JON, 1983. *Japan: The Coming Social Crisis* (Lotus Press Ltd., Tokyo).

YAMAMURA, YOSHIAKI, 1986. 'The Child in Japanese Society', in Stevenson, Azuma, and Hakuta, (eds.), *Child Development and Education in Japan* (W. H. Freeman and Company, New York).

YAMASHITA SHINICHI, 1988. 'The Future of Broadcasting in Japan with Special Reference to NHK' (paper presented at the Nissan Institute of Japanese Studies, University of Oxford, 4 March 1988).

YANAGI, TATSUO, 1983. 'Jugyōchū no Jidō.Seito no Kōdō ni taisuru Kyōshi no Atsukaikata no Nichibei Hikaku (A Comparative Study of Japanese and American Teachers' Treatment of Pupils During Class)', *Tōkyō Gakugei Daigaku Kaigaishijo Kyōiku Centre Kenkyū Kiyō*, No. 2, pp. 55–77.

YOKOSHIMA, AKIRA, 1977. 'Tenkōsei no Tekiō ni tsuite no Kangaekata (Views on the Adjustment of Transfer Children)', *Utsunomiya Daigaku Kyōiku Gakubu Kiyō*, 27/1, 139–53.

YOSHIDA, TEIGO. 1981. 'The Stranger as God: The Place of the Outsider in Japanese Folk Religion', *Ethnology*, 20/2, 87–99.

ZADANKAI (General Discussion), 1987. 'Sayōnara Eigo Complex (Good-Bye English Language Complex)', *Chūō Kōron*, No. 6, pp. 286–95.

ZENSEIKEN JŌNINIINKAI, 1975. *Gakkyū Shūdan Zukuri Nyūmon (An Introduction to Creating School Groups)* (Meiji Tosho, Tokyo).

ZEUGNER, JOHN F., 1984. 'What can we learn from the Japanese? The Puzzle of Higher Education in Japan', *Change*, January/February 1984, pp. 24–1.

Index